How to Build a Successful Virtual Assistant Business

Written by:

Janice D. Byer, CCVA, VAC, MVA
Elayne Whitfield-Parr, CCVA, VAC, MVA, PREVA

Notice of Rights

Notice of Liability

The authors and publisher have made every effort to ensure the accuracy of the information herein. However, the information contained in this system is sold without warranty, either express or implied. The information in this system is general in nature and not intended as a substitute for professional, legal or financial advice. Neither the authors, Virtual Business Solutions, Mediamage Business Solutions, nor it dealers or distributors make no claim as to the success of any business, promise of revenue to be generated, or amount of time to achieve results set forth in this publication. Nor will they be held liable for any damages to be caused either directly or indirectly by the instructions contained in the system, or by the software or hardware products described herein.

Printed in Canada
Published by CVAC.ca

ISBN: 978-0-9809676-2-3

Table of Contents

Foreword

This is *the* time to become a Virtual Assistant (VA)! Working from home is no longer relegated to unachievable dreams. Becoming a Virtual Assistant is now a reality for anyone with administrative experience, a computer and the support to make it happen. Elayne and Janice's new book is that much needed support for Virtual Assistants worldwide and is a welcome addition to this emerging and exciting industry.

When I first became a Virtual Assistant, it was a tough struggle from start-up to success. It was a time-consuming mission to find even the smallest tidbit of information to answer the tiniest of questions I had revolving in my head regarding starting up a virtual assistant business. There were few, if any, resourceful books or other social networks to satisfy my quest to learn more on this topic. Then along came Elayne and Janice who were one of the first contributors to my success as a VA. It was their organization, Canadian Virtual Assistant Connection (CVAC) that I first joined after a long hard search on the internet for more information on this unknown term "virtual assistant." It was at CVAC that many of my questions were finally answered. This led me onto the path of eventually leading a worldwide network of Virtual Assistants as well as becoming a major spokesperson in the VA industry, a feat I never would have dreamed possible at that time. Kudos and many thanks to Janice and Elayne for their contribution to my success and for now taking it one step further and authoring, *How to Build a Successful Virtual Assistant Business* to further help others just like me make a mark for themselves as a Virtual Assistant.

This book demystifies the questions every Virtual Assistant will have when developing their business. Most of all, it challenges the Virtual Assistant chapter after chapter to operate and build a successful Virtual Assistant practice no matter who they are or where they are located. It can be achieved by each and every individual by simply following this book from start to finish. By paying careful attention to the following pages, you will have the opportunity to unravel the (not so) complex steps to building a successful Virtual Assistant business. You'll read about the important business planning stages, setting up your office, developing your service list, marketing for new clients, training and certifications, balancing business and family life, not to mention the marvelous resource tools found within this book. The reader can view this as a "how-to" manual or strategic business planner. Either way, it will benefit both new and veteran VAs in developing their dreams of obtaining a successful Virtual Assistant business.

Had this VA resource book been around when I was starting out, I know my journey would have been not only considerably shorter but much less stressful. I wish all Virtual Assistants the success in building their new Virtual Assistant business. Trust me, from one VA to another, this book will be a resource that you will be regularly taking down from the library shelf for a long time to come. Make sure it is reachable on your bookcase!

Tawnya Sutherland, CIMBS

Founder of VAnetworking.com, the Original Virtual Assistant Networking Forum since 2003 and Author of the Virtual Business Startup System (VBSS). A Certified Internet Marketing Specialist, Tawnya also runs Mediamage Business Solutions helping her clients turn their website clicks into cash.

Introduction

Although the term "Virtual Assistant", also referred to as a VA, is still very new to the business community, there are thousands of home-based administrative workers around the world who now refer to themselves as VAs. The opportunities for the professional services offered by these VAs are endless.

Our dream for this book is to help those who have administrative or VA-related service skills to start, operate and build a successful Virtual Assistant practice, no matter where they are located and no matter what their gender is.

How to Build a Successful Virtual Assistant Business includes information and tips to help aspiring and established VAs with every aspect of starting and building a Virtual Assistant business. From naming your business, to upgrading your skills, to expanding your business, we have put together everything you need to know based on our combined years in this industry and the input of successful VAs worldwide.

As we are both Canadian-based VAs, we have also included a chapter to help with the legalities of registering and operating a business across Canada. We wish we could include information from every country on the ins and outs of working there, but that would mean a series of country-specific books. Maybe one day we will do that, but for right now, 95% of this book includes information that any VA can use to become successful. For information on registering a business in your specific country, we recommend visiting some of the websites listed in the VA Organizations area of our Resources section near the end of this book.

Being a Virtual Assistant is an exciting and highly rewarding career. The Virtual Assistance industry works hard to help the term "VA" become recognized in all business circles. Our wish, along with VAs around the world, is to change the question from "what is a VA?" to "who is your VA?" and with the professionalism that we have witnessed in this industry, that won't take long to happen.

So, welcome to a fast-growing industry that allows you to have the freedom of working from home (or *virtually* anywhere), be your own boss, and assist the many entrepreneurs and business professionals around the world who need to concentrate on running their businesses while you handle their non-core tasks.

We hope ... no, we know this book will become your VA encyclopedia and we look forward to seeing you become successful by growing your business beyond your wildest dreams.

Sincerely,

Janice & Elayne

Acknowledgements

Janice's Acknowledgements - Firstly, I would like to thank my family for their support while working on this book. There were countless evenings and weekends when I had my laptop in front of me and they completely understood how passionate this project was and is to me. Thanks to my husband, Randy and my daughter, Megan for being so patient with me.

Secondly, I want to thank all of the VAs out there who helped us with their input and tips to add to this book. The discussion lists from all of the organizations to which we belong were a huge asset when it came to researching what needed to be included. So, thanks to every VA for being helpful and passionate about the success of our industry.

And finally, I want to thank Elayne for being an awesome business partner in the Canadian Virtual Assistant Connection, a great co-author on this book and a wonderful friend! Thanks for just being there, Elayne, no matter if the discussion was business or personal. I am so glad we decided to write this book and I look forward to working on more projects with you in the future!

Elayne's Acknowledgements - It's amazing to me that I am where I am today, doing what I love to do and being so completely happy with my life. I want to thank all of those who played a role in getting me here.

Thanks to my family and friends who believed in me and supported me during those first tough months. Thanks also to everyone who has continued to support me over the years as I have grown my business. Not once have I ever received a word of complaint when I started up my computer on a family vacation or downloaded email when we were out on a secluded island in Georgian Bay. It's amazing where you can access email, isn't it? My husband, Tim, has been a true inspiration and an amazing source of strength and support. Thank you to Tim, Taylor, Cameron and Braedan for your love, patience and support. And thank you for expressing your pride in me so often.

Thanks to the incredible VAs from around the world as you have been a true source of inspiration to me. Thanks to everyone who ever offered me advice or asked for advice from me – both have been of great value to me. Thanks especially to the members of CVAC – what a wonderfully diverse group of women and men who are intelligent, successful and completely supportive of each other. These individuals are what make our industry so exceptional.

I would like to offer a special thank you to Caley Walsh who has worked with me at Executive Assistance for the past five years. I truly couldn't do what I do without her. She is an unbelievable mix of intelligence, wisdom, patience, and unparalleled administrative abilities. And last (but not least) to my partner, Janice Byer. Janice has been an inspiration to me since I began this journey and I'm proud to have had the opportunity to partner with such a brilliant and extraordinary woman. She is such an integral part The Canadian Virtual Assistant Connection and the VA industry as a whole. My life is better for having known her. I am looking forward to years of growing CVAC and am truly honoured to be a part of her life, both professionally and personally.

What Is a Virtual Assistant?

Definition

A Virtual Assistant, also known as a VA, is an entrepreneur and business owner who takes pride in offering various forms of help for tasks that are generally related to keeping a business running smoothly. Their services are readily available for fellow business professionals, but they are also suitable to anyone who may be in need of some administrative or other related assistance. VAs work from their own offices: usually home offices. They are virtual partners to their clients.

That description may still seem a little vague because it is difficult to best describe what a Virtual Assistant is or does since the services offered and expertise of VAs vary so much.

Most VAs offer assistance with such tasks as word processing, spreadsheets, and other administrative duties. These types of services generally make up the core of any VA practice. However, these services aren't JUST what VAs offer since the quality and experience put into each service is far more than simply "typing a letter." Most VAs have a specialty that includes, or is in addition to, their core services.

VAs are generally experienced in administrative tasks that are necessary to keep any business running smoothly. However, some have more advanced skills in certain services than others. For instance, one VA may be extremely proficient in providing the design of customer-catching marketing material using desktop publishing software, while another VA can do wonders with contact management information in the form of a database. These are some ways that VAs specialize in core tasks.

Administrative tasks aren't the only specialties offered by VAs. The range of services with which to aid fellow business professionals is endless. These can include web design, graphic design, concierge services, ghost writing, and so much more. VAs can even help with everything from travel arrangements to personal shopping.

With that being said, you can see that a VA possesses the skills and expertise to provide professional results for their clients. Most VAs have been in the administrative field for many years and bring that experience to life in the way they run their practices and in the projects they perform for their clients. They take pride in offering their expertise to others in need of their services and communicate with these clients via telephone, fax, snail mail, email and other forms of online communication and technology.

Some VAs will occasionally visit a client's office to perform tasks, but the majority of Virtual Assistants work from their own offices, thus, giving credit to the 'virtual' reference in the term, Virtual Assistant.

Benefits of Becoming a Virtual Assistant

The Virtual Assistant industry is extremely unique. It is made up of entrepreneurs from around the world who come from many different walks of life and are really just one big family.

But as a big family, we do have our "issues" with one another. Sometimes things don't always run smoothly. However, we still communicate in our hours of need by sharing and learning since this is a vital part of what makes this industry work so successfully.

The VA industry also has the benefit of being like an "equal opportunity employer." Although 96.8% of those practicing today are women[1], the number of men entering this field is increasing daily.

VAs who start their practices now are finding it easier to build their client lists than those who began their businesses five or more years ago. This is because the benefits of utilizing the services of a VA are becoming easier to grasp by our target markets, therefore more fellow business professionals are open to the idea of contracting a VA.

Since its inception, the VA industry has received a fair amount of publicity, which has increased its exposure. This recognition in the media has also helped individual VAs to have their written material accepted by publications, another great benefit of being a VA.

> "*Benefits of having your own business*: Now that I have had to enter the job market on a full-time basis for the short term I hope; I really miss working for myself. I didn't care that it was me doing all the work I found it challenging. I miss the days of waking up, getting dressed and making the two-minute commute to my office. I would spend all day working on the one project, and take a break whenever I wanted. Work through a project with no interruptions except for the dogs wanting to go out. It was great! I didn't miss the water cooler chit-chat because I was able to get out and network with other likeminded people. I was able to connect with other professionals. The freedom and independence to be your own boss was wonderful and a great high, not to mention a great ego boost."
>
> *Francesca Frate, Owner/Operator*
> *AdminConcepts - Your Administrative Connection*
> *http://www.adminconcepts.net*

Other advantages of being a home-based Virtual Assistant are:

- You have the freedom to be as creative as you like.
- You can be home for the children when they need you.
- You don't have to worry about office politics.
- You can provide a non-biased view to your clients.
- You can save money on child care expenses.
- Your target market isn't limited to just your local area.

---

[1] VAnetworking.com's Virtual Assistant Survey, 2008 (www.vanetworking.com)

- You have the freedom to schedule your time as needed.
- You can determine your own fees as opposed to someone else determining your pay rate.
- You have the freedom to choose if you would like to work with someone or not.
- You don't have the added expense of requiring a 5-day-a-week business wardrobe
- You can work in the comfort of your own home and in whatever outfit you choose (although we do recommend getting dressed … you never know who will stop by).
- You will build relationships with many talented business professionals.
- You will have access to a multitude of resources on the Internet.
- You will revel in the feeling of accomplishment for everything you do!

Downfalls of Being a VA

The benefits of being a VA definitely outweigh the downfalls, but yes, there are a couple of issues that VAs must face and conquer.

Most VAs work from home. Working from home can produce feelings of isolation which can have a negative effect on yourself and your business. A great way to learn to overcome these feelings is by joining various VA organizations, which include email discussion groups that can give you ideas on ways to beat any feelings of isolation.

Another downfall, which is easily overcome, is ensuring that you stick to a schedule and realize you are the only one responsible for everything that happens in your business. When working from home, it is very easy to take time off to handle personal matters. Being your own boss does give you that privilege, but you need to keep this type of activity to a minimum.

And finally, you may find it a challenge to do everything that needs to be done to build your business as well as keep up with your client work. But, it can be done as you can tell by the number of successful Virtual Assistants who are practicing today.

> "*Difficulties with being self-employed*: Finding time to market when you are busy. Finding time to market when you aren't as busy. Learning how to stay motivated even when you don't feel like it and realizing that the buck stops with you."
>
> *Francesca Frate, Owner/Operator*
> *AdminConcepts - Your Administrative Connection*
> *http://www.adminconcepts.net*

Who can benefit from the services of a VA?

In short, anyone needing help with the core tasks of running their businesses is someone who can benefit by utilizing the services of a VA. Whether it is administrative tasks or other services that VAs offer, working together with a VA can be highly beneficial to entrepreneurs and business professionals.

Here are just a few features & benefits of working with a VA:

Feature: Virtual Assistants work on a contract basis.
Benefit: This means that the client doesn't need to worry about the added expenses that are generally associated with an in-house employee. These include payroll expenses such as source deductions & company benefits.

Feature: Virtual Assistants bill only for time worked.
Benefit: Clients do not need to worry about paying salaries for times when an in-house assistant may be sitting idle. They also don't have to worry about providing vacation time or vacation pay.

Feature: Virtual Assistants work from their own home offices.
Benefit: Clients don't have to provide office space or equipment; an expense that many small businesses can do without.

Feature: Virtual Assistants have fully-equipped offices.
Benefit: This allows the client to get help with almost any task that an in-house assistant generally performs. They do not need to worry whether or not the assistant has the proper peripherals or software.

Feature: Virtual Assistants have many years of experience in their given fields.
Benefit: Clients receive the expertise they need in order to handle their projects without having to train someone. And, there is no need to worry about spending valuable time reading through dozens of resumes and deciding who would be best to handle the work.

Feature: Virtual Assistants can offer full-service assistance with the help of others in the industry.
Benefit: If a client has a task in which their VA is not specialized, they don't need to waste time shopping around for someone else to handle the project. VAs work closely with other VAs and can sub-contract any projects that need a specialized touch.

Feature: Virtual Assistants build relationships with their clients.
Benefit: Clients can be assured that after working closely with a VA, common tasks and how a client likes things done will be a given to the VA. They will begin to know what and how tasks need to be performed without the client explaining it over and over again.

Feature: Virtual Assistants are available on an as-needed basis.
Benefit: This allows the client to have occasional projects done by simply contacting their VA when they need them. There is no need to worry about having a staff member available for a particular task. When clients need help, a VA is ready.

Feature: Virtual Assistants handle the overflow for clients.
Benefit: The client can concentrate on generating company revenue and other necessary tasks that keep a business running smoothly.

What kinds of clients work with VAs?

Virtually anyone can be a client for a VA. However, most VAs do have specific client target markets in which they often specialize.

Most VAs work with small business professionals, but that is a fairly broad spectrum. To expand on that a little, VAs work with coaches, speakers, attorneys, accountants, real estate agents, doctors, students, authors, non-profit organizations, and other service and product suppliers. In addition, VAs work with other VAs.

Unfortunately, not all prospective clients even know about VAs and how much they can help an organization in streamlining their business. So, it is our job to find those prospects, show them all the benefits of working with a VA, and then keep them coming back for more. You will learn more about this throughout the book.

How do you know if you are cut out to be a VA?

Just because you have a computer and can type does not make you a Virtual Assistant. And, just because you have years of experience in the administrative field does not mean you have the skills to run your own VA practice.

A VA works independently, and thus, must have the skills to be a business owner; not just a secretary. A VA is a business owner and does not work FOR her clients, she works WITH them. She plays the role of a partner to her client and takes pride in helping the client's business become successful. It is a win/win situation for all parties.

Having many years of experience in the administrative field is a great start to becoming a VA, but this does not necessarily mean you are cut out to be a business owner. Being a VA involves taking control of how you run your business and how others perceive your business. If you do not have the skills to be a business owner, then starting a VA practice may not be for you. Almost everyone wants to have the freedom to work from home, but there is more to it than just setting up your computer at the kitchen table and hoping that typing projects will come your way.

Let's look at some of the reasons why people consider starting a home-based business, in particular a VA practice:

- They want to be home with the children and watch them grow.
- They are tired of working FOR others and all the politics that can come along with it.
- They have had enough of the competition in the administrative field and trying to land a job that will sustain their lifestyles.
- Their former job no longer exists as the result of company restructuring.
- They want to make money from home while having the freedom to schedule their own workdays.
- They may be ill and cannot obtain a job due to their circumstances.
- They have the notion that if they can type, they can make money doing it.

If these are your main reasons for considering starting your own business, you may want to do some rethinking. These are only partial reasons for having the desire to start your own business. There are two other very important aspects necessary in making your dream a reality:

You must have an extreme passion and desire to be your own boss; and
You must be highly proficient in your skills, while knowing that these skills will give a helping hand to your fellow entrepreneurs, resulting in an income that can sustain your lifestyle (or more!)

Are you ready to work from your home?

Okay, now we have determined why you want to start your own VA practice. It must be time to go ahead and get started, right? Wrong!!!! Now you need to look at whether you have the discipline and passion to work long hours to get your business off the ground and provide the quality of services that are in demand while still keeping your family running smoothly.

Starting any home-based business takes an extreme amount of discipline and dedication. You have to juggle your home life and your business in such a way that there is as little negative effect on your family and your day-to-day life as possible. And, you have to make sure that you have the personality traits required to make your business successful.

First and foremost, you must be sure to have the commitment to make a home business a successful venture. Just because you work at home does not mean you can go off and do whatever strikes your fancy on any given day. Sure, being a home-based business owner does give you that freedom and flexibility, but if you do not schedule yourself and stick to that schedule (as best you can), you may find that you are not putting as much effort into building your business as is required, and thus, your new business will suffer. You need to be disciplined and realize that you alone are responsible for building your business. No one else is going to do it for you.

Effects on Your Personal Life

You don't want your personal life to suffer. When you start your own business, you will spend a lot of time trying to make it soar and the extra effort that you have to put into it can be cause for concern when it comes to your family. Children who are at home during regular business hours may feel left out or ignored while you are trying to accomplish all the tasks that you need to do in building and running your business. It may be time to consider arranging some kind of childcare for the kids.

You may be lucky enough to have children who are old enough to attend school full time. But if they are still too young for school, this means they are around the house during the day and may be trying to get your attention when you are trying to concentrate on work. Although childcare is an expense you were probably hoping to do without when you decided to work from home, it may also be the answer to your dilemma of keeping the children entertained when you are trying to get work done.

You don't have to have them gone all day, or even every day, but you could consider having them visit a babysitter's home a few days a week or see if your local community has any kind of children's programs in which you can enroll them. This will give you at least a little bit of a break from the constant "Mommy!!!" during the day.

Organizing your day so you can build your business and still have time for your family can be quite tricky. During the start-up phase of your business, you may be tempted to work in the evenings to get caught up on marketing your business or completing that extra project for a client. But, there is no need for you to be super-mom all the time. Be sure to set aside some time for family and other extra-curricular pursuits. You may find yourself suffering from burnout if you work too much. And, in the long run, that will have a negative effect on your business.

"Starting your business: Don't let the naysayers stop you. There will always be people in life who will tell you not to do something and they'll be the first ones at your door saying "I told you so." The only person you have to or should listen to is the little voice inside of you telling you to go for it. If you don't try you'll always be wondering what would have happened had you given it your best shot. If the business doesn't take off you'll have grown as a person because you gave it your best shot."

Francesca Frate, Owner/Operator
AdminConcepts - Your Administrative Connection
www.adminconcepts.net

Making the Decision

Do you like the work?

Probably...no, definitely the most important question of all. Do you like working at your computer? You'll be spending an unbelievable amount of time doing just that, so if you don't like it, you'll be miserable and ultimately that will be reflected in the success of your business.

Do you have the skills?

You will hear over and over in our industry, "Having a computer does not make you a VA." For that matter, having significant administrative or secretarial experience doesn't make you a VA either. A VA is equally skilled at all the areas necessary for a successful practice...and more:

- Administrative
- Typing
- Sales abilities
- PR abilities
- Marketing skills
- Verbal and written communications skills
- Etc.

Do you have what it takes?

Some characteristics are essential qualities to running your own business. In approximate order of importance:

Drive

Drive encompasses many attributes including, but not limited to, energy, self-motivation, initiative, dedication, commitment, ambition and being tireless in the pursuit of success. You simply **must** have drive in order to make a success of owning a business (or super amazing luck!).

Simply put, the more you invest in your business in terms of time, energy, creativity etc., the more successful your business will be. If sitting back and waiting for your new business line to ring sounds like part of your plan, you might want to re-think your decision.

> "*Inspiration to keep going when things are tough*: I had the great honour of attending a seminar at which J. Merelle Rodrigo was the speaker the one phrase that she said that really stuck with me was "*If it is meant to be, it is up to me*." When you are the business everything falls on your shoulders. You can't blame anyone else and you have to be the driving force. Give yourself pep talks, celebrate the triumphs and learn from the mistakes."
>
> *Francesca Frate, Owner/Operator*
> *AdminConcepts - Your Administrative Connection*
> *http://www.adminconcepts.net*

The Ability to Think

Hopefully the ability to think sounds ridiculous to you. If it does, then that's probably because the ability to think is ingrained in you. In order to be a success you must be able to think your way through your new venture. **Creative thinking** will play a large roll in your marketing efforts and **critical thinking** will enable you to know what plans to go ahead with and the ones that might be better left for later or perhaps discarded all together. **Analytical thinking** will help you to solve problems and discover solutions outside your own abilities. We can't possibly be experts at everything, but if we're thinking, we can always find a way around our weaknesses.

Good Interpersonal Relationship Skills

Starting your own business doesn't mean you won't have to deal with difficult people anymore. Unfortunately, it also means politics will not become a thing of the past. Now you'll be dealing with these types of people because you need their business or want to avoid burning a potentially lucrative bridge. Remember that there are just as many difficult clients as there are bosses. You will always have colleagues (fellow VAs), subcontractors, suppliers, and others on whom you can rely. It is nice to have the power to control the people you deal with and those you don't, but now your immediate earnings will be directly related to your decision to keep or cut loose that difficult person.

The truly successful VA is positive and cheerful, emotionally stable and socially conscious. Building strong relationships with your clients, colleagues and even your competitors is key to building a strong, professional reputation and a strong professional reputation is key to building a successful business.

Communication Skills

Communication encompasses many different mediums. Verbal, written, facial expression and body language are all methods of communication.

You must be able to communicate effectively in all areas. Poor grammar and telephone etiquette are not acceptable. For example, writing 'you're' in an email when you should have written 'your' could mean the difference between getting the job and never being considered again.

Your body language must back up your message. When presenting your 30 second speech to a potential client you must look them in the eye, put your shoulders back and smile.

The better you are able to communicate and deal with different (and sometimes difficult) personalities the better off you'll be.

Deal well with....	And they will...
Bankers	lend you money
Subcontractors	work harder...for less
Suppliers	provide product or services at low cost and with quick turn around times
Customers	hire you, keep you and provide referrals for you
Colleagues	subcontract to you and/or refer you.

Technical Abilities

Technology seems to change every day. The savvy VA keeps up with the changes, knows how to implement them, and has a superior support structure on which she can depend to help her when something comes up with which she is unfamiliar.

Basically, you must have an all-encompassing knowledge of your market, the services you are providing and the products you need to provide those services.

Can you afford to start a VA practice?

It can _almost_ be guaranteed that the day you open your doors there will NOT be a line-up of clients ready to hire you.

There are two ways to go about starting your practice: full-time or part-time. Pros and cons of both will be covered later in this book.

Either way, there are certain requirements in terms of equipment or supplies that are necessary to any VA, and these are not inexpensive. We'll get into the details later, but suffice it to say that you'll probably need approximately $2000 to start up your business if you're starting with nothing. You may already have a computer, printer, etc., in which case the start-up costs will be less.

Running your own business means that sometimes you make less and sometimes you make more. Do you have some savings, family who will help out financially, or another income provider in the home to fall back on during the uncertain start-up phase?

"Always remember your online 'persona'. You wouldn't go out to meet your clients in sweats and torn clothing, nor should your appearance online appear shoddy. Ensure your website is as you would want your store shop to appear; clean, informative and free of typos and grammatical errors. This also extends to any time you present yourself online including chat rooms and forums, try to maintain as much professionalism as you can. Remember, your next client may be reading your forum entries and if you can't be bothered to appear coherent and intelligent, why should they be bothered to hire you?"

Kate V. Kerans
Kerans Virtual Assistance
http://www.yourvirtualparalegal.net

The Reality of a VA Practice

It is important to understand that, in addition to the above noted qualities, you walk into this venture with your eyes wide open.

- It is hard work to be successful.
- Long hours can be tiring – are you physically strong?
- It is sometimes lonely working by yourself.
- The fear of failure can be occasionally overwhelming.
- The kids will still get sick.
- The dog will still chew your shoes.
- Company will come to visit or stay and you'll HAVE to work.
- Vacation time can be hard to come by.

Summary

As you can tell, starting and developing a thriving VA practice is not for everyone since... it's not easy!   The statement that covers it best is: *You're about to embark on the journey of starting your own business.* You will be an entrepreneur as well as a business owner and the nature of your business is to provide administrative and other support services to small businesses.   First and foremost you are now a business owner.   If you're considering a VA practice then you ***probably*** have the administrative or secretarial skills but the real question is, "**Are you prepared to be a business owner?**"

And the answer is....

Yes, you've got it all and you are seriously committed to starting a VA practice; you are ready to **be a business owner.**

Remember that a positive attitude is half the battle and keeping it through the occasionally tiring and stressful start-up period is often tough to do.

Given that you possess all of the qualities listed above, the following pages will provide you with everything you need to launch a successful VA business.

Business Registration & Licensing

Name Your Business

When devising the name of your business you must clearly define the message you want to deliver. Then you can reduce it to a single theme or image and create a name that conveys that theme. Distinctiveness is the key to a great name and it will give the name its marketing value and effectiveness.

Type of Business Entity

In Canada, we have three basic choices: proprietorship, partnership or corporation.

Proprietorship

The simplest form of business is a proprietorship. All you need to get started is a business license and a service to sell. When operating as a sole proprietorship you and your company are, essentially, one and the same. This means that your company's liabilities are your liabilities and the profit from your company is your income. You'll need to pay taxes on that income at your personal tax rate. You are entitled to deduct all the same expenses from your income as would an incorporated business. Your company's fiscal year is the same as your personal tax year; usually January 1 – December 31. You can register your sole proprietorship at your local Ministry of Consumer and Commercial Affairs.

In Canada, a sole proprietorship can be operated legally under the individual's name. If you operate a sole proprietorship under your given name, i.e. Susan Browne, you are not required to register your business. However, if you operate under a modified name, such as Susan Browne and Associates or Susan Browne Designs, the Business Names Act requires that you register your sole proprietorship.

If the new business is to be a sole proprietorship or a general partnership, it's still a good idea to file the business name with the Registrar of Companies. Sole proprietorship and partnership registration do not protect your business name; others can register and use the same name. To protect your business name you need to incorporate your business, and/or apply for a trademark.

Business Registration and Licensing

To Register Your Sole Proprietorship (By Province):

To register a sole proprietorship or partnership in **British Columbia**, you must reserve a name. First go to http://www.fin.gov.bc.ca/registries/corppg/forms /0708BFILL.pdf (*see Appendices*) to fill out your application for name approval ($30) and then fill out a 'Declaration for Proprietorship or Partnership Registration Form' and submit your declaration and fee. You will need to obtain a 'Declaration for Proprietorship or Partnership Registration Form' (*see Appendices*) (can be obtained from: http://www.fin.gov.bc.ca/registries/corppg/forms/0707FILL.pdf), ensure that it is

properly filled out, and then submit this form along with a fee of $40. You must have your name approved prior to filing your declaration.

A fairly new, convenient way to register your business in British Columbia is to use the province's One-Stop Business Registry. (This service is not currently available through the Internet, so you must go to a location that hosts a One-Stop Business Registration station to register your business). There are a number of workstation locations in Vancouver. You can find the location nearest you by going to: http://www.bcbusinessregistry.ca/introduction/sites.htm.

In **Alberta** you can reserve your business name by filing a declaration form. The form asks you to provide basic information about the company and its owner. A declaration of trade mark form, for example, will require you to include:

(a) the company's type
(b) the company's name and address
(c) the owner's name and occupation
(d) the company's starting date
(e) the name of the officer authorizing the declaration

In Alberta, registering a business name is necessary if you will be operating a sole proprietorship under any name other than your own. A copy of the Declaration of Trade Name form (*see Appendices*) can be found at http://www.servicealberta.gov.ab.ca/pdf/Forms/REG3018.pdf. Once the form is filled out, it must be filed with an authorized service provider.

These are private sector firms - such as accounting firms, legal firms or search houses - authorized by the Alberta government to examine your application to ensure that it meets legislative requirements. The authorized service provider processes the request and issues a proof of filing to verify that the registration has occurred.

An important point to remember is that fees charged by private sector firms are not government regulated; so, shop around for the best price. Make sure that the service provider is authorized and the fee is consistent with the area's other service providers.

In **New Brunswick** you must go to the Corporate Affairs Branch of Service New Brunswick, where you will be given the necessary paperwork to complete. The contact details are:

Corporate Affairs Branch
Service New Brunswick
432 Queen Street
P. O. Box 1998
Fredericton (NB) E3B 1B6
Telephone: (506) 453-2703
Fax: (506) 453-2613

You will also be required to apply for a Business Number (BN), which you will use for harmonized sales tax (HST); corporate income tax, import/export taxes and payroll deductions, where applicable. For an information booklet regarding Business

Numbers, visit http://www.ccra-adrc.gc.ca, or call Canada Customs and Revenue at: 1-800-959-5525. You can also complete this form (*see Appendices*) online by going to: http://www.cra-arc.gc.ca/tax/business/topics/bn/menu-e.html.

For a home-based business you should also be aware that certain zoning restrictions might apply. To find out what regulations apply to your jurisdiction, contact your local municipality at the number listed in your telephone directory, or call 1-800-668-1010

You can check that your desired business name has not been taken by requesting a list of private sector name search firms. Once you have chosen a name, you will be required to pay a fee in order to reserve all legal rights to the name.

Once you have confirmed your business name you must submit your paperwork, namely the Form 5: Certificate of Business name (*see Appendices*) to the Corporate Affairs Branch of Service New Brunswick:

Corporate Affairs Branch
Service New Brunswick
432 Queen Street
P. O. Box 1998
Fredericton (NB) E3B 1B6
Telephone: (506) 453-2703
Fax: (506) 453-2613

Certificate of Business name may be found online here:
https://www.pxw1.snb.ca/snb7001/e/1000/CSS-FOL-45-3502E.pdf and
Additional Information form may be found here:
https://www.pxw1.snb.ca/snb7001/e/1000/CSS-FOL-SNB-45-0015E.pdf

New Brunswick and Nova Scotia have what is known as a reciprocal registration agreement. This means that if you have a business registered in one of these provinces, you don't need to register it in the other to do business in that province.

The first step in business registration in **Nova Scotia** is to reserve your business name. To do this, you need to submit your chosen business name and other pertinent information to the Nova Scotia Registry Of Joint Stock Companies, which will conduct a name search. The cost for the name search is $48.99 (inc. HST) for Atlantic Canada Fee or $61.24 (inc. HST) for a Canada-wide search. If the name search is successful (i.e. the business name is deemed appropriate and distinctive), the business name will be reserved for your use for 90 days. If it's unsuccessful, you'll need to file another Name Reservation Request and go through the procedure again.

Nova Scotia now offers online business registration services; you can submit your Name Reservation Request (*see Appendices*) online at http://www.nsbr.ca.

There is no legislation at this time in **Newfoundland** governing the registration of business names, sole proprietorships or partnerships. That means you can open your sole proprietorship or partnership business in Newfoundland without registering a name and, most importantly, without shelling out a dime.

There is one rule, however, that these types of businesses have to follow. Sole proprietorships and partnerships are not permitted to use the words 'incorporated', 'corporation'; 'limited' or the abbreviation of any of these words in their names.

For more information:

Registry of Companies
Commercial Registrations Division
Ground Floor, East Block
Confederation Building
P.O. Box 8700
St. John's, NF.
A1B 4J6
Tel: 709-729-3317
Fax: 709-729-0232

All businesses must register their business name with the Companies and Personal Property Security Branch of the Ministry of Consumer and Business Services unless you are a sole proprietorship operating under your own name with nothing else added.

In **Ontario**, registering the name of your business is easy because you have so many different access options. For instance, you can register your business name through the public office of the Companies Branch in person or by mail. (Forms are available from the branch or at local Land Registry Offices across the province.) The fee for registering a business name by mail or in person at the Companies Branch is $80. If you register in person, you'll receive your Master Business Licence (proof of business name registration) immediately; if you register by mail, you'll receive it in 6 to 8 weeks.

You can also register your business name at any of the Ontario Business Connects Workstations or register online at the Ontario Business Connects Web site (http://www.gov.on.ca/ont/portal/!ut/p/.cmd/cs/.ce/7_0_A/.s/7_0_252/_s.7_0_A/7_0_252/_l/en?docid=STEL02_038758). Whether you register your business name at a workstation, or via the Web site, the fee is the same; $60. Your business registration is valid for five years, after which time you need to renew your registration.

Computer workstations are located throughout the province (commonly found at business help centres), which allow you to apply for Business Name Registration, Name Search, Retail Sales Tax Vendor's Permit, Employer Health Tax (including self-employed), and Workplace Safety & Insurance Board.

Another option is Business Registration Online (http://www.cra-arc.gc.ca/tax/business/ topics/bn/bro/menu-e.html) which is a one stop, online, self-serve application that allows you to register for a Business Number, as well as for four major CRA programs (Corporation Income Tax, Goods and Services / Harmonized Sales Tax, Payroll Deductions, and Import-Export accounts).

You can now register or renew an Ontario sole proprietorship or partnership or register or renew a business name with the Ministry of Consumer and Business Services on the Canada Customs and Revenue Agency (formerly Revenue Canada) website at: http://www.businessregistration.gc.ca. You can also register for a Business Number (HST and payroll taxes are sub-sets of the BN), and register for CCRA programs at this address.

If you plan to open your VA practice in **Quebec**, and the business name will not be including both your first and last name, you need register the business within 60 days after beginning operations. The only instances where you don't need to register is if it will be a joint venture or if you plan to operate as a sole proprietor under your own full name (business registration in Quebec allows additions to the business owner's first and last name; other provinces do not.)

Although you don't have to register a sole proprietorship in Quebec, you can if you want to. Registered businesses are automatically included in the business register maintained by the Registraire des entreprises (REQ), making the existence of these businesses a matter of public record.

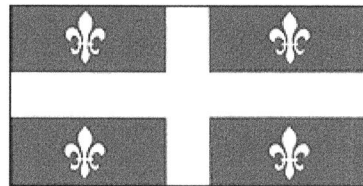

As most VAs will register as a sole proprietorship, we will cover the procedures you will need to follow here. For other entities, such as a partnership or corporation, we recommend searching online for the procedures needed to register them.

Registering a sole proprietorship in Quebec is fairly simple; you file a Declaration of Registration form (along with the applicable fee) at an office of the Registraire des entreprises (REQ) in Montréal or Québec City. English versions of the form are available to use but you MUST also fill in the French version of the form in order to register.

Also, although the forms are available on the Registraire des entreprises Québec website (http://www.registreentreprises.gouv.qc.ca/en/demarrer/formalites-immatr iculation.aspx), currently the Declaration of Registration cannot be filed electronically. You must fill them out, sign them, and take them to an REQ service counter in Montréal or Québec City, to one of the many courthouses in Québec or mail your business registration form to:

Registraire des entreprises
Direction des entreprises
P.O. Box 1364
Québec City, Québec
G1K 9B3

The fee for submitting a Declaration of Registration for a Natural Person (to register a sole proprietorship in Quebec) is $32.00. You also have the option to pay a higher priority fee of $48.00 to expedite the process if you wish.

Once you have registered your business, you will also have to file an Annual Declaration (re-registering your business in Quebec each year). For a sole proprietorship, the regular fee for filing an Annual Declaration is $32.00. (Note that no annual registration fees are due the year following registration with the Enterprise Registrar unless the registration follows a striking off.)

Registering a business in **Saskatchewan** is straightforward. The registration process is required of any person or corporate entity who conducts business under a business name in the province. Administered through the Corporations Branch of Saskatchewan Justice, the legal structure of a company registered in the province may take the form of a sole proprietorship, a partnership, a corporation, or a non-profit corporation.

A Business Name Registration Kit (*see Appendices*) may be downloaded from: http://www.justice.gov.sk.ca/Default.aspx?DN=17002098-70af-4d5d-9a75-fc68067b35ed

Forms must be typed or completed in ink and then forwarded to the Corporations Branch with the appropriate fees. Fees are payable to the Minister of Finance, in cash, cheque, money order, Visa, or MasterCard. Forms may be mailed or faxed. The faxed copy should include an attached client authorization form for payment. The schedule of fees is as follows:

Name Search $50.00
Registration (paper) $65.00
Registration (electronically) $55.00

All businesses and non-profit organizations operating in the **Northwest Territories** must be registered. For a sole proprietorship this fee is $50.00. You must provide a business registration when opening a business bank account.

Businesses operating in the **Northwest Territories** must register and attach a copy of the Certificate of Compliance to the Business Licence application. More details can be obtained by writing or phoning the Workers' Compensation Office.

Employer Services
Workers' Compensation Board
5014 -- 49th Street
3rd Floor Centre Square Mall
Box 8888
Yellowknife, NT X1A 2R3
Toll Free 1-800-661-0792
Tel. (867) 920-3888
Fax (867) 873-4596
Email: yellowknife@wcb.nt.ca
Web site: www.wcb.nt.ca

If your business is to be established within a community that has Hamlet, Village, Town or City status then you must also obtain a **business licence** from the local municipal office. Costs of municipality business licences vary by municipality and by type of licence.

If you intend to establish your business in a community that does not have municipal by-laws you must receive a business licence from Consumer & Corporate Affairs, a division of the Department of Municipal and Community Affairs. The communities that **do not** have their own municipal by-laws include:

Deline
Dettah
Enterprise
Fort Good Hope
Fort Liard
Fort Providence
Fort Resolution
Jean Marie River
Kakisa
Lac La Martre
Lutsel K'e
Nahannie Butte
Paulatuk
Rae Lakes
Reliance
Snare Lake
Trout Lake
Tsiigehtchic
Tulita
Wrigley

More details can be obtained by writing or phoning Consumer & Corporate Affairs.

Consumer & Corporate Affairs
Department of Municipal and Community Affairs
Government of the Northwest Territories
5th Floor Northwest Tower
5201 -- 50th Avenue
Box 1320
Yellowknife, NT X1A 2L9
Tel. (867) 873-7125
Fax (867) 920-6343
Web site: http://www.maca.gov.nt.ca/forms/forms.html

In **Prince Edward Island** if an individual or a partnership carries on a business and uses a business name the business name is required to be registered under the Partnership Act.

If an individual carries on a business but uses his or her own name (with no other words added) there is no requirement to register.

A business name should be registered before it is used. A person wishing to register a sole proprietorship is required to have the Consumer, Corporate & Insurance Services Division conduct a computerized name search of the proposed name prior to registration. The fee is $40.00. If your proposed name is taken or too similar to an existing business you will have to come up with a new name and request another search. Before investing in a NUANS name search you may try this simple and free name search which can save you time and money before you start the official NUANS search. It can be accessed here: (http://www.gov.pe.ca/corporations/index.php).

Following a successful NUANS search you will need to complete the Declaration for Registration of a Business Name form (*see Appendices*) which can be found here: http://www.gov.pe.ca/forms/pdf/78.pdf. This form, along with the $60.00 fee, is then sent to the Consumer, Corporate and Insurance Division office.

There are two steps to registration in **Manitoba**. First, you must file a Request for Name Reservation. You can register online here: https://direct.gov.mb.ca/bsi/coo/servlet/ca. mb.gov.coo.presentation.servlets.OrderServlet. (It usually takes about 24 hours to clear a name). Second, if the proposed name is available, you must file the appropriate forms within ninety (90) days or it will be necessary to file new reservation forms.

Once you have reserved your name you will need to complete and file the Registration of a Business Name form. This form is to be sent to the Companies Office along with the $45.00 fee. You can get the Registration of a Business form (*see Appendices*) here: (http://www.companiesoffice.gov.mb.ca/forms/bnr_e.pdf).

Consumer and Corporate Affairs
Companies Office
Room 1010 - 405 Broadway
Winnipeg, MB R3C 3L6
Telephone: (204) 945-2500
Toll free in MB: 1-888-246-8353
e-mail: companies@gov.mb.ca
Website: http://www.gov.mb.ca/cca/comp_off/index.html

In the **Yukon Territories** a name search must be done to verify availability of the business name before you can register as a business. Registration should also occur before obtaining a business licence. To register a business in the Yukon it will take approximately 24 hours for a name to be searched and for registration to be completed.

Department of Justice
Corporate Affairs
3rd Floor, Andrew Philipsen Law Centre
2134 2nd Avenue
Box 2703
Whitehorse, Yukon Y1A 2C6
Phone: (867) 667-5442
Fax: (867) 393-6251

Municipalities normally require that your business premises be licensed to conduct business within its municipal boundaries in accordance with the bylaws. In some instances, persons may be required to obtain licences in municipalities in which they do not maintain premises but do carry on business. For example, persons involved in direct sales to the consumer should contact each community in which they are doing business. If your business is located in an incorporated municipality (city, town, village or district), obtain a business licence from the municipal business licence office. Please refer to the chart below.

It takes approximately three days to process a business licence.

Yukon Incorporated Municipalities:

Village of Carmacks
Box 113
Carmacks YT Y0B 1C0
Phone: (867)863-6271
Fax: (867) 863-6606

City of Dawson
Box 308
Dawson City YT Y0B 1G0
Phone: (867)993-7400
Fax: (867)993-7434

Village of Haines Junction
Box 5339
Haines Junction YT
Y0B 1L0
Phone: (867)634-2291
Fax: (867)634-2008

Village of Mayo
Box 160
Mayo YT Y0B 1M0
Phone: (867)996-2317
Fax: (867)996-2907

Town of Watson Lake
Box 590
Watson Lake YT Y0A 1C0
Phone: (867)536-7778
Fax: (867)536-7522

Village of Teslin
Box 32
Teslin YT Y0A 1B0
Phone: (867)390-2530
Fax: (867)390-2104

City of Whitehorse
4210 Fourth Avenue (By-law office)
Whitehorse, YT Y1A 1K1
Phone: (867) 668-8316
Fax: (867) 668-8386
Town of Faro
Box 580
Faro YT Y0B 1K0
Phone: (867)994-2728
Fax: (867)994-3154

Any communities not on the chart above are considered to be in an unincorporated area. If you wish to operate your business in an unincorporated area of the Yukon, a business licence is not required.

Operating a business from home requires a business licence and meeting the zoning by-laws controlling property uses in your municipality. There may be restrictions on the use of the land in your home area. For more information about your area, contact your local municipality office.

The Business Licence Applications are available in the Bylaw Services Department of the City of Whitehorse. These applications must be completed and paid for in the Bylaw Services Department. *If the business is going to be run out of your residence, you will be required to complete a supplementary form called a Development Permit.* The Development Permit applies to any residence that is being used as a business. (There is a one time fee for the Development Permit as long as the business continues to be operating from those premises.)

Once the application has been completed and paid for, the application is then taken upstairs to the Planning Department (867) 668-8335. The application is left there along with the Development Permit and once it has been signed off by both the Planning Department and the Building Department it is returned for final approval, typing and distribution. This process typically takes about three days if the paperwork if filled out correctly.

Following are the regulations for running a home-based business in the Yukon which will affect your VA practice:

Specific Use Regulations

The specific use regulations shall apply to all development unless otherwise exempted in this section. Where these regulations may be in conflict with any regulations in a zone or the general regulations, the specific use regulations of this section shall take precedence.

6.1 Home Based Businesses, Minor

6.1.1 All minor home-based businesses shall be accessory uses and must comply with the following:
a. a minor home-based business shall be conducted only within a principal building and no exterior storage or operation of the home-based business shall be permitted;

b. no variation from the residential character and appearance of land or buildings shall be permitted and no external structural change to any principal building or structure for the purpose of accommodating a home-based business shall be permitted;

c. no offensive noise, vibration, smoke, dust, odours, heat, glare, electrical or radio disturbance shall be produced by the home-based business and, at all times, the privacy and enjoyment of adjacent dwellings shall be preserved and the home-based business shall not adversely affect the amenities of the neighbourhood;

d. the minor home-based business shall not generate any vehicular traffic in excess of that which is characteristic of the neighbourhood within which it is located; and

e. an accessory building may be used for minimal storage purposes for the business. A minor home-based business may not be operated from an accessory building. (Bylaw 98-48 passed 99-01-25)

6.1.2 No person other than residents of the principal residence shall be engaged in the minor home-based business.

6.1.3 The home-based business shall not occupy a required parking space and no parking of commercial vehicles larger than 4500 kg gross vehicle weight on or about the site is allowed.

6.1.4 No retail sales shall be permitted in a minor home-based business.

6.1.5 The operator of a minor home-based business may attach one non-illuminated fascia sign to a maximum size of .3 m2 to the principal building advertising the business or, in the case of a RC zone, at the entrance to the driveway.

The process of registering your Business/Trade Name in **Nunavut**, has three main elements:

First is the Name Search. A Nunavut Business Name Search Report should be obtained. This is a search through the Corporate Registry Office records that will determine whether another business is using the name you have selected and where that business is located.

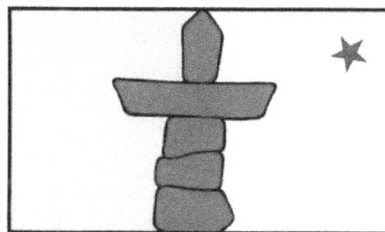

Second, Registration of your Business Name is completed with the Corporate Registry Office.

The third element is the fee to register your Business Name and expedition of your Business License.

Name Search & Reservation: $ 61.24
Registration Fees:$55.00
Our Service Fees: $39.99
GST (6%):$2.39
Total:$ 158.62

To register your Sole Proprietorship in Nunavut, visit http://www.corporateregistries.ca/Nunavut_business_name_registration_service_Order_Form.html. The form accepts Interac and Paypal for the fees. Or call 867.975.6590 for forms and information. The time to process the registration is generally 6 days.

Business Plan

You don't necessarily need to write out a formal business plan, although you do need to plan your business. Planning your business is 100% thinking, analyzing, investigating, choosing and decision-making.

Some benefits of producing a business plan include:

- the process of preparing a business plan will force you to think about your business, research some options, recognize opportunities and risks, and test some of your assumptions;
- a business plan will help you identify the cash needs of your business;
- a business plan can be used to raise funds from banks and investors;
- a business plan provides a benchmark against which to compare the progress and performance of your business.

It is a good idea for all businesses to prepare and regularly update their business plans. There is definitely research to be done, questions to be answered, decisions to be made, goals to be set and plans to be made. Here we go...

TIP: There's a great interactive Business Planner on the web at: http://www.canadabusiness.ca/ibp/ - it's yours for the taking; in English and French.

Elements of a Business Plan

Executive Summary

Business Description

Fictitious VA is a new business located in Your city, Province scheduled to begin operations on September 1, 2004. *Fictitious VA* will be a sole proprietorship, owned by *V*alerie *A*rnold. *Fictitious VA* will provide permanent or temporary part-time business support services to small and medium-sized businesses. Fictitious VA will provide all necessary administrative help to assigned clients such as correspondence, invoicing, data base management, special promotions, direct mail campaigns, telephone solicitation, sourcing and pre-qualifying potential prospects, Internet research (including MLS searches for Real Estate agents). Our mission is to provide our clients with temporary or permanent part-time assistance, replacing an on-site assistant, virtually.

*V*alerie *A*rnold has previous experience as an assistant to several sales executives in the advertising, sales (non-technical and technical) and real estate fields. She has extensive experience in direct marketing, marketing, business development, sales and management and has taken the Canadian Real Estate Course.

Initially *Fictitious VA* will be located in the home of *V*alerie *A*rnold where there is ample office space to accommodate up to three employees.

Ownership and Management

Fictitious VA is a sole proprietorship, owned by *V*alerie *A*rnold. As the business expands it will become incorporated.

*V*alerie *A*rnold has a Bachelor of Arts degree from the University of Western Ontario. Her area of concentration was the Administrative and Commercial Studies program. Over the past 15 years she has completed courses in Print Production, Professional Writing, Managing People, and Time Management, various software packages including Microsoft Word, Excel, PowerPoint, CorelDraw, Print Shop Pro Publisher, various fax software packages and Local Area Networking.

Ms. Arnold's experience in marketing and direct sales will provide the expertise necessary to convey *Fictitious VA*'s message to the marketplace.

Additional staff will be obtained as client demand warrants.

Key Initiatives and Objectives

Fictitious VA is currently in the process of obtaining a $10,000 loan to finance the start up of the business and the purchase of the necessary fixed assets (computer, printer, fax, copier and office furniture). Our key objective during the first 12 months of operation is to develop a strong and consistent client base in order to realize a profit at the end of each month.

Marketing Opportunities

There is currently no real competition for *Fictitious VA* in the local area while there does appear to be great demand. There is great and growing competition within the cyber community. We will concentrate on introducing the concept of our company locally and on the Internet along with its name into a new and emerging market while providing outstanding quality and service to our clients.

Competitive Advantages

Our key competitive advantages are:

1. virtually no direct competition presently in the market.
2. increasing demand of office services to small businesses.
3. low distribution costs using technology and the Internet for distribution of finished product.
4. low overhead costs as *Fictitious VA* will be a home-based business.

Marketing Strategy

Our target markets will be small office or home-based businesses in the area and internationally via the internet. Specific business types that will be targeted are salespeople (area representatives and satellite offices), real estate agents, interior designers, landscapers and private health care professionals (massage therapists, chiropractors, aestheticians, etc.).

With the inclusion of the 'virtual assistant' as part of *Fictitious VA* the market segments are virtually limitless. Self employed, home-based offices, small offices and even large companies who want to occasionally outsource administrative duties to minimize their overhead will use *Fictitious VA*.

Fictitious VA will rely largely on its web presence and its corporate brochure. The brochure will be used in a direct mail campaign targeting small and home-based business. This brochure will also be distributed at networking functions and will be available for downloading from our web site.

Confidentiality and Recognition of Risks

Confidentiality Clause

The information included in this business plan is strictly confidential and is supplied on the understanding that it will not be disclosed to third parties without the written consent of Valerie Arnold.

Recognition of Risk

The business plan represents our best estimate of the future of *Fictitious VA*. It should be recognized that not all major risks can be predicted or avoided and few business plans are free of errors of omission or commission. Therefore, investors should be aware that this business has inherent risks that should be evaluated prior to any investment.

Business Overview

Business History

Fictitious VA is a new business located in Your city, Province scheduled to begin operation on September 1, 2004. *Fictitious VA* will be a sole proprietorship, owned by *V*alerie *A*rnold. *Fictitious VA* will provide permanent or temporary part-time business support services to small and medium-sized businesses. Fictitious VA will provide all necessary administrative help to assigned clients such as correspondence, invoicing, data base management, special promotions, direct mail campaigns, telephone solicitation, sourcing and pre-qualifying potential prospects, Internet research (including MLS searches for Real Estate agents) Our mission is to provide our clients with temporary or permanent part-time assistance, replacing an on-site assistant, virtually.

*V*alerie *A*rnold has previous experience as an assistant to several sales executives in the advertising, sales (non-technical and technical) and real estate fields. She has extensive experience in direct marketing, marketing, business development, sales and management and has taken the Canadian Real Estate Course.

Initially *Fictitious VA* will be located in the home of *V*alerie *A*rnold where there is ample office space to accommodate up to three employees.

Vision and Mission Statement

Our mission is to become a pioneer and leader in this, as yet, uncharted market. We will succeed by providing our clients with invaluable support in order to enable our clients to reach a higher level of success.

Objectives

1. To obtain a bank loan of $10,000 to cover the start-up costs and initial operating costs for *Fictitious VA*.
2. To develop and maintain an Internet web site to outline our services, attract 'virtual' clients and facilitate file transfers and other web-based services.
3. To secure three new clients per month by networking, marketing and direct sales activities.
4. To generate a net profit of $ 20,000 in the first year by developing a strong client base and providing excellent quality and service.

Ownership

Fictitious VA is a sole proprietorship, owned by Valerie Arnold. As the business expands it may become incorporated.

Location and Facilities

Fictitious VA will operate from the home of *V*alerie *A*rnold in order to keep the initial overhead costs low. The home, located at 111 Any Street in City, Province has a large office space that will accommodate up to three employees. The home is presently equipped with one computer, colour printer and fax capabilities. The office is wired for two telephone lines and cabling for Internet connection. Administrative and secretarial needs of *Fictitious VA* will be covered by *V*alerie *A*rnold until such time as additional outside help is necessary.

Once financing is secured, additional computers and photocopier and fax machine will be purchased.

As *Fictitious VA* grows consideration will be given to acquiring office space.

Products and Services

Description of Products and Services

Fictitious VA will offer support services to small businesses, the self-employed and remote or home office employees.
Secretarial:
General office: Preparation and distribution of general office correspondence as well as more complex documents such as spreadsheets. Faxing, mail, email and message service.

Specialized: Transcription, manuscripts, resumes and presentations
Desk Top Publishing: letterhead, business cards, logos, brochures and newsletters
Marketing: direct mail campaigns, bulk mailing, address labels, telemarketing, and newsletter distribution
Database Management: update and maintain database, provide reminder service for appointments, and noteworthy client events such as birthdays
Internet Research: general or specific information research including MLS searches for realtors.
Resume consult and prepare resumes and cover letters
Basic Accounting: bookkeeping, payroll, invoicing and bill payment
Event Planning: conferences, meetings, trade shows, seminars, receptions, dinners and galas
Travel Planning: individual or group travel including provision of detailed itineraries
Proof-reading: spelling and grammar check

Key Features of the Products and Services

Fictitious VA will specialize in the small business and remote office markets offering full service, permanent, part-time assistants with a full range of skills. This will provide a creative, innovative and affective solution with the increase of home office and remote office employees.

Fictitious VA will provide many services over the Internet increasing its target market from the local area to the world.

We will outsource, where necessary, large print jobs, colour print jobs, binding and other services that require a major equipment cost until such time as it becomes cost effective for us to purchase such equipment.
The Service:
Initially all services will be handled by **V**alerie **A**rnold. As demands for our services increase, subcontractors will be engaged with varying areas of expertise. All initial marketing programs and pieces will be developed and implemented by **V**alerie **A**rnold.

The Future

We will continue to expand our services based on client needs. We will continue to research new products and services that will allow us to offer our clients the most up-to-date technology available.

The purchase of colour scanners, printer and copiers will be investigated over time as demand requires.

Production of Products and Services

All production of our finished products will be done by staff at *Fictitious VA*. Initially functions such as high-quality colour copies and binding services will be outsourced.

New employees will provide new in-house expertise as demand from clients indicates.

Future Products and Services

We will continue to expand our services based on client needs. We will continue to research new products and services that will allow us to offer our clients the most up-to-date technology available.

The purchase of colour scanner, printer and copier will be investigated over time as demand requires.

Comparative Advantages in Production

Our comparative advantages in production are low overhead and the use of technology to deliver much of our finished work.

Industry Overview

Market Research

To fully understand the market and determine the feasibility of this venture we researched the Internet for similar businesses and spoke with local home-based workers and small office businesses.

The general trend of home-based workers is increasing as companies down-size while finding it necessary to maintain a local presence. With advances in technology, remote employees are able to maintain contact with their head offices yet require local administrative assistance. Sales professionals will be deliberately targeted as many are operating autonomously, developing and implementing their own marketing programs yet requiring the need to meet head office targets and quotas.

Size of the Industry

There are no office service companies presently operating in the Barrie area. The 'virtual assistant' market is just beginning to emerge on the Internet with a world-wide target market.

With the increase in home-based businesses and remote or home offices the need for virtual and local administrative assistance will continue to grow.

Key Product Segments

Fictitious VA will offer support services to small businesses, the self-employed and remote or home office employees.

Secretarial: General office: Preparation and distribution of general office correspondence as well as more complex documents such as spreadsheets. Faxing, mail, email and message services.

Specialized: Transcription, manuscripts, resumes and presentations.

Desk Top Publishing: letterhead, business cards, logos, brochures and newsletters

Marketing: direct mail campaigns, bulk mailing, address labels, telemarketing, and newsletter distribution

Database Management: update and maintain database, provide reminder service for appointments, and noteworthy client events such as birthdays

Internet Research: general or specific information research including MLS searches for realtors

Resume: consult and prepare resumes and cover letters

Basic Accounting: bookkeeping, payroll, invoicing and bill payment

Event Planning: conferences, meetings, trade shows, seminars, receptions, dinners, galas

Travel Planning: individual or group travel including provision of detailed itineraries

Proofreading: spelling and grammar checks

Key Market Segments

Key target markets for *Fictitious VA* will be small office or home-based businesses in the Barrie area. Specific business types that will be targeted are Sales (area representatives and satellite offices), Real Estate, Interior Design, Landscaping, Private Health Care (massage therapists, aesthetics), Building Contractors, Electricians, Plumbers, Business Consultants to name a few.

With the inclusion of the 'virtual assistant' as part of *Fictitious VA* the market segments are virtually limitless. Self-employed, home-based offices, small offices and even large companies who want to occasionally outsource some of their administrative duties to minimize overhead will use *Fictitious VA*.

Purchase Process and Buying Criteria

The buying process for our services will vary by type of client and by type of service.

Price

Fictitious VA will offer a multi-tier pricing structure.

Quality

Fictitious VA will provide top quality work and fast turn around times. We will build up a variety of references and make these available to potential new clients. Our company's success will depend on repeat business based on high quality output in terms of both product and service.

Service

One of our key 'selling features' will be the ability of our clients to have a permanent part-time assistant while paying only for the time that assistant spends on their work. Clients using this service will be assigned an assistant who will come to know their preferences and personality. This will allow the client to determine and develop, over time, the exact working relationship he or she requires.

Description of Industry Participants

We found no direct competition in the local market. There are several 'Virtual Assistance' companies on the Internet offering various administrative services. Most of these are one person companies offering services that are limited to the capabilities of that individual.

Key Industry Trends

The demand for office services is increasing as companies downsize and outsource work that was historically done in-house but is outside of their core competency. Corporate downsizing combined with advances in technology have also resulted in an increase in employees operating from home offices in order to provide a broader local presence. These home office employees continue to require local administrative assistance.

An additional outcome of corporate downsizing is that many people who have been laid off are starting their own home-based or small businesses, but have come to rely on a high quality of administrative assistance that they are unable to provide for themselves.

Industry Outlook

According to our research, *Fictitious VA* is a pioneer in an emerging industry. Experienced business people starting up their own businesses will recognize the importance of a professional image for their company and understand the cost effectiveness of outsourcing these services.

Marketing Strategy

Target Markets

Our target markets will be small office or home-based businesses in the Barrie area. Specific business types that will be targeted are Sales (area representatives and satellite offices), Real Estate, Interior Design, Landscaping, Private Health Care (massage therapists, aesthetics).

With the inclusion of the 'virtual assistant' as part of *Fictitious VA,* the market segments are virtually limitless. Self employed, home-based offices, small offices and even large companies who want to occasionally outsource some of their administrative duties to minimize overhead will use *Fictitious VA*.

Description of Key Competitors

There is no direct competition to *Fictitious VA* in the Barrie area.

There is growing competition in the 'Virtual Assistant' market across the Internet.

Analysis of Competitive Position

Our prime competitive advantage is that there is little, if any, competition presently in the marketplace.

As the 'Virtual Assistant' market is not our primary interest and this option is offered to our clients to expand our market rather than define it, fierce competition in this area will not be vital to our success.

All Virtual Assistants operate over the Internet with their key marketing tool being their web site. *Fictitious VA* will have a web site online as soon as possible to compete in this market.

Each Virtual Assistant offers services that they are capable of providing. In many cases these services will be limited compared to the varied strengths that *Fictitious VA* plans to secure.

Another key competitive advantage is the experience and abilities of **V**alerie **A**rnold. Ms. Arnold has a Bachelor of Arts degree from the University of Western Ontario concentrating on the Administrative and Commercial Studies program. Her experience as both an assistant and a manager uniquely qualify her to provide the calibre and professional administrative assistance that is required.

Ms. Arnold has spent the past seven years working in the ever-changing computer industry while attaining knowledge of advances in technology and gaining experience in several software programs that will provide her clients with the expertise necessary to advise and fulfil administrative needs.

Pricing Strategy

Fictitious VA will offer a three-tiered pricing structure:
   Hourly Rate: Clients will be billed $35.00 per hour for general and ongoing administrative support. Assistants will keep detailed time sheets that will be provided to clients on a bi-weekly basis. Billing will be calculated in 10 minute

increments. Clients will also be 'charged-back' all stationery and incidental costs such as photocopies, faxes and long-distance telephone calls.

Special Projects: Quotations for special projects will be provided based on the estimated time and the complexity of the project.   All incidental costs associated with the project will be included in the estimate.

A la carte: *Fictitious VA* will offer a general document 'menu' with standard pricing for letters, faxes, photocopies, résumés, etc.

Promotion Strategy

Fictitious VA will employ various promotional strategies simultaneously:

Web Site

This will be developed and posted on-line as soon as possible. The web site will convey our corporate image in addition to listing our services and providing a means of communication to our clients.

Brochure

A corporate brochure will be immediately developed outlining our services and fee structure. The brochure will also highlight our past experience and level of expertise. The brochures will be distributed through personal networking and targeted direct mail.

Direct Mail

Fictitious VA will use a personalized and targeted direct mail approach to various groups such as Real Estate Agents, Insurance Agents, Consultants, Interior Designers, Landscapers, etc.

Networking

Fictitious VA will join local business associations in order to promote services and secure new clients.

Management and Staffing

Organizational Structure

Fictitious VA is a sole proprietorship that will be run and managed by the owner, **V**alerie **A**rnold.

As the client base increases, staff will be hired with experience matching the needs of our clients.

Management Team

Valerie **A**rnold has a Bachelor of Arts degree from the University of Western Ontario. Her area of concentration was the Administrative and Commercial Studies program. Over the past 15 years she has completed courses in Print Production, Professional Writing, Managing People, Time Management, various software packages including Microsoft Word, Excel, PowerPoint, CorelDraw, PrintShop Pro Publisher, various fax software packages and Local Area Networking.

Ms. Arnold's experience in marketing and direct sales will provide the necessary skills to convey *Fictitious VA*'s message to the marketplace.

Ms. Arnold has recently re-located to the Barrie area to start her own business.

Staffing

As the client base grows, additional staff will be hired. The demographics of the client base will determine the skills and level of experience and expertise necessary. New staff will be paid an hourly rate commensurate with their level of education, experience and skills. Once the company has over three employees, a health benefit program will be investigated. Training will be ongoing in regard to software and technology so that *Fictitious VA* is always able to provide clients with the latest and greatest in office technology.

As staff is hired, Ms. Arnold will assume a management role concentrating on marketing of services and growth of the company.

Labour Market Issues

Fictitious VA will use the local business schools placement programs in addition to classified advertising in the local Barrie newspapers to find qualified employees.

Employees will be required to sign a non-competition agreement stating that they will not work with clients of *Fictitious VA* one year following the end of their employment at *Fictitious VA*. A lawyer will provide an appropriate contract for this purpose.

As *Fictitious VA* grows, opportunities to advance will be available to our employees. We will always promote from within where possible.

Implementation Plan

Implementation Activities and Dates

*V*alerie *A*rnold is in the process of obtaining a $10,000 loan to start up *Fictitious VA*. This loan is intended to cover initial start-up costs and the purchase of necessary fixed assets, specifically computer, printer, copier, fax machine, scanner, office furniture and paper cutter.

During the first two months the web site will be developed and the corporate brochure will be produced and distributed via direct mail campaign.

Financial Plan

PRO FORMA INCOME STATEMENT

PROJECTED CASH FLOW STATEMENT

PROJECTED ANNUAL CASH FLOW STATEMENT

PRO FORMA BALANCE SHEET

RATIO ANALYSIS

> Note 1: Revenue Assumptions
>
> Note 2: Assumptions Regarding the Collection of Sales Revenue
>
> Note 3: Cost of Sales Assumptions
>
> Note 4: Sales and Marketing Assumptions
>
> Note 5: Property and Utilities Assumptions
>
> Note 6: Operations Assumptions
>
> Note 7: Banking and Other Assumptions
>
> Note 8: Wages and Other Assumptions
>
> Note 9: Other Sources of Funding
>
> Note 10: Other Uses of Funding

Setting Up Your Office

Your office is a place where you will spend a great deal of time while running your VA practice so you need to ensure that it is both comfortable and fully equipped. The last thing you need during your busy day is to have to go from location to location to work on your equipment or to find necessary files.

If you don't have the option of a designated room in your home for your office, you can always do a nice set-up in the corner of your living room or dining room. Just be sure it is an area where you will not have to move everything in order to serve dinner.

When setting up your new office, you need to have the mindset that you are now "the boss" so your office should reflect that, well...as best that your budget will allow. Even though you may never have a client or associate visit your home office, you should have it arranged in a professional manner just in case the need arises. This may not be a reality at the start of running your business, but you can begin with the basics and then add new pieces as time goes on and, again, as your budget allows.

No matter where in your house you set up shop, you need to make sure that you can separate your area, in some way, from the family area of your home. Even if you are sharing a room for both business and family life, there are steps you can take to try to keep each area as its own. Putting up a screen or makeshift wall is a great way to form a semblance of separation. But, we do still recommend that you try to have your own office in a designated room and we will continue this section of the book with a designated office in mind.

Essentials:

Now that we have determined that you need your own space, which, by the way, you may outgrow some day, let's move on to the essentials you will need. If possible, try to acquire ergonomically correct essentials, such as your furniture and computer equipment. These items can make a huge difference in your comfort level which, in turn, will mean you can perform you work much more effectively.

1. <u>Furniture</u>

You will need to have a desk or work area large enough to hold all of your equipment and paperwork. You will also need to have a chair that you feel comfortable enough to sit in for several hours at a time.

Other furniture required will likely include filing cabinets, storage shelves, and a spare chair for your clients. You may even want to consider a small table that can be used to lay out information during a meeting.

2. <u>Computer</u>

Your computer is the most essential part of your office and your VA business. You must have a fast computer with plenty of space for the various software you will need and the files you will store. It is important that you keep it up to date in order to provide your clients with the best service and outcomes.

The parts of your computer will vary, but you should try to include a CD/DVD drive and preferably a DVD writer drive so you can copy files onto DVDs for clients and use it to back up your files on your computer.

It is highly recommended that you have a cable connection or DSL Internet access. However, if you are situated in an area where neither of these are available, be sure to have a high-performance modem and keep your computer maintained (i.e. disk cleanup, defragment, etc.) to help increase the speed of your dial-up connection.

Graphic, video and sound card preferences and performances depend on the reason you will need them. Most computer packages come with sufficient graphics and sound cards for normal use. However, if you plan on doing a lot of graphic work, you may want to consider a higher quality graphics card.

And, it is recommended to have at least 1gb of RAM. This will help your computer's performance when you are running numerous programs at once.

For a more detailed explanation of How to Buy a Computer can be found beginning on page 47.

3. <u>Peripherals</u>

One thing to remember when you are researching the peripherals you will need is the cost of replacement components. Be sure to check how much it will cost you to get new ink cartridges for your printer or a fax film for your fax machine.

A **colour printer** is essential in a VA business. You may not think you will need it for basic word processing projects, but being creative in your work means you will be adding colour to your documents. You also need to have a good quality printer to provide your clients with a presentable hard copy. The printer should also be able to print as quickly as possible since there is nothing worse than waiting forever for a project.

If you think you may have a need to print pictures, you should consider getting a **photo printer**.

You will also need a **fax machine** or a fax program on your computer. Faxing is a part of business and you need to be able to accept and send faxes.

Your **telephones** are also very important in your business. If you have to use the same phone for both your fax machine and your Internet connection, be sure to install Call Waiting software on your computer. Of course, if you have cable access, you will not have to worry about this.

Try to have a separate phone for your business line. If you use the same phone line for both your business and your personal life, be sure that everyone in the household knows that during regular business hours, the phone is to be answered only by you.

Be sure to have an **answering machine** with a professional message on it connected to your home phone line. Conversely, you can purchase the call answer option that your phone company offers. The nice part is that most of these options can be personalized to suit your needs.

A **scanner** is also another valuable piece of equipment to have in your office. It can be used for many purposes to help you run your business more smoothly and it also allows you to offer scanning services to your clients. We recommend a flatbed scanner which allows you to scan books without having to tear the pages out, a drawback of a sheet fed scanner.

A **photocopier** can also be an asset, but it you have a scanner; you can use it to make necessary copies.

All of the above pieces of equipment can also come in **all-in-one** machines. Some have 3 features, such as a printer, scanner (either flatbed or sheet fed) and a copier, and others also include a fax machine.

Many factors will affect your decision to either get several individual pieces or an all-in-one version. Such deciding factors will include your needs, your available space and your budget.

4. Software

Software is ever-changing and evolving, so you will have to continually stay as close as possible to the top of cutting-edge technology without actually going broke. We aren't saying that you need to run right out and buy the latest version of software as soon as it is released, however, you do need to make sure your arsenal of software includes everything that you will need to get the job done properly.

First and foremost for a VA is some type of office suite. The number of individual programs of the suite you need to use will depend on the services you offer. There will definitely be numerous types of software you will use.

As a VA, the most important software is your **word processing** software. There are several on the market with the most widely used one being Word. You can get office suites that mirror Microsoft programs, but Word is the most popular word processing software on the market and the most compatible with other available software.

Database programs are also an essential; not only for client work, but also to organize your own office. They are a great tool for keeping track of contacts and to develop mailing lists. Microsoft's Access is the most readily available database software and is included in the MS Office Suite. Keep in mind that there are also others, such as ACT.

Spreadsheet software is widely used as well, with MS Excel being the most popular. Not only used to develop spreadsheets, they can also be used to create databases in order to keep track of important information.

Email programs are essential and have a wide range of uses. Of course, you can use them to receive and send email, which you can customize with the various add-ons that are available. You can also use them to schedule yourself and your clients. The most widely used are Outlook and Outlook Express but there are others, such as Eudora.

A word of warning…Outlook Express has a history of being vulnerable to viruses so be sure to keep a virus checker running to scan incoming emails.

Anti-virus software is an absolute must. As most of us are already aware, viruses are emerging every day, and you need to stay protected or you risk losing everything on your computer. Be sure to keep your virus definitions up to date and it is also recommended that you scan your computer for viruses at least a couple of times a week. As mentioned above, be sure to have your anti-virus software scan ALL incoming emails. Even if you trust the source of the email, they could acquire a virus and not even know about it and, in turn, may pass it on to you unknowingly.

Two of the most widely-used anti-virus software programs come to us from both Norton and MacAfee.

We would also recommend **security or firewall software.** You would be amazed at how many people have the capabilities to hack into other people's computers. You may think they only hack into computers of big corporations, but that is no longer the case as small and home computers are now becoming the spot of choice for hackers to attack.

Again, Norton has popular security software, including Norton Security which also includes anti-virus software. There is also a good one available called Zone Alarm.

Other essential software to your business is an **accounting** program. It allows you to keep track of your income and expenses, produce invoicing for your clients, and have everything in one place when it comes time to transfer your files to an accountant for your tax returns or when your business becomes large enough that a specialist should be looking after your bookkeeping.

Some of the most popular accounting programs include QuickBooks and Simply Accounting. These are very user friendly and great for small businesses.

Now, back to office suite software. Others that you will need will include **desktop publishing** software. MS Publisher is the most popular choice and has a fairly easy learning curve. One thing to remember is that if you are sending your design to a commercial printing company, you need to find out what programs they can use since many cannot convert a Publisher file to print.

Other software that you may need will depend on what types of services you are offering. **Slide show presentation** software, such as PowerPoint, can benefit your own business and also allow you to offer presentation development services to clients.

Others include PDF creators and readers, graphic design software, and web page design software. Again, the services you offer will have a direct impact on the software you choose to purchase and use.

We have put together a large list of the many types of software programs that VAs have mentioned using in their own businesses. You can find it in the Appendices.

5. Calendars

A wall calendar is a must for easy access to dates. One with big squares for each day makes it easy to jot down appointments.

A day timer is also an invaluable tool. Unlike a wall calendar which is good for short notes, a day timer allows you the room to jot down information in more detail.

6. Office Supplies

A trip to Staples or any other office supply store will provide you with everything to stock your office. Suggestions to keep on hand include:

- backup supply of inks & ink cartridges
- paper, in various sizes, weights, colours quantities
- envelopes for both regular mailing and for couriers
- pens, pencils, highlighters, and other drawing apparatus
- labels to fit various envelopes and shipping containers
- stapler, staples & stapler remover
- sticky notes and note pads
- paper clips, bulldog clips, ruler
- letter opener and postage for both Canada & the U.S.

Non-Essentials

1. Miscellaneous Equipment

There are other pieces of non-standard equipment which, depending on the services you offer and the types of projects your clients need, you may need to acquire; for instance, a **typewriter**. Word Processing software is usually used for most tasks that involve typing but some printed material may require the impact that a typewriter offers (i.e. three-part carbonless forms, etc.).

Another piece of electronic equipment that you may need is a **calculator**. If you plan to offer bookkeeping services or any other services using numbers, you should consider a calculator that has a print-out tape capability.

In order to keep your office organized, you should consider various forms of storage, such as **CD/DVD storage units** for your software or computer backup files and **filing boxes** for older files or in place of filing cabinets.

2. Gadgets

A great little gadget for your desk is a **Rolodex**, preferably one that will allow you to place in business cards rather than having to re-write the information out on separate cards. Using a little hole punch will allow the cards to fit directly into the Rolodex.

A **headset** for your telephone is another useful item. If you spend a great deal of time on the phone or if you are trying to type while talking on the phone, you will find that a headset considerably reduces the strain on your neck and shoulders, not to mention your ear.

Miscellaneous Tasks

Now that you have all of the essentials, you move onto:

1. Making Your Space Your Own

Add pictures of your family and mementos that will help to inspire you and bring a smile to your face. Give your office a homey feeling but keep in mind that this is also a place of business so don't go overboard.

Because it is a place of business, be sure to display your business accomplishments. If you have certificates or awards, put them up on your walls.

2. Make Sure Your Space is Well Lit

Be sure that your office has plenty of lighting, especially in your work area. Fluorescent lighting is a great source for overall lighting. If you find that your computer area is still not bright enough, try using a desk lamp beside your computer.

Brightening or dimming your computer screen can also help if you find you are straining your eyes. Another consideration is an anti-glare screen.

3. Getting Connected

Contact your phone company and arrange to have them come in and install your phone lines for your business telephones. Also, arrange for your Internet connection with your Internet Service Provider (ISP).

4. Choosing Your Decor

Keep the colour scheme in the lighter tones. Light colours help to produce a calming atmosphere, which can reduce your stress levels. However, as your office will be well traveled by you, as well as your family and your visitors, be sure that you have a darker (but not too dark) colour for your carpeting. Better yet, use a low-pile carpet, tile or hardwood flooring. All of these will help to keep the evidence of high traffic to a minimum.

No matter what you decide to include in your office, be sure that you set it up in an organized fashion. Keep the clutter to a minimum and be sure that everything you regularly use is at arms' reach. This will result in your day running more smoothly. Be sure that the atmosphere is professional, not only for the appearance for your visitors, but also because it will help to keep you grounded and in a business state-of-mind.

5. <u>Safety in Your Home-Office</u>

While working in a home office, you need to be aware of safety concerns. Do not list your home address on your website or other marketing materials. For a nominal fee you can get a post office box to handle your mail. Only give out your address to people with whom you are directly dealing.

If you need to meet with a new client, try to choose a location that is both professional and safe. Your local executive suites will usually have offices or small meeting spaces available for hourly rent. This is in inexpensive way to present a very professional image in a safe environment.

If this is not an option due to lack of availability or financial concerns, then you may want to opt for meeting in a public place such as a restaurant or coffee shop.

It is not recommended to ever invite a stranger into your home or go to visit their home-office. If it is necessary to have someone that you don't know to your home office, there are things you can do to provide some measure of security:

1. Ask a fellow VA to call you, periodically, during the meeting time to ensure you are comfortable with the situation.
2. Set up MSN with the video camera powered up so a fellow VA or other personal friend can keep an eye on the situation.
3. Invite another person to be there during the meeting.

How to Buy a Computer

Your computer is the most important part of your office and VA business. You need to have a system which operates quickly with plenty of space for the various software programs you will need and the files you will store. It is essential to keep your computer up-to-date in order to provide your clients with the best possible service and outcomes.

When choosing a computer, there is more involved than simply walking into a store and picking one that looks cool.

1. Your first step is to decide "when" you need a computer. If you are just beginning your business, the fact that you need a computer is a given. However, if you have been in business for a few years and have been using your computer for some time, you will probably find at some point that it's time to get a new one. Most of us will know when this is since our computers start to lag.

Examples of such experiences are when your software doesn't work with your current operating system or when the fan or CPU decides to call it quits. These signs and perhaps others are an indication that you may be ready for a new system.

2. You then need to decide if you want to get a desktop computer or a laptop. If you tend to travel to clients' offices, a laptop may be the better choice. Or, if you are just starting out and don't have an office set up yet, a laptop may be a good choice so you can move it around. Keep in mind that your budget will influence your purchasing decision and, as laptops are generally more expensive than desktops (and harder to upgrade), a laptop may not be an option.

3. You next need to choose where you want to shop. Keep your eyes open for flyers from computer stores as well as online savings. Purchase your computer from a reputable store or website or from someone who has been referred to you by a trusted source. If you or someone you know has the ability to build a computer, you can pick up the parts and it may not cost as much as a pre-made computer. However, you probably won't get the warranty that you would get from a computer store and/or manufacturer.

Now that you have made the decision to shop for a new computer, you need to decide what options to include with your computer. Some of the features you need will depend on what you will be doing with your computer.

1. CPU – Your processor is the part of your computer that will offer you the speed you need to accomplish your tasks. The faster the better however, the faster the more expensive. By today's standards, you need to have a minimum of 2.4 to 3.0 GHz in order to run the various office software. If you plan to run graphics, web design or video editing software, you may want to consider a higher CPU rate. If possible, a dual core processor would be a tremendous asset as would increasing your computer's speed.

2. RAM – Random Access Memory... the part of your computer that runs your programs. The more programs you run, the slower your computer will be, so you need to have sufficient RAM to keep things running smoothly. A minimum of 2gb of RAM is required for most software applications; however, many people have 4, 8 or more GB of RAM on their computers.

   There are different "types" of RAM. Many pre-built computers come with DDR RAM these days with the most common being DDR3.

   Also, when you are choosing your computer, ensure that your RAM is expandable. You may need to upgrade your memory at some point without actually getting another new computer so be sure you can expand your RAM. (Don't you wish we could do that with the memory in our heads, especially as we grow older?) ☺.

3. Hard Drives – This is the "space" on your computer that will hold your software and files. As software applications continue to advance and include more features, they get larger and as you work on images and graphics, they will take up more room. This means you need to be sure you not only have enough room for what you have now, but also for what you will add during

the next few years. You can, of course, add more hard drives later on, but why bother when you can add a good size hard drive now? Aim for a

minimum of 500GB (which may seem excessive, but you would be surprised at how fast that fills up).

4. Secondary Drives – Also called Optical Drives, these are the CD and DVD drives that you will need. Most of today's systems include a DVD burner that can usually handle both DVDs and CDs. However, you need to ensure that the burner supports both +R/RW and –R/RW DVDs. You also want to be sure the speed is fast enough since a 4x drive just won't cut it. You need to have at least 16x the recordable speed with even higher numbers providing faster recording speeds (and a higher price). If you feel that you don't need a DVD burner, try a CD burner with a DVD player... a CD-RW/DVD combo drive. Also, if you plan to copy from CD to CD or DVD, you need to consider having two optical drives.

5. Video Card – Deciding on the extent of the video card you need will be determined by what you want it for and how you will be using it. If you plan to do video playing or recording or you plan on working with software such as Flash, you want to have a video card with a high performance. Also, if you have a digital LCD screen and/or you want to use multiple screens, you should ensure that your video will be able to handle it. Video cards are constantly changing, so choose one that will be adequate for your needs in the future (at least 128mb of memory that supports the current and future versions of DirectX) and be sure to constantly check for driver updates.

6. Monitors – Once again you have a multitude from which to choose. Monitors come in a full range of sizes, from 15 inches all the way up to 55 inches (the largest size at time of printing). Also available are LED (Light Emitting Diodes) and LCD (Liquid Crystal Display) monitors. Both are flat screen designs and provide great clarity and colour. Not to mention, as they grow in popularity, prices are dropping. When purchasing any monitor, look for at least a 22" screen that is capable of displaying 1280x1024 pixels.

Dual Monitors is also a good option if you have the budget for it as it will highly increase your productivity speed. You'll have to make sure your audio card supports dual monitors.

7. USB Ports & Firewire – Many peripherals that you will attach to your computer (i.e. printer, webcam, keyboard, etc.) will have USB cables. As a result, you need to make sure that you have plenty of USB (4 - 6 ports minimum). Firewire is also popular these days, although it is not as readily available as USB. You should have at least one or more.

8. Peripherals and other devices – Of course, there are a number of other peripherals available on the market for your computer. What you decide is important will be more a matter of preference and individual taste than necessity (i.e. printer, keyboard, webcam, etc.).

Deciding On and Developing Your Services

A vital step when developing your business is to decide which services you will offer and how you can build upon these services.

A majority of VAs have many, many years of experience. While acquiring these years of skill, many have also honed their expertise in specific services known as **Core Services**. These are the services around which your marketing efforts should centre. They will be your prime revenue generator, and as such, should be the ones to which you give the most attention.

Other tasks with which you have experience should also be included in your arsenal of services. Remember that these are considered your **Secondary Services** and should not be the services on which you will concentrate your marketing efforts.

While running your business, your main concentration will be on your Core services. However, you should also feel free to accept projects that may involve a service in which you do not have experience or which lay at the more advanced end of the secondary services that you offer. If you find that a situation similar to this arises, remember that there is a huge network of fellow VAs available to you who have various and unique specialties they can offer you. We take pride in being able to take the administrative load off the shoulders of our clients, so be sure to 'practice what you preach' and outsource to a fellow VA any of those tasks that are over your head.

With that being said, the following is a large list of services that are being performed by VAs all over the globe:

General Word Processing: This is the most common service offered by VAs, and is the one needed by the majority of VA clients. Examples – memos, letters, and manuals.

Enhanced Word Processing: This service goes beyond simply typing and formatting documents. With added skills, you can produce more intricate documents, such as spreadsheets.

Desktop Publishing: Applying your creativity using desktop publishing software can allow you to produce eye-catching documents, such as business cards and newsletters.

Transcription: Tape, midi, and phone transcription will require that you have some type of transcription machine. You may be able to get away without this type of machine, but if you are going to specialize in transcription, investing in a professional machine will be worth the cost. Examples include medical and legal transcription.

Writing: This service has many facets and has the added bonus of utilizing your unique talents to help increase your own exposure. As a service, you can assist in business, technical, academic and even ghost writing while also providing editing services.

Database Creation & Management: Most VAs can provide basic contact management database for clients. However, some have the expertise to specialize in the creation of intricate databases that allow for everything automated, including report generation and inventory management.

Bulk Mailings: You may need to create a database in order to offer this service. It can involve everything from printing documents and labels to stuffing envelopes and making a trip to the post office.

Bookkeeping: Another specialized service, bookkeeping, can be offered to your clients to help keep their accounting needs in order. This may involve creating and mailing invoices, keeping track of payables and receivables, and paying your clients' bills.

Phone Answering: Being in the same time zone as your client can be beneficial when you offer this service, but it's not a necessity. It may involve the need to acquire new phones, phone lines, or an add-on phone line with a special ring. The needs of each client will differ and may require you to be available during regular business hours.

Office Management: This service has no definite description, as each circumstance is unique. It involves most tasks that an in-house assistant offers and that are listed here as individual services, such as answering phones, providing word-processing, and even some amounts of design-work or bookkeeping.

Website Design: Creativity is an essential trait of web design. This service can include designing and maintaining websites, search engine optimization and submitting a client's site to directories and search engines.

Email Management: When a client is planning to take a holiday, no matter what other services you offer, be sure to let them know you can keep their incoming email organized. For example, you can weed out the junk and provide a response to those who require it. Your client simply needs to forward an email address to you. At your end, you can designate a folder in your email program where all their email will go, thus keeping it organized and available if your client calls and wants to know "what's new?"

Marketing/Advertising: As a small business professional, you have dealt with your own share of marketing, so why not offer some help to your clients as well? If you have a background or specialty in the marketing or advertising field, then this would be a beneficial service to offer.

Internet Research: Providing results from online inquiries can involve personal research, business-related research or academic research and may require special formatting.

Graphic Design: Specialty software and a creative outlook are needed to produce such images as a company logo that can be used in both print and online applications.

Proofreading/Editing: Proofreading can involve visually reading through documents to locate spelling, grammatical and formatting errors. Editing goes a step further and involves inputting the necessary content to keep the story flowing smoothly.

Translation: If you are lucky enough to be able to speak and write in another language besides English, then be sure to let your potential clients know you have that skill.

Presentation Preparation: Provide your clients with either print or media presentations that will help enhance their marketing or teaching efforts. Desktop publishing software can be used to produce printed presentations. However, PowerPoint allows you to not only produce a slideshow presentation, but to also have the option of printing the slides so your client can provide handouts.

Computer Training/Tutoring: As you run your business, you will acquire skills in various software applications. This knowledge can allow you to offer assistance to clients and others. You can also help clients with the day-to-day operation of their computers by passing on some of your experience to them. This service can also be a specialty if you have expertise in such applications.

Photocopy Service: Most VAs can offer a few copies here and there by using a scanner and a printer, but you will definitely need to invest in a good photocopier or lease one if you want to do bulk printings at an economical rate.

Meeting & Event Planning: Your target market when you offer event or meeting planning will be larger companies or associations. You could also offer smaller gathering assistance for such events as weddings or parties. Event planning includes the ability to organize venues, arrange accommodations, and co-ordinate any catering or event add-ons.

Public Relations: This service allows you to assist your clients with their exposure. As small business owners, we must tackle our own publicity, but that does not make us experts. This service is best offered by those who have training and a great deal of experience. This service can involve everything from writing and distributing press releases to arranging radio and television show appearances.

Scheduling: Organizational skills are a must for all VAs but never so much as when you offer scheduling services. As your business builds, you will not just be keeping track of schedules for the odd person. You can expect to be keeping the lives of many people organized and running smoothly.

Resumes & Cover Letters: You will be required to know the various forms of resumes that are commonplace for the target employers of your clients. A necessity for your client will be multiple copies and electronic formats, such as putting these documents on CD.

Fax Services: You will need to be aware of long distance costs if you are going to offer outgoing fax services. Costs for fax machine supplies and maintenance needs will affect your rates if you offer an incoming fax service.

Scanning: Scanning of graphics and content is something that every VA should know how to accomplish. OCR scanning is a convenient and time-saving task in comparison to having to retype any large amounts of text. In addition, scanning graphics gives you the opportunity to use pictures and logos in your correspondence. Once you have mastered scanning, offering it as a service is the next logical step.

PDF Conversions: You will need either the full version of Adobe's Acrobat PDF Writer or a PDF printer driver or software. The full version offers all options for creating interactive PDF documents. The other available drivers and software available that produce PDF documents may not allow you to create full interaction. Such products that you can create in PDF include newsletters, registration forms, and even ebooks.

There are many, many more services available which can be offered by VAs to their clients. Basically, any service that you can offer to help alleviate some of their workload which may be taking them away from doing tasks that generate revenue is a good service and one they will soon learn they can't live without.

Having all of these skills is great, but you also have to be prepared to **keep your skills at a level that will compete with others** offering these services. Keeping track of the latest software available and most widely used skills is a must, and you need to keep them current.

Taking **online courses** or reading ebooks and tutorials can help in upgrading your skills. There are many Internet-based training and educations facilities. (See our Resources section)

Subscribing to specific **newsletters** is also a great way to hear the latest. There are many industry-specific and technical newsletters that keep track of changes in technology, new products and services.

You can also subscribe to **daily tips** for the software or hardware you are using. **News feeds** can also be an important resource.

Staying informed at **online forums** will show, right from the trenches, what others are using and how these resources help to improve the services they offer. This is especially true on VA **email discussion lists**.

Specialty industries require Specialty Services

There has been great discussion within the VA industry regarding niche marketing. A niche market is a specialized targeted market. There are two schools of thought. The first is that by selecting a niche market you are limiting yourself as to the clients you will market to. The other argument is that by setting yourself up as a generalist you actually limit the clients you attract because general advertising doesn't 'speak' directly to anyone in particular. By selecting a specific target market you will use language that your market will relate to. In this chapter we will discuss the benefits and ways to target a niche market.

The niche industries that can use the help of a virtual assistant, and the targeted services you can provide them, are endless. Everyone from authors to coaches to lawyers, and all kinds of entrepreneurs in between, can take advantage of the services that VAs have to offer. With so many industries out there, you can improve your chances of success by thinking about offering specialized services that focus on the greatest needs of the specific industry that your talents can best be used in... your niche market.

For instance, if you spent the past several years of your administrative career working for a law firm, you have gathered a multitude of experience in the various tasks that need to be performed for the attorneys in that firm. There are countless attorneys out there who have their own small practices and need the occasional (or ongoing) assistance with their administrative tasks that you can now target.

In every industry, entrepreneurs generally need to concentrate on working on client tasks and projects which often means that they let important aspects of their own businesses slide. A Virtual Assistant can help business professionals to keep their businesses organized by offering everything from the basic administrative tasks to web design (because every business needs a website to sustain success). However, there are also specific services that each industry could use help with so we have included some of those services below.

Also, when thinking of targeting any industry, you will need to get your information in front of them in order to not only share how you can help them but also to educate the industry on the value of working with a Virtual Assistant. The following are just some of the associations, organizations and websites that you may want to consider becoming a member of (if they allow members from outside the industry), offering seminars and webinars to, writing articles or contributing to their blogs or publications, all in an effort to educate their members on the advantages of working with a Virtual Assistant. It is also a great way to get your name in front of the members so they have someone to turn to when they realize the benefits of having their own VA.

Accountants

Specialized services:

- bookkeeping
- creating spreadsheets
- designing graphics
- developing and maintaining databases of clients and contacts
- design and keep their company website and blog updated
- help with network marketing campaigns
- receive and address emails inquiries
- produce and implement marketing initiatives
- etc.

Industry Associations, Organizations & Websites:

- American Accounting Association - http://www.aaahq.org/
- Australian Society of CPAs - http://www.cpaaustralia.com/
- British Accounting Association - http://www.bham.ac.uk/
- Canadian Institute of Chartered Accountants - http://www.cica.ca/index.aspx
- Federation des Experts Comptables Europeens - http://www.fee.be/
- IA International - http://www.accountants.org/
- International Federation of Accountants - http://www.ifac.org/

Artists

Specialized services:

- Research appropriate galleries for a showing
- Arrange all details of the gallery showing
- Set up EBay auctions to sell art
- Make travel arrangements for artists
- Maintain artist's website to include new artwork, testimonials, sales, etc.
- Develop marketing and network marketing campaigns

Industry Associations, Organizations & Websites:

- Artist Universal - http://artistuniversal.com/
- Artists Helping Artists - http://www.artistshelpingartists.org
- Artists in Stained Glass - http://www.aisg.on.ca/
- Highlands Art Union - http://www.highlandsart.com/
- International Fine Art Guild - http://www.fineartguild.com/
- International Plein Air Painters - http://ipap.homestead.com/
- Nature Printing Society - http://www.natureprintingsociety.info
- Oil Pastel Association International - http://www.opai.org/
- More can be found at http://www.artshow.com/orgs/

Architects

Specialized services:

- Handle printing of important blueprints
- Courier required documents to anywhere in the world
- Arrange in-person and virtual meetings with clients
- Answer and respond to incoming emails and phone calls
- Design marketing material

Industry Associations, Organizations & Websites:

- American Society of Architectural Illustrators - http://www.asai.org/
- Architectural Association of Ireland - http://www.aai-ireland.com/
- ArchiwebSA - http://www.saia.org.za/
- Building Designers Association of Australia Ltd. - http://www.bdaa.com.au/
- Canadian Center for Architecture - http://cca.qc.ca/
- New Zealand Institute of Architects - http://www.nzia.co.nz/
- Organization of Women Architects and Design Professionals
- The Royal Institute of British Architects

Attorneys

Specialized services:

- Develop specialized databases of clients, contacts
- Work with law related documents
- Electronic filing of documents
- Maintain attorney schedules
- Arrange in-person, phone and virtual meetings
- Dictation and transcription

Industry Associations, Organizations & Websites:

- ALFA International - http://www.alfainternational.com/
- All China Lawyers Association - http://www.chineselawyer.com.cn/
- ALPHA Universal - http://www.alphauniversal.org
- Eurojuris International - http://www.eurojuris.net/eng/default.asp
- European Women Lawyers Association - http://www.ewla.org
- European Association of Attorneys - http://www.aeuropea.com
- Global Affiliation of Independent Lawyers - http://www.tanandtanlawyers.com
- International Bar Association - http://www.ibanet.org
- International Law Association - http://www.ila-hq.org
- International Lawyers Network - http://www.iln.com

Authors

Specialized services:

- Digital and analog dictation/transcription
- Fact checking and other researching
- Coordinate your peer and audience review
- Research potential publishers
- Prepare the manuscript to publisher requirements
- Review final proof / printers proof
- Get the copyright registered
- Register ISBN number
- Create virtual book launches and book tours
- Organize Social Marketing Campaigns
- Coordinate promotional activities
- Track your book sales

Industry Associations, Organizations & Websites:

- Canadian Author's Association - http://www.canauthors.org
- International Association of Aspiring Authors - http://www.associationofaspiringauthors.com
- International Association of Writers - http://www.associationofwriters.com
- American Author's Association - http://www.americanauthorsassociation.com
- Australian Society of Authors - http://www.asauthors.org

- The Society of Authors - http://www.societyofauthors.org
- American Institute of Architects (AIA) - http://www.aia.org

Building/Construction

Specialized services:

- Bookkeeping
- Answering emails and phone calls
- Mass mailings
- Event planning
- Helping with project management including scheduling, estimating, job cost accounting, prime and subcontract preparation, DEQ compliance, permitting
- Dealing with vendors

Industry Associations, Organizations & Websites:

- Confederation of International Contractors' Association - http://www.cica.net
- International Construction Information Society - http://www.icis.org
- Canadian Construction Association - http://www.cca-acc.com
- Design Build Institute of America - http://www.dbia.org
- National Association of Women in Construction - http://www.nawic.org
- Construction Association of Mexico (CMIC) - http://www.cmic.org

Coaches

Specialized services:

- Scheduling
- Ezine and Newsletter Design and Management
- Teleclass and Webinar Assistance
- Transcription
- PowerPoint Presentations
- Contact Management
- Copywriting and Editing
- Marketing and Publicity

Industry Associations, Organizations & Websites:

- International Coach Federation - http://www.coachfederation.org
- International Coaching Council - http://www.international-coaching-council.com
- International Business Coach Institute - http://www.businesscoachinstitute.org
- Worldwide Association of Business Coaches - http://www.wabccoaches.com

- Professional Coach & Mentors Association -
  http://www.pcmaonline.com
- Association of Coaching - http://www.associationforcoaching.com
- American Federation of Coaches - http://www.americanfedcoaches.org
- International Association of Coaches - http://www.certifiedcoach.org
- More links can be found at http://www.mentors.ca/coachorgs.html

Doctors/Dentists

Specialized services:

- Scheduling appointments & meetings
- Travel Arrangements
- Phone or Email Reminders
- Contact Management
- Researching
- Creating Invoices
- Record Maintenance
- Paper work and reports
- Desktop publishing (flyers, documents etc.)
- Proof Reading

Industry Associations, Organizations & Websites:

- Association of International Physicians and Surgeons of Ontario -
  http://www.aipso.ca/
- World Medical Association - http://www.wma.net/
- Canadian Association of Physicians Assistants - http://www.caopa.net/
- Canadian Medical Association – http://www.cma.ca
- Australia Medical Association - http://www.ama.com.au/
- American Medical Association - http://www.ama-assn.org/
- New Zealand Medical Association - http://www.nzma.org.nz/
- More links can be found at http://www.wma.net/e/members/list.htm

Insurance Agents

Specialized services:

- Arranging Conventions
- Diary Management
- Digital Transcription
- Electronic Forms
- Grant Writing
- Invoicing
- Newsletters
- OCR
- Payroll
- Phone-in Dictation
- Presentations
- Procedural Documentation

- Proof Reading
- Time Management
- Transcription
- Travel Arrangements

Industry Associations, Organizations & Websites:

- Insurance Canada - http://www.insurance-canada.ca
- Association of Online Insurance Agents - http://www.aoia.com/
- American Insurance Association - http://www.aiadc.org/
- Association of Risk and Insurance Managers of Australia - http://www.arima.com.au/
- Insurance Institute of London - http://www.iilondon.co.uk
- National Association of Insurance and Financial Advisors - http://www.naifa.org/

Realtors

Specialized services:

- Real Estate Transaction Coordination
- Blog Creation & Maintenance
- Social Media Marketing
- Listing Marketing
- Create CMAs
- Top Producer management
- Lead Follow-Up & Tracking
- Pre-listing & Broker Price Opinion
- Create Just Listed and Just Sold cards
- Real Estate Design Services
- Drip E-Mail Campaigns
- Autoresponders
- Create newsletters
- Contact Database Management
- Manage FSBO and/or Expired programs
- Online Transaction Coordination
- Write and place ads

Industry Associations, Organizations & Websites:

- National Association of Realtors - http://www.realtor.org/
- Canadian Real Estate Association - http://www.crea.ca/
- International Real Estate Federation - http://www.fiabci.com/
- Real Estate Institute of Australia - http://www.reiaustralia.com.au/
- Real Estate Institute of New Zealand - http://www.reinz.org.nz/

Speakers

Specialized services:

- Marketing and Promotional Materials
- Web Design
- Social Media Set Up and Management
- Direct Marketing Campaigns
- Venue research and negotiation
- Travel Arrangements

Industry Associations, Organizations & Websites:

- Canadian Association of Professional Speakers - http://www.canadianspeakers.org/
- National Speakers Association - http://www.nsaspeaker.org/
- American Speaker's Association - http://www.speakersbureau.com
- American Seminar Leaders Association - http://www.asla.com
- International Association of Speakers Bureaus - http://www.iasbweb.org

Determining Your Rates

How much should you charge?

One of the most difficult decisions you have to make is how much to charge your clients. There are several questions to ask yourself when you are trying to determine how much to charge:

First and foremost, **how much is your competition charging?** You want to be sure to stay competitive. By doing a little research, you can find out what others in the VA industry are charging. But, you don't want to charge less than the average going rate or you may be viewed as not experienced enough to provide the professionalism that your potential clients are looking for and that your competitors offer; which brings us to the next consideration when deciding on **your rates.**

What is your experience? Your education and positions you held while out in the workforce as well as your experience as a VA and small business owner will help to determine what your rates will be in comparison to the range of pricing that current VAs charge. If you are a fairly new Virtual Assistant and your work experience is limited, you may choose to charge lower on the scale of rates. However, if you have been an administrative assistant for many years and have an expertise in a particular service, your logical choice would be to charge more...charge what you are worth.

What kind of shape is your local economy in? Although you offer your services virtually, your local market is going to be the hardest to convince that you are worth every penny. You don't want to charge more than what your local market is willing to pay.

"*Anything about the income you make as a VA (good or bad)*: If you are willing to work hard you can make money as a VA. I don't know that you would make the same if you were working for someone else. I've always been a one-person operation and like working that way. I like that I can limit the number of clients that I can deal with and am able to build not only a working relationship but also a personal one with my clients.

It's frustrating seeing that some VAs price themselves too low. They under estimate their value and themselves. Many people interested in starting a VA business do so because they think it is so easy and all you need is a computer and some skills. If you are dedicated and willing to put forth an effort to promote yourself and continually educate yourself, I feel that you can make a decent living as a Virtual Assistant."

Francesca Frate, Owner/Operator
AdminConcepts - Your Administrative Connection
http://www.adminconcepts.net

How should you bill your clients?

There are different ways to bill your clients. The way in which you bill and receive payments from your clients is your choice and should be determined by what is best for you and your clients. Each situation and client relationship will be different, and may even require unique financial arrangements.

First, let's take a look at the various ways that you can keep track of what you do for each client and how you will bill them.

1. **Hourly:** For this form of tracking and billing, you will need to keep track of each minute that you work on a client's project. Then you add it all up when it comes time to invoice your client. How you choose to keep track is again your choice. Some VAs choose to write down each time they start and stop working on a certain project while others choose to use time-tracking software.

2. **Quotation/Contract:** Some projects will require that you provide a bulk figure quotation and then sign a contract outlining what you will be doing and how much you will charge for it. Be sure your contract is specific regarding what is involved in the project and the details. Also, be sure to note that if any additions to what was agreed upon are required, you will bill for these over and above your quote.

3. **Retainer Billing:** When providing a client with the option of a retainer agreement, he or she will provide you with a lump sum and, as the work is done, you will deduct the time spent from the retainer fee. Some clients prefer to pay you this way and then receive an invoice from you when the retainer amount is running low.

   You may also choose to hold restrictions on your retainer agreement. For instance, you may choose to hold a retainer fee for a certain amount of time and, if that time runs out but the retainer fee doesn't, that amount then becomes yours and the balance of the account goes to zero. After all, when you take on a retainer, your client is essentially telling you that they will have enough work for you over the time period to match the retainer. And, as you are assuming you will be doing that amount of work over the period, you may pass up other assignments that you will not have time to do. Therefore, you may lose income. That income is the retainer fee.

4. **Monthly Fee:** If you have steady clients whose administrative tasks you most handle, charging a monthly fee can help you both. This enables your client to budget, as they will know what they will be charged each month. For you, this means not having to worry about keeping track of the time you spend on each of his/her projects. Some months you may do more than the agreed-upon estimate and some months you may do less.

   However, it may be a good idea to keep track of your time simply to evaluate if you are both on track with what has been agreed. If you find that you are working more than was expected when the fee was established, it may be time to revisit the issue with your client.

5. **Bartering:** You may want to consider this option, especially during the start-up phase. Many times you will need a product or service that may be out of your budget. If you can arrange to exchange your services for those needed products, you can save money and also increase your skill level and portfolio.

When should you bill?

Another aspect when deciding how to bill your clients is deciding when to build your clients. This will be something that both you and your client will decide upon. Whichever is most convenient for your client should be the first consideration. As well, for some of these options you should make sure you have a signed contract outlining what is expected and when and how payments will be made.

For **retainer** clients, you will either bill your clients when the money has run out or when the retainer period has ended.

For **quotations or contracts**, you may require a deposit at the beginning of the project and the balance when the project is completed. If the client is new, you may choose to be sure that payment has been received before you hand over the final outcome. If the project is large, it might be a good idea to split the payments over a pre-determined time period.

For **hourly** clients, you have several options. You can bill them based on time elapsed (i.e. weekly, bi-weekly, monthly, etc.), at the end of a project, or when a certain dollar figure has been reached.

If you charge a **monthly fee**, you will bill on the same date each month. More often than not, you should bill at the end or beginning of the month. However, if it is more convenient for your client, consider billing mid-month.

What type of payment methods should you accept?

Most of your clients will be able to provide you with a business cheque, but when you first start working with a new client, you may want to make sure that there are no problems with any payment. After all, you know as much about them as they do about you. It takes time to build trust and a relationship.

If you are leery about accepting a business cheque, you may choose to accept other forms of payment. These can include a certified cheque, money order, credit or debit card, or even cash.

Be sure that both you and your client understand how payment will be processed before beginning any projects. A misunderstanding regarding preferred payment methods could cause unwanted problems. It might be a good idea to have something in writing, including that you require the balance of the fee be paid to you prior to handing the project over to your client.

Should you provide a contract?

In short, yes! Contracts are the insurance policies of the business world. Whether you compile the contract (which is recommended) or your client does, it is a means of ensuring that everyone understands exactly what is required by the client and what will be supplied by you.

Information that you may want to include would be: both yours and your clients contact information, total contract price including payment schedule, currency of payment, and payment methods, length of the contract, exemptions or additional services and of course, an outline of what services will be included.

Templates of contracts can be found in various locations on the Internet or you may be able to get them from your fellow VAs. You may also want to draft up your own contract templates and adjust them as needed for each project. If necessary, view contracts from other sources to get ideas.

If you are providing a variety of services for your client (i.e. web design, word processing, etc.), you can consider having a contract for each service or set of services. You may offer different rates for different services so a contract for each will help to keep the details clear.

What about all the extras you provide?

Well...that depends. Certain tasks and extras with which you provide your clients will be all part and parcel of the services you provide.

However, sometimes there are aspects of a project that crop up and may be over and above the agreed-upon fee.

Extras can include postage, freight, printing costs, phone and long distance charges, traveling expenses, and even consulting charges. If you find that you are spending a great deal of time typing explanatory emails or consulting with your client on the phone, you may want to consider adding this time to your fees.

Should I be adding taxes to my invoices?

As you are providing a service and not a product, you are not required to pay the government provincial retail sales tax. If at any point you decide to sell a tangible product, you will need to register for a sales tax number. This is something that you can investigate further if you do decide to sell a product. As most VAs are only selling a service, we will not go into any further detail regarding sales tax.

However, every business needs to consider a Goods & Services Tax (GST) or Harmonized Sales Tax (HST) number. When your business begins to gross $30,000 per year, you must register for a GST/HST number and you must remit GST/HST payments to the Canadian government.

Prior to reaching the $30,000 mark, whether or not you register and file GST/HST remittances is your choice. There are pros and cons to starting early or waiting until later.

As soon as you register for a GST/HST number, you must submit regular remittances. During the start-up phase of your business it may not seem like a benefit for you to collect and remit GST/HST. However, think of all the expenses that you have during those first few years of business. For every purchase, you will be paying GST/HST. Why not claim that on a remittance? And, as you will not be billing a huge amount of GST/HST, you may receive rebates for the first little while. Once your expenses level off and your billing increases, you may soon have to pay out GST/HST with your remittance.

Speaking of which, one of the main drawbacks of charging GST/HST when you start your business is that you will have to charge GST/HST to your clients. This could also be an advantage, as your regular clients will pay GST/HST right from the start of your relationship and will not have to deal with a price increase from you, in the form of GST/HST, when the time comes.

One other disadvantage of early GST/HST registration is that you will have to do all the paperwork necessary and submit regular remittances. Again, this could be an advantage, as it will help keep your bookkeeping updated and you will not have to worry about that huge pile of paperwork that would otherwise have to be entered at the end of the year.

What should you look for when thinking about banking needs?

Now that you have figured how and when to ask for money, it's time to figure out where to put it and what types of accounts you should be using.

Many of us have dealt with the same bank for our personal needs for many years. However, does this mean they can offer the small business solutions that your company needs? Each financial institution offers different products and caters to different target markets. Don't be afraid to shop around for a banking facility that can provide you with both excellent solutions and high-quality customer service.

When choosing your financial institution, you need to take into account the following:

- Is online banking available?
- Variety of business loans available
- Ease of using alternate branches, if necessary
- Location, as you don't want to travel to do your banking
- Do they offer merchant account services or other ecommerce solutions?
- Can they offer what you will need for future growth?

Get to know the staff at your bank, everyone from the tellers to your business advisor and even the bank manager. The more comfortable both of you are with each other, the better your chances of being able to obtain any loans, lines of credit, or other financial assistance that you may need to obtain to help grow your business. If you have difficulty in building a relationship with your bank, it may be best to consider finding a bank that will cater better to your needs and provide you with higher quality customer service.

Your business manager will help you in deciding what type of account is best for your business. There are certain aspects of the accounts that need to be kept in mind when choosing the one for you. These include:

- the rate and frequency of interest accumulated
- any service charges or fees
- added features to the account (i.e. bank cards)
- any minimum balance requirements

Market & Marketing

Two of the most important and widely-used words in the vocabulary of a small business owner are **Market** and **Marketing**. From the very first day we use some form of these two words in almost every aspect of running our business.

Target Market

Rule Number One...don't just start a business on a whim. Be sure that you research the viability of your business and to whom you will sell your services...your target market.

The ongoing success of Virtual Assistants currently making up the industry, and the quick success that many new VAs experience, are proof that this industry is viable. Success can be had if you follow the lead of others and work with them in the industry.

However, all VAs have different target markets from the many business sectors. The various sectors that you may choose to promote and offer your services to include industry, product and service sectors. The needs of each of these sectors will differ greatly and it is generally recommended that you have some experience with businesses from your chosen sector. Most VAs have client bases that are largely made up of companies in the service sector.

Your specialty may also affect your target market. If you have a knack for producing legal papers, your target market will more than likely be lawyers or those in the legal profession. If you break that market down even further, such as criminal lawyers or family lawyers, you are now getting closer to determining your niche market.

> "*Market Your Strengths:* You must have marketable skills that you can confidently sell to potential clients. There are many different services that a VA can offer, but you will be much more successful if you work within your strengths and market them confidently, instead of trying to 'be everything to everyone'. Offering only services that you are very skilled at speeds up your workday."
>
> *Tracey D'Aviero*
> *Virtual Assistant*
> *http://traceydaviero.blogspot.com*

No matter who your target market is, you need to ask yourself an abundance of questions in order to determine how to best service these clients. Some of these questions include:

- What do these customers buy?
- What are the specific needs and wants (economic, spiritual, social, etc.) of your target market?
- What evidence do you have that these needs exist?
- When do these customers buy? Is there a specific time of year that they would need your services more than others?

- Who in the company makes the decisions on the services that they may need help with?
- Where are your customers located?

Marketing Environment

One of the reasons why many VAs are successful is because they have determined their marketing environment. They have researched major social forces for which they cannot control including demographics, trends, economics, and specific laws and policies relating to their industry and target market. By analyzing these external market influences, it is easier to become familiar with any threats and opportunities that can arise.

The following are some of these social forces and examples of what they encompass:

Current economic conditions, including interest rates, inflation rates, personal income tax levels, employment rates, income levels, stable to growing community, population base stable or seasonal and expected economic changes.

Technological or scientific advances that can have positive or negative effects on your industry. You also need to consider upgrades that are available for your current technology, enhancements in the services you offer, and advancements that will streamline both your business and that of your clients'.

Laws and policies that can have an effect on your business also need to be considered. These include tax laws, intellectual property laws, copyright and even employment laws.

Political climates can also have an influence on how you market your business. Your business is more likely to succeed if you are aware of whether or not government regulations and consumer confidence are on your side.

Demographics, and knowing how they change, can have the highest influence on if you can sustain the building and success of your business or not. These influences include market size, age, sex, family size and household composition, ethnic mix, education, occupation, and religion.

Current trends can affect your company's future growth. For instance, the VA industry is the buzzword on the small business front. How valuable does your target find you now and down the road? And, what new trend will come along that will hamper your company's growth?

Industry, product or service sector growth patterns, whichever is your target market, can fluctuate. With careful research, you can determine if your market's growth pattern is increasing, holding steady or declining.

Knowing your marketing environment can also influence your marketing strategies and how you will promote your business. Therefore, you need to stay on top of what is happening with your target market and what factors influence its business and buying decisions. As your marketing environment changes, so should your marketing strategies and efforts.

Create Your Corporate Image (Your Brand)

Before you begin to get your marketing material designed, you need to think about and create an image for your company. Often referred to as your brand, a corporate image needs to portray what you want everyone to think of when they think of your business. This can include your company name, tag line, logo or a combination of all

of these factors that will identify your services and differentiate you from your competition.

When establishing your image, you want to be sure that your brand achieves the following:

- gets your message across clearly
- establishes your professionalism and credibility
- invokes your loyalty
- motivates your potential client to want to learn more and/or buy
- builds a solid reputation as an expert in your industry

Your brand is communicated through your company using every form of contact that you have with clients and contacts. Whether it be in the phone call you make, the business card you hand out, or the website you put online, your clients and prospects need you to understand their requirements. Your brand will be how you will convince them that you do understand their needs and that you are an expert in your field.

There are two basics that will not only help develop your brand, but will probably be used in the majority of your marketing endeavours:

- Your company logo
- Your tagline

These will be used more than anything else in your business, so you want them to be recognizable. For example, Nike… everyone knows their logo (that little checkmark kind of swish) and their tagline (Just Do It). When developing your logo and tagline, shoot for the success that Nike has had with theirs (or even half the success they have had would be great :-).

<u>Creating a Great Logo</u>

A great logo design will be the main aspect of your brand. You probably spent many hours deciding on a company name, so now you want to have a logo that is fitting to your company name and sticks in your potential client's mind. The following are just a few tips to help you in designing a high impact company logo:

- Ensure your logo is original. You can research to see what your competitors are doing and other successfully branded companies, but your logo needs to be original.
- Use an easy to read font.
- Choose a graphic that is appropriate for your business and the brand you are attempting to establish.
- Your logo needs to stand the test of time. You don't want to use an image that won't be recognizable or fashionable (so to speak) in ten years.
- Keep your logo looking strong and balanced.

- Ensure your logo looks good in both colour as well as black and white.
- Your logo needs to be scalable. It must be larger for such things as a poster or your website, but smaller for such items as your business card.

Don't rush the design of your company logo. Be sure that what you or your logo designer creates really says, "That's it!" to you. You may want to run it by your associates first to get some input.

<u>Creating an Unforgettable Tag Line</u>

Your tag line may not be used in as many marketing pieces as your company logo, but you still need to take time in deciding how you want it worded and the effect you want it to have on those around you. A tag line should be short and sweet... at least 3 words and no more than 7 to 10 words. When crafting a tag line, keep in mind the following:

- Express your business's most important benefits... words that you want your target audience to remember.
- Take the time to create an effective tag. Don't rush this process. It could take as long as the time used in designing the logo.
- Your tag line should flow and appear to be a natural addition to your brand and business.

Marketing

Now that we have determined to whom you are going to market and have decided on your company brand, it's time to figure out exactly how you are going to get your message out there. What techniques can you use to get noticed and build your client base?

Marketing endeavours will be the most important aspect of your business. It is a never-ending necessity. After all, if we don't market, we don't get clients, and without clients we don't have a successful business. So coming up with new ideas will keep your eyes peeled and your marketing efforts fresh. Eventually you will notice the marketing potential in almost everything you see and hear. It's all a part of being a business owner and having the responsibilities of making and keeping a successful business.

<u>Printed Promotional Material</u>

Your promotional material must reflect you, what you offer, your dedication to perfection, your ethical practice, and your professionalism. It is important that you tell as much as possible without giving away too much information to give potential clients the urge to learn more. You want them to contact you for more information and that is when you can make the sale.

Some of the most common forms of promotional material and what should be printed include:

- Business Cards
  - Include as much of your contact information as possible, with your name and phone number (and even your email address) being the most prominent.
  - Include your website address.

- o As home-based business owners, you may prefer not to include your street address, as it will become available to anyone who has your card.

- o Try to include a listing of your services, especially your specialties. Not all company names can effectively spell out the types of service you can offer, so highlighting your specialties is a good way to bait the hook.
  - o If you hold any certifications, be sure to include a mention of them on your card. Whether it is a one-line sentence or just abbreviations, make these visible yet not overpowering.
  - o An optional inclusion on your card is your tag line. If you are trying to brand yourself and your business by your tag line or what it represents, this will be a necessity. However, if space is an issue on your card, you may want to omit this information.
  - o Include logos of prominent organizations to which you are a member (i.e. Chamber of Commerce, Board of Trade, etc.), space permitting.
- Brochures
  - o Again, your contact information needs to be prominent. Clients must be able to reach you, so be sure you include as many options as you can (i.e. phone, fax, email, pager, cell phone, etc.) without sharing more than you feel comfortable.
  - o List all the services you offer, if possible. If space permits, a brief description of your specialties would be a recommended inclusion. Show them what you can offer to make their business lives run more smoothly.
  - o List your Features & Benefits. You need to show potential clients what's in it for them.
  - o Testimonials give an added touch to any of your marketing materials. At first you may not have any or very few to include. But, as time goes by and as your happy client base grows, testimonials will come and should be included. And, if you choose to design and print your own brochures, you have the freedom to print as little or as many as you need, plus you can change the style and/or wording anytime without worrying about losing money in wasted stock.
  - o Again, include your credentials… certifications, memberships, awards and anything that shows your professionalism.
- Portfolio
  - o Include your contact information, testimonials, services, features & benefits and credentials. Some credentials may rate a separate sheet in your portfolio, such as your certifications or awards.
  - o Distributed less frequently than most pieces of marketing material, the added bonus of a portfolio is that it can include actual samples of your work. Bear in mind that portfolios are best saved for distribution to those who show a genuine interest in working with you.
  - o Samples of your work are a must. In the administrative field, it is not always easy to show others what you can do with your computer, but there must be samples of your work that you can include. Even if you need to, include the marketing material you have already developed for yourself.
  - o If you write articles, include a few in your portfolio.

- o This may even be where you want to include your pricing schedule, if you have one. Many VAs have set rates for specific tasks which can be outlined in a price sheet. Certain tasks may require a unique quotation, so you should mention that on your price list.

- o Include copies of any media clippings regarding yourself and/or your business.
- o You may also want to include your resume, showing your experience in your specialty, especially if you are in the start-up phase and don't have as much to include in your portfolio as you would like.

Word of Mouth

Promotional material is one way of highlighting your talents in hard copy form. But it is not enough to get people to recognize your name and know you as a person... the person behind the business and talents. So, you need to get out there and make "personal appearances."

There are a variety of ways for people to see and know the face behind the name:

- Networking
  - o This is the best form of word of mouth. Not only do you get to personally talk to others who are in your target market, it also gives them a chance to hear what you have to offer, right from the VA's mouth.
  - o Check with your local Chamber of Commerce or Board of Trade. Most hold regular networking events and often it is not required that you be a member in order to attend a few meetings.
  - o Other types of organizations also offer organized networking events. Ask your fellow local business associates if they know of any such events and what their procedures are. Some groups will require that you be a member while others welcome everyone. Remember that most of these types of events will have a cost on top of the price of your meal.
  - o Prepare a 30-second 'schpeel'. At all networking events you will have the chance to tell others what you can do for them. Give as much detail in as little time as possible. Depending on the event, you may even have the opportunity to stand up in front of everyone and tell them how you can help them.
  - o Every chance you get, tell others about your business. They may not necessarily need your services, but perhaps they know others who do and will remember you when the time comes.

- Online Discussion Lists
  - o Find online groups that offer an email discussion list to help members share and learn from each other.
  - o Join industry-specific email discussion lists. These not only give you a sounding board and source of assistance if you need it, they are also a great place to inform others of the services that you can offer to other VAs should they have a project that requires a different expertise than theirs.

- o Join small business communities that also have a way for their members to communicate with each other. Again, these are a great way to learn what is new and are an ideal place to find new clients.

- Volunteer
    - o What better way to show others that you really do care than to offer your expertise to organizations or individuals? This also allows you to

        give something back and allows you to build relationships with others which could be beneficial to you in the long run. Not to mention, volunteering can help you to get out and be with other like-minded people. It can help you relieve some of your working stress as well as make you feel good inside knowing you are helping out where help is really needed. Doing something out of the goodness of your heart has an overwhelming way of making you feel all 'warm and fuzzy inside'.

"When you decide you are serious about becoming a VA, tell everyone you know. It seems like such a little thing to do, but it can make a huge difference. Think about how many people you know and how many people they know and so on and so on and so on (like the Pert commercial). It is a huge market, so be sure you don't miss out on a free opportunity to land that valuable first client."

Kate V. Kerans
Kerans Virtual Assistance
www.yourvirtualparalegal.net

Website

Another wonderful way of promoting your business, and a necessity for all virtual professionals, is your website. This is your version of a "brick and mortar" storefront.

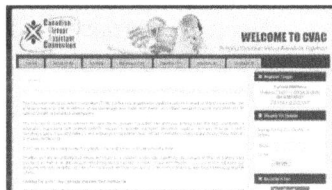

How and who you choose to design your site is very important in determining how you will be perceived by your target market and others. As a business website, you don't want to overdo the fancy graphics and flashy animations. The main purpose of your site is to bring in clients and it should reflect your professionalism and creativity but not distract anyone from that main purpose.

Now, that doesn't mean you can't offer more than just a listing of your services. Many Internet surfers want to get something for free. As a VA, there aren't a lot of services that you can offer pro-bono from your website, but you can offer resources for your target market. This can include a list of helpful links, a collection of related articles, an archive of your online newsletter, or any other helpful information that your site visitors will appreciate.

You also need to make your website interactive. Offer a survey, feedback form, or a quotation request form. These can all be coded to send responses directly to your email inbox.

Complete and easy-to-follow navigation also needs to be forefront in your plans for your website. If your site visitors cannot find what they need with just a few clicks, they may end up leaving your site to find others that are easier to get around.

Once you have your website designed, it is time to mention it everywhere you possibly can and whenever you correspond with anyone. How many emails do you send in one day? Well, every one of those emails is a perfect place to mention your company name and website.

Creating a great website is a lot of work. Writing original copy is also a lot of work. But it's worth it. Research other VA sites to determine the kind of information that you want to include on your website. Remember to write everything in your own words. The internet is not as small as you might think and it's easy enough to find websites that have 'borrowed' your content to use as their own. Once your website is up you might want to occasionally check to see that no one else out there is using what you worked so hard to create.

One way to do this is to try to find a sentence on your website that has a unique combination of words. Search for that sentence enclosed in quotes on Google Blog Search and Yahoo Search (it indexes fresh content more quickly than Google).

Another way is to use Copyscape, http://www.copyscape.com/. This is a free service that allows you to enter your domain and it will search to see if other domains are using similar copy.

If you do find that someone else is using your copy there are several steps that you can take. The first step would be to write a friendly email advising them that their copy is exactly the same and yours and letting them know that you understand how this can happen when researching from other sites. Ask them to change or remove your copy. If you approach them nicely they will usually comply. In the event that they don't comply you can send them a stronger 'Cease and Desist' letter

A Cease and desist letter should be a formal and specific letter that gives as much information as possible and sets deadlines/ultimatums that you are prepared to follow up on. It's important to remember that this is your hard work you're defending and you have every right to protect it vigorously. This letter should reflect that.

A cease and desist letter usually contains four key elements:

1. All pertinent information about the infringement including the URLs of your pages as well as their copied pages
2. A list of things you want them to do (usually either give you proper credit as the author or remove the plagiarized text)
3. A deadline by which the recipient must meet those demands and
4. What will happen if they aren't met (usually including possible legal action and a complaint filed to their website host)

Most plagiarists don't expect to get caught and, when they do, they generally go along with the demands to avoid escalation. Many will do so silently, never writing back and others will write back to apologize or make excuses. Some do make excuses saying that they didn't mean to copy the work or that someone else gave it to them. There are also those who vehemently deny having plagiarized and may even accuse you of plagiarizing their work. If this is the case there are steps you can take:

- Provide a link of the Google Cache to prove that Google spiders discovered your content earlier.

- If you are site is mentioned in the Web archives (archives.org), share that information with the web host.

- Inform them about the Google Page Rank of your site - a site which indulges in copyright violations is generally a new site with no or a low page rank.

Signature Lines

Your email signature should not be too long. If you belong to email discussion lists, some will have rules about what can be included and how long your signature can be. It seems that most do not like any more than six lines, so by pre-developing your signature line in your email program, you can have those six lines automatically included at the end of all your emails.

This feature on your email program allows you to have several signature lines. This allows you to have many signatures that can be used as needed.

Now, what should you include in those six lines? Your name is not considered to be a part of your signature line, so you put it there in addition to the lines. The first line should be your company name, followed by your website address (URL) on the second line.

You could include your email address if you have room, but you already have your email address in the header of the email, so it makes more sense to use that space for other things.

If you have a tag line for your business, include it here. You could also include where you are located (city & province). If you have a specific group of people requiring more contact information, you can also include your phone number and full address.

If you have a special offer, you can include information and/or a link in your signature line. The same holds true if you are selling an ebook or something else. Include the information about it and where people can go to buy it.

Your signature line is also the perfect place to promote your newsletter (if you write one). You can also include any links to organizations to which you belong and would like to promote.

Write Articles

One of the most under-used forms of marketing a business that doesn't require forking out your hard-earned money is writing articles. The only real requirements in order to write articles are your expertise and your time.

Writing articles helps you to be recognized as an expert in your field. You might be questioning, "What can I possibly write about?" Well, what do you know a lot about?

Is there something in your business or personal life that you do really well, that you have a passion for, a subject that you know and understand well, or that would help enlighten others? Share this knowledge and write about it.

Writing articles when you are not familiar with the subject can take more time than if you are already familiar with the topic, but the rewards of researching and providing the most up-to-date information will far outweigh the time it takes to write about it.

The following are just some ways to come up with article topics, either those you may have experienced before or those you will need to research in order to compile:

1. Article ideas can pop into your head at any time of the day or night, but are soon forgotten. Think about having a notepad, micro-cassette recorder or PDA handy in your home, office and even beside your bed to record ideas. As you are watching TV, reading the newspaper or industry magazine, jot down any ideas and also be sure to carry a notepad with you when you go out. Don't throw away your list of ideas; file it safely where you can find it as it could very well come in handy when you decide to write your next article.

2. Take your cues from those you deal with daily. When speaking with clients, acquaintances, or anyone, if they happen to mention a problem or say they would like to know more about something, take note. There's an article just waiting to be written. Do some research and put together a knowledgeable article or list of tips that can be shared. Someone will be thanking you later.

3. Current social, economic and environmental happenings, as well as current trends, can also be the subject for an article. How do these conditions affect your business or affect other businesses? How can your business provide a solution? Remember that most editors don't want articles to be blatant advertising, so make sure you don't come right out and sell your products or services.

4. Another source for article ideas can be the discussion lists, message boards and chat rooms to which you belong. Use the ongoing discussions as your research for your article. Summarize what is being discussed and be sure to give credit where it is due.

    If you are going to use the discussion verbatim, be sure to ask for permission and quote that person specifically. Most will accept it as another great opportunity to get free exposure.

5. You can also write opposing opinions or follow-ups to other articles you have read in newsletters, newspapers or magazines. If the article was in one publication and you are writing a follow-up that will appear in another publication, be sure to include a synopsis of the item to which you are responding. However, if you are doing the article for the same publication, make reference to the original article (i.e. date published, title, & maybe the author). Editors may omit this information when printing your article or they may add more to it.

6. If you seem to be having writer's block and can't come up with an idea for an article, try doing a survey of your contacts to see if there is any subject they would like to know more about. You could ask your fellow discussion list

members and that may even generate an ongoing discussion for use as opinions in your article. Again, if you are using 'word for word' ideas or opinions, authorize their use with the originator before publishing.

With all the wonderful ideas you will gather and the informative article you will put together, we will now need to cover where you can publish your article.

1. First and foremost, your own website is a great place to start. Every article you write should be archived on your website. Even if a particular article is referring to something in your personal life as opposed to your business life, it needs to be archived on your website where it can be seen by those wanting the information or who may be looking for articles on that topic. It will also be indexed by search engines who return to spider websites for new content.

   Design a new article page on your site and divide your articles by category. Interested people can then scan through the sub-headings to easily find articles relating to a subject in which they are interested. Include a note about how everyone is welcome to use the articles as long as they leave your contact information in place. Speaking of which, don't forget to have your bio/contact information on all of your articles on your site so if someone simply pulls one from your site, they will have your name to include.

2. Research publications whose readers are your target market are also good places to publish articles. They generally keep databases of editors who accept article submissions. Be sure to keep that database up to date. Your article will either be "returned to sender" or filed under "G" very quickly if you don't personalize it to the right person. It is not always easy to find the name of the editor, but do your best to ensure exposure of your written material.

   Also, if possible, check to see if there is a preference on how the editor would like to receive submissions. Although most publications will accept work via email, some may have specific requests, such as if they would prefer the article to be directly in the body of the email or sent as a Word attachment, a PDF attachment or perhaps even some other preference. If the preference is not known, play it safe and put the article directly in the body of the email.

3. There are many websites that will allow you to submit your articles for others to use in their publications. Many editors will go to these kinds of sites to get their content when they are in need of an article on a particular subject and don't have anything handy to use. Some of these sites include:

   http://www.1st-in-home-businesses.com/
   http://www.ideamarketers.com/
   http://www.goarticles.com

   You can do a search online and probably come up with more.

4. Share your articles with others on your discussion lists, forums and chat rooms. Keep the announcements of new articles to a minimum or don't announce them at all if the list protocol says "no blatant advertising". However, if a discussion is ongoing or a question is asked on a subject that

you have done an article on, then briefly mention it and provide a link to it where readers can learn more on the subject or include the article under your signature lines of your post.

5. Have others pass on your article. We all have associates and friends online and they have friends and associates as well. Ask people to distribute your articles (or a link to them) to anyone that makes a plea for information on a subject about which you have written.

6. If you find out that anyone is looking for content for their website or newsletter, offer your articles or offer to write a new article.

7. Introduce your articles in your own newsletter and include a note stating that others are welcome to use it in their publications or on their website. Also, include a link to the rest of your articles so your readers have a larger selection from which to choose.

As mentioned earlier, writing articles can portray you as an expert in your field. It doesn't require a budget, but it definitely requires your time. You WILL have to work hard in order to offer information that is both correct and informative. Before you know it, you could be writing a book :-)

"Marketing your business: To this I say you have to constantly be marketing and networking. When you're standing in line at the bank or in the checkout line, strike up a conversation with the person behind or in front of you. Keep your ears open for an opportunity to introduce yourself. When I lecture about becoming a VA I always recount the following story.

My husband and I were just finishing our breakfast at a neighbourhood restaurant. Three men came and sat down at the table next to us and started talking about business and how you need to have a business plan. Right away my ears perked up, I looked at my husband and said should I give them my card they may need someone to type up the plan for them. He wasn't sure, but I was already pulling out 3 business cards one for each the men sitting at the table. I asked the waitress if she knew them (I thought maybe she could introduce me or give them my card); she didn't. So I got up with my cards in hand walked over and said, "I'm sorry, I don't usually listen to other people's conversations, but I heard Business Plan, and right away my ears perked up. So I thought maybe you might need someone to type it up for you and make it look professional.

They accepted my cards and thanked me. One gentleman even complimented me for being so pro-active and taking the initiative to introduce myself. He told me that was good business.

So you see you have to constantly be marketing."

Francesca Frate, Owner/Operator
AdminConcepts - Your Administrative Connection
http://www.adminconcepts.net

Social Networking Overview

It's been around for quite a few years now but Social Networking has recently been getting a huge amount of exposure and talk time in almost every circle. Whether you use it for business or for just keeping in touch with friends, the many social networking avenues that are out there can make communicating with others easy and less expensive than long distance phone calls. They allow you to touch base with people you may have never had the opportunity meet or speak with before.

What exactly is Social Networking?

If we look at the definition of the two words (courtesy of www.merriam-webster.com) that make up the phrase "social networking", that's a start.

> Social: *tending to form cooperative and interdependent relationships with others of one's kind; the interaction of the individual and the group*

> Networking: *the exchange of information or services among individuals, groups, or institutions ; specifically : the cultivation of productive relationships for employment or business*

Put those together and you have "interaction of individuals to cultivate productive relationships for employment or business". If we then add the spin of the need for everyone to be on the computer and conversing that way, you have what is now the buzz phrase on the Internet today... social networking.

Social networking, as mentioned, has been around for a long time. Business owners have long known that they need to network with other like-minded individuals and businesses in order to gain contacts and visible, professional relationships. Now, with the constant increase of people using the Internet, online networking is gaining huge momentum. Whether it is through a chat feature or on one of the many social sites that are available, connecting with others for business or personal has never been easier.

What are the Benefits of Social Networking?

The number of social networking sites online is growing rapidly as entrepreneurs learn that communicating with others around the world is highly beneficial to them and their businesses. Those who are looking to increase their business networks can take advantage of the many benefits that social networking offers and help grow their exposure to their target markets.

The benefits of being involved in social networking include:

1. As mentioned, growing your network of professionals that will help you to build your business.
2. Meeting others from geographical locations that would otherwise not have been possible.
3. Not only make new business contacts but also make new friends.
4. A platform where you can share your expertise and help others.
5. Learn of new and beneficial assets to help your business (ie. Software, websites, upcoming events, etc.).

6. Cost effective as most social networking sites and memberships are free.
7. The ability to communicate with others no matter what time of day it is in your area or what time of day it is in other parts of the world.
8. A great way for you to market and increase awareness for your products or services around the world.
9. Using social networking to keep in touch with your trusted circle of friends and colleagues.
10. Being able to ask a question about something you may be considering getting to get feedback from others, whether they like or dislike it.
11. Ask for recommendations for software, hardware, or anything else you can think of.
12. Find out what your target market needs and how you or some of your contacts can meet those needs.
13. Allows you to discover a multitude of other opportunities.
14. Allows you to gain recognition and establish your presence with your skills and knowledge.
15. Allows for opportunities in business collaboration and joint ventures.
16. A great starting point for marketing new products or services or events.

Popular Social Networking Websites

There are hundreds of websites online that offer a variety of means of social networking. Some are targeted and specific to particular industries, trends or hobbies while others are more open to just about anyone joining and then using their memberships to connect with people and businesses of interest to them. There are also different levels of interactivity that each has and based on your needs and your own personal choices, you can find several that will help you to accomplish what you need.

Paramount to being successful in social media and seeing the results of your connections and communications is preparing a social media strategy to build your "brand", share helpful information, provide customer service and satisfaction and find and establish targeted connections for future opportunities.

The "Rule of Thumb" in social media etiquette is:

50% Business: sharing content, thoughts, ideas, "tips"

30% Personal: (business related) your experiences, how you helped a client, new applications, programs, websites, etc.

20% Sales: buy my book, pick up this free report, check out my eBook on tips, free consultation, see my video, etc.

AND...
   ❖ DO - Create Complete Profiles

   ❖ DO - Choose a limited number of ideal networks

   ❖ DO - Grow your connections

- ❖ DO - Participate & promote Invitations

- ❖ DON'T - Be selfish - networking is all about sharing

- ❖ DON'T - Have unrealistic expectations

- ❖ DON'T - Give up

- ❖ DON'T - Market all the time

- ❖ DON'T - Forget to network locally

The following are just a select few that are being used by small business owners to help get network with colleagues, associates, target market and even family and friends:

Twitter (www.twitter.com) - this is one of the most popular social networking sites today. It is categorized as a micro blogging site that you can access on your computer, through your cell phone and in conjunction with other social networking sites. You register on the twitter.com website and create a profile for yourself. You can then find friends and colleagues on Twitter and "follow" them which, in a nutshell, means that whenever they post a "tweet" (a maximum 140 character post to tell people what they are doing, what or whom they recommend, etc.) it will show up on your Twitter page. Others, in turn or just by searching the Twitter database for contacts they would like to hear from, will want to follow you. You can set this option to let you know each time someone wants to follow you (which can be time consuming as you are notified of a new follow request and then have to click on a link to either accept or deny them) or set it so anyone can follow you (you are notified of the follow but you don't have to accept it or you can click on the link, learn more about the person who is following, and decide if you would like to follow them as well).

Many people use separate stand-alone applications to receive Twitter updates from their contacts. The applications automatically update tweets from others at a time frame that you determine. Some also allow you to pre-program your tweets to automatically broadcast to your followers your updates. And still others have even more neat features to make the tweeting process more enjoyable and productive. Some of these applications include:

- Tweetdeck – www.tweetdeck.com
- Tweetlater – www.tweetlater.com
- Twirl – www.twirl.com
- There are hundreds of other applications that can be used for & with Twitter. By doing a search of "twitter applications" in a search engine, you can find more than enough to suit your needs. There is also a huge list of applications at http://www.squidoo.com/twitterapps

We recommend joining Twitter, getting a few people to follow and adding more as you go along, allow people to follow you automatically, and then just watch what people are doing to learn how you should act and proceed on Twitter.

Facebook (www.facebook.com) – this is another popular social networking site that allows you to develop a complete profile of yourself and your business but it is kept private until you confirm those who want to become friends with you on there. You can share pictures, videos, great links and so much more on your Facebook page and can update people on what you are doing by updating your status. You can also send private or public (using the "wall") messages to your contacts.

Facebook offers a multitude of features that are both fun and functional. By exploring Facebook and getting messages from others, you will see many of these fun features and can add them to your own profile.

Linkedin (www.linkedin.com) – this networking site is used mostly by business professionals who want to increase their network of line-minded individuals. It allows you to create a comprehensive profile, including your educational background, and share it with others. Like Facebook and other social networking sites, you have to confirm those that request to be linked to you and you need to update your status so people know what you are doing or plan on doing. LinkedIn is based on forming relationships and connections. Through your first level of connections with the people you know, you can make additional connections with the people they know. It just builds from there.

LinkedIn also offers Groups. LinkedIn Groups can help you keep in touch with people that share your interests. Once your profile is complete search for groups (by clicking on the Groups link on the left side of the page when you're logged in) that interest you and join them. Your membership usually needs to be approved but once it is you have access to all the other members of the group and you can start networking.

To learn more about Linkedin and how to use it, simply read the help files or visit http://www.linkedintelligence.com/smart-ways-to-use-linkedin/ which includes a great list of how to use Linkedin.

Plaxo (www.plaxo.com) – this is another social networking site that is used primarily by entrepreneurs and other business professionals. Like Twitter and other social networking sites, you can take Plaxo with you on your cell phone. You can share photos, videos and resources; you can connect your Plaxo account to your blog and synch it with your Outlook calendar; and you can share your content with such sites as YouTube, etc.

As mentioned, there are hundreds of social networking sites out there. You can do a search on any search engine to find more, including this Wikipedia site (http://en.wikipedia.org/wiki/List_of_social_networking_websites) which has a huge list of these sites. We recommend asking around with your colleagues and associates to see which sites they feel are most beneficial to be a part of. Also, as you get invitations from your online friends, you will soon see which ones are being used by those you want to connect with.

Thank you to Diane Coville of Alternative Office Assistance (www.alternativeofficeassistance.ca) for her social networking expertise and input ensuring accuracy in this Social Marketing Overview section.

Organization is the Key

As Virtual Assistants, our purpose in the business world is to help our clients to have some form of organization in their businesses. However, if we can't stay organized ourselves, how can we expect to help others accomplish the same thing?

Cut Down the Paper Trail

Having an organized office is not only important for appearance sake (if you have clients or contacts who visit your office), it is also essential in helping run your business smoothly.

Paper and sticky notes scattered here and there are a common site on almost every desk, but you need to keep the excess to a minimum.

Filing Cabinets

These are one of the most essential pieces of furniture you will have in your office and you can get them in designs that will compliment the rest of your office. Although there are many ways to produce and save documents on our computers, there will still be a multitude of paperwork that needs filing.

Use a system that will be the most efficient when filing away important documents. Have those documents that you would use the most at your fingertips. If you have a file drawer in your desk, you should keep client and other frequently used files here since they are easily accessible. Have other documents that are still used, but not as often, in files that are in close proximity. Other less frequently used files can be located in an area even farther away from your work area, or perhaps even in another room.

Storage Shelving

Every office needs to keep a certain supply of office necessities. However, as Virtual Assistants, we tend to keep even more items than the average office of an entrepreneur. Since we do work for a number of companies, not just one, we need to keep stock for the occasions when items are needed for the various projects that may crop up.

Due to the amount of supplies we need to have on hand, it makes sense to keep these items, along with other items such as books, in shelving in our offices where we can easily access them. And don't forget, if you have a closed-in shelving system, this will help to keep dust down on your supplies.

Password Software

So… where do you keep all those usernames and passwords that you use for your business? How about all the ones you need to use to do work for your clients?

For some, there is a collection of sticky notes or pieces of paper hanging around our desks. Conversely, we may keep that information tucked away in the client's file. Although this would seem to be a great way to keep all of a client's information in one place, it can actually be an inconvenience and take time to look for every time you need it.

One solution is to acquire software that will hold all of these passwords in an easily-accessible location. There are a few on the market that can be found by typing in *password storage* (or something similar) into any search engine. A simple one that is currently available is Password Keeper which is available for download at http://www.passkeeper.com.

Another solution would be to develop a spreadsheet or Word document with columns for the username, password, the client's name, the URL where you will need to use this information (log in page), and any other comments that you may need to remember regarding that password.

Rolodex

We all have many people that we regularly keep in touch with during the course of running our businesses and, for each of these, you probably have a business card lying around.

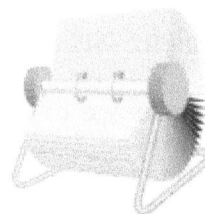

One way to keep this contact information organized is to put it all into a Rolodex. There are many different kinds of Rolodexes that are available, and each has its advantages. Some allow room for basic information of hundreds of contacts, while others hold more detailed information of fewer contacts.

There are Rolodexes with index cards on which you will need to transpose the contact information and others that simply allow room for you to place in the business cards of your contacts by using a hole punch.

No matter which type you choose, Rolodexes are a great way to keep contact information in an easily accessible location.

PDAs & Smartphones

Another great little gadget which can help you organize the information of your contacts is a PDA (Personal Digital Assistants) or Smartphone (ie: Blackberry, iPhone). Again, there are a wide variety on the market from which to choose, some being more expensive than others and some having more features.

PDAs and Smartphones not only allow you to keep contact information handy, they also have such features as a calendar, memo pad, and even a web browser. They are a great way to keep many aspects of your life organized.

Scanning

Another way of reducing the piles of paper on your desk is to scan printed documents that you did not produce and save them as electronic files on your computer.

<u>Paper Shredder</u>

Last but not least, the good old paper shredder is an invaluable tool.   Recycling paper is the right thing to do in order to help with our environment, but sometimes you will have documents that should not be seen by others, even years after they were originally produced.   These confidential documents need to be torn up, and a shredder is the quickest and most efficient means of destroying them.

Paper shredders come in various sizes and can handle different quantities of sheets. You also have the option of one that does straight cuts or one that does crisscross cuts. You can even use the shredded paper as packing material if you need to ship something.

Time Management

Now that we have taken care of the paper that can clutter up your desk and office, let's work on managing your time.

<u>Setting Your Office Hours</u>

The first thing to do to help in managing your time is to set regular office hours. This will help you establish a routine.   Be sure to inform others of these hours in order to avoid interruptions during your off hours.

<u>Day Timer</u>

If you do not have an electronic device (PDA) to keep track of your schedule, we highly recommend getting a Day Timer. You can choose whether you prefer to have individual pages by day, week, or even by the month depending on how busy your schedule is. Be sure to make all of your entries in pencil as it is common for anyone's schedule to change, sometimes more than once.

Some Day Timers even include an address book and you can replace the calendar pages every year so be sure to purchase one with a high quality case/cover as you will probably have it for many years.

"Organize, Organize, Organize! - If you are going to be successful at running your VA business from your home, you will need to be able to manage your time so that you maximize your productivity. This becomes essential as you build your client base. I try to schedule time for everything I do, for both home and business - and that way nothing gets missed, and everyone gets their fair share of my time (including me!)."

Tracey D'Aviero
Virtual Assistant
http://traceydaviero.blogspot.com

To Do Lists

This is another essential task that you need to perform in order to manage your time effectively. Write down every project and task that needs to be done. If you have several projects that need to be done for a particular client, be sure that you list them all so nothing gets forgotten.

Generally, once you have a To Do list started, it will constantly be changing. When a project is complete, you will cross it off your list. When a new project surfaces, you will add it to your list. As this list will be ever changing, writing it on a piece of paper may not be the most efficient use of your time (and paper). You may choose to use NotePad or Word to keep track of your ongoing tasks, but remember to have either of these handy so you can view your list when you needed.

Organizing Emails

We all receive hundreds of emails a day. It comes with having your email address in various locations online. Most of these emails will be spam but some will be important and some sort of action will need to be taken at some point.

One of the first steps you can take is to set up folders in your email program to hold the various emails. For instance, set up a folder for your clients and then set up sub-folders and name them "To Do."

The next step is to set up a rule (which is an available feature in most email programs) to send incoming emails from that client to automatically be redirected to that folder.

You can also set up Rules to move spam email directly into your Deleted Items folder. Of course, spamsters are always changing how they send emails so doing this may seem like a never-ending task which takes time. In the long run, it will save you time that you would normally spend deleting those emails.

Another advantage of using folders and rules is that you can reroute any emails that come in from email discussion lists and then scan through them when you have time.

One other way of deleting unwanted emails all in one shot is by disabling the detail screen of emails. Then, on the list of emails that have come in, highlight those that you want to delete and then just hit the delete key once.

Flagging emails can also help to determine which emails need a response. When you have read the email and want to respond to it at another time, simply apply a flag to it (i.e. in Outlook, click on Tools, Flag for Follow-up). You can then choose how you want to categorize the follow-up by adjusting the flag's properties. As you answer the email or perform the task that the saved email represents, be sure to move it to its designated folder or delete it.

Establish Priorities

Now that you have your To Do list and have categorized your email, you need to prioritize your tasks. You recorded each of these tasks because they hold some form

of importance to you, but there are some that will be more urgent than others. For instance, if you have a project that needs to be ready by a specific deadline, it and any email associated with it, should be handled first.

You will find that your day is filled with constant interruptions and small tasks that need to be done right away, so you need to account for them when you are prioritizing. Don't let those small tasks overtake your schedule. Some things can wait and you can schedule them into another day. Your To Do list and email Flags will be highly beneficial when establishing your priorities.

You also want to be careful to keep a handle on procrastination. We all have a tendency to put things on the back burner for a little too long and before you know it, time has run out to get the project or task done.

Speed Dial

And then there is the amount of time that you spend dialing the phone and fax, not to mention searching for the phone number. For all those people who you talk with on a constant basis, add their phone numbers into your speed dial feature. Then all it takes is the push of one button to reach them.

Time-tracking Software

As your business grows, keeping track of the time you spend on client work can begin to be overwhelming. We have all tried several options to keep track of time spent on assignments, from spreadsheets laid out on paper to tables designed in a word processor. Many techniques have been tried, but most start to become a burden as the paperwork builds up and the amount of space being taken up on your computer grows by having a larger program open.

By using a quick online search or by asking those on email discussion lists, you can get an entire list of wonderful little software programs to help you keep track of your time. The advantage is that these programs use up very little of your memory. They are also fairly simple to use, both in starting and ending each session and in producing reports of the time you worked. A couple of clicks and things are done.

Not only can time tracking software help you keep track of the time you spend on client's projects, it can also help you to determine how long it takes you to do other tasks involved in running your business and on volunteer initiatives.

By keeping track of the time involved in every project, you have a better idea of how long it may take you to do a similar project the next time it arises. This is extremely beneficial when you must provide an accurate quote for future projects.

Getting and Keeping Clients

Clients are the most important asset of any business; not just a virtual assistance business. Without these valued clients we would be out there working for someone else rather than enjoying the passion of being independent business owners.

Thus far, we have covered a great deal about how to attain clients. Now we will concentrate on keeping those clients. First and foremost, you need to make every client feel like they are number one! This is the key to keeping your clients happy and coming back again and again for your assistance. There are a number of ways to do this:

Keep In Touch

As was mentioned in the *Organization is the Key* chapter, you need to keep in touch with your clients. This not only puts your name in front of their eyes, but it also shows that you care about them for more than just being an income for you.

Say thank you to your clients. When they sign a contract, when you start to perform tasks for them or upon completion of a project, send your client a thank you note. You can personalize it by using handwriting for both the message on the card and the address on the envelope.

On birthdays or other special occasions important to your clients, be sure to acknowledge them. **Send them a card** in the mail or an e-card to their email. Even a small gift for clients who are extremely special would definitely not go unnoticed.

TIP: Use www.sendoutcards.com. SendOutCards offers a simple and professional way for businesses to follow up with their customers, vendors and associates. You choose a card online, write your message and they print and mail it out on your behalf.

For the rest of the year, be sure to send your clients and contacts a **newsletter or company updates**. Newsletters are the preferred form of keeping in touch because they show your recipients the talents you possess and your willingness to share valuable resources with others. You will be showing your clients that you want to help them improve the exposure of their businesses by mentioning them in your newsletter in one form or another. You can include a customer profile every issue or add them to a list of links or resources and you would be surprised by how much they will appreciate even a little mention.

"I replied to an ad in the paper for an administrative assistant. I suggested that perhaps due to the nature of what the ad said that I felt having a VA might be a really good fit. The gentleman replied almost immediately and said he thought it was a great idea. After meeting with him and discussing all the details, I was hired. This was very exciting, but sadly as it turned out, he was one the worst clients for payment. It took him over one year to finally pay all my invoices, but he did manage to do it."

Denise Hill
Divine Design Creative Services
http://www.divinepresskits.ca

Customer Service at Its Best

Another way to keep clients happy is to offer the best customer service you possibly can. It is your duty to always keep their needs and wants in mind and cater to them.

Always respond to their requests in a timely fashion. If you cannot perform the task that they need done right away, at least respond to their request so they are aware that you have received it and will take care of it as soon as possible.

Maintain Professionalism

No matter how close a relationship with a client becomes, always remember to treat them with respect by continually maintaining a professional attitude and reputation.

When meeting with your clients, dress the part of a professional entrepreneur. Although most of our clients know that we work in a relaxed atmosphere in our homes, it is always best to keep a professional appearance.

Always be courteous to everyone, whether you want to be or not. There will be times during the course of running your business that you will come in contact with those who test your patience. However, by being courteous and respectful, those with which you experience conflict will not have the upper hand. You will be the one with more professionalism, and that will be noticed by everyone, including others who may be aware of the conflict you may have had. Keep a handle on any anger and ensure that your attitude is portrayed as patient and respectful. They won't be expecting that, and it may help in calming the situation.

If your conflict is with a valued client, make every effort, while maintaining your professionalism, to smooth the waters. Your client will respect a calm resolution to the problem rather than defensive remarks or tactics.

Honesty Builds Trust

Always be honest with your clients. If you are unable to complete a project on time, let your client know. It is better to be honest and earn their respect than to ill advise your client of a situation and lose their respect when you do not live up to their expectations.

On the same note, always keep your word. If you promise to do something for your client, whether in a certain time frame or not, be sure to stick to that promise. Again, if you can't meet a deadline or temporarily forget something you were supposed to do, let your client know of the delay. And, do your best to not let it happen again.

Each of the above suggestions is essential if you want to build a trusting relationship with your clients. Trust is vital to any relationship, and it is one of the most influential reasons why clients come back.

Go Above & Beyond The Call of Duty

Everyone has the ability to be respectful of his or her clients and to build honest relationships with them, but it is the person who goes the extra mile for their clients that will get the most recognition. Don't just do what the client wants; give them more than they need. If you are supposed to design a spreadsheet, do so by adding some input of your own. For example, colour-code the cells or highlight the results. Of course, as you work more with a client, you will get a sense of whether they would welcome your input. Do not go overboard if you have a feeling that they would not appreciate it.

Be sure to address problems or conflicts with your clients in a timely manner and keep them posted on the progress. Do not put off problems or give clients excuses. Face problems as they arise and don't let them accumulate.

Promote Your Clients and Their Businesses

As was mentioned in the Keep in Touch section at the beginning of this chapter, people like to see their company getting free exposure, so spread the word about your clients whenever possible.

You can do this by adding their website address to your list of resources on your website or in your newsletter. Have a portfolio of your work on your website and include a sample or screen shot of what you have done for clients. Include testimonials from your clients on your site or in your newsletter and be sure to give the name and company name of your client. Write an article and include information about your client that is pertinent to the article.

Any good businessperson knows that free publicity, especially to your target market, can help boost your exposure. This means the likelihood of increased clients counts, and thus, increased sales.

Remember, as Virtual Assistants we take pride in working WITH our clients and helping to build their businesses. Not only do we have to attain and maintain our own clients; In turn, we have to work with them to help them attain and maintain their clients.

> *"Getting your first client*: I felt like I had arrived. That at last I was in my element - that someone recognized my true worth.
>
> *Firing your first client*: Like I was in control."
>
> *Francesca Frate, Owner/Operator*
> *AdminConcepts - Your Administrative Connection*
> *http://www.adminconcepts.net*

Others Can Help You Get New Clients

Now that we have covered some of the ways in which we can keep our clients happy and thus keep them coming back, we should look at how those happy clients can help us get other new clients.

Testimonials

Many of your happy clients will offer words of appreciation and praise in either a verbal or written form. Be sure to ask them if they would mind if you use their words as a testimonial. This can not only help to show your potential clients about your skills and how pleased your current clients are, it can also be an excuse to solicit the testimonial by telling your clients you will include it in some form of your marketing and have their contact information as part of the testimonial.

If you are in need of a testimonial but do not have one on hand that you haven't used already, or if you need a longer, more detailed testimonial than you currently have available, be sure to ask your clients if they wouldn't mind writing one. You could even offer to write it for them, have them approve what you have written, and then sign their name to it.

Referrals

More than likely, your clients will mention you and your services when they come across someone who may need you. This is a great compliment for what you do, and a definition of the relationship you have with your client.

However, as part of your marketing efforts you should ask clients to spread the word about you and pass your name on to others.

Link Exchange

Exchanging links with your clients, and anyone whose business compliments yours, is beneficial to everyone all the way around. As a show of good faith and to pad your portfolio, include your client's website information. However, that doesn't mean your client will have a link to your site from theirs. So, why not ask them if they would add your website address to their site? Relevant link exchanges can help show your popularity to search engines and potential clients and thus increase your placement in the search engines and your exposure in other forms.

Letters of Reference

At some point you may have a potential client who would like to hear words from your current clients that show how you can provide the best services. That will be the time to ask a client for a letter of reference. Again, you could write the letter yourself and then get the client to approve it and sign it. However, a letter of reference will be more true to heart if the client writes it.

Dealing With a High Maintenance Client

Clients are the reason why we start our VA businesses. We strive to help each client with their overflow and build relationships with them. If we are lucky, they become a regular part of our routines and some even become good friends.

However, the longer you are in business, the more likely you will find yourself working with a client who leaves a little (or a lot) to be desired. You may find yourself wondering if working with this client is really worth the aggravation. Well, with the right planning and patience, as well as the ability to negotiate, you can turn a not-so-happy business relationship into a successful and prosperous one for both you and the client.

Have a Contract

No matter whom you are going to be working with or how much your intuition tells you that things will run smoothly, anything can happen. Things can start off well (or they may be bad right from the start) and then go downhill from there. In order to try and avoid any misconceptions of what is expected of you and them, it is best to have a contract outlining what you will be doing for the client and what their role is as well. This will help to cover both of your virtual derrieres should any issue arise. Be sure that both of you sign and date the contract and that each of you has a copy.

Negotiate

If a problems arises and you both stick to your guns about how the problem should be resolved, it is time to step back, take a deep breath and then negotiate with your client. If you explain your reasoning behind why or how you did a task for your client, they may understand and realize that your experience and desire to contribute to their success is the reason behind your actions, and that it may be good for them.

However, they also know their business better than you do and what is best for them, so you will have to give in and go with their wishes if they are adamant about how things should be done. You never know, you may learn something new from them and pass that on to other clients in some form in the future.

Ask for Help

One reason you may feel that a client is high maintenance may be because you do not have the expertise that they require for a certain project. You want to be in control of what you are doing for a client, but frustration sets in if you feel you can't provide the best service.

If you find yourself in a situation where you fear the relationship with your client is strained because you don't have the skills they require for a certain project, this is when it is time to ask for help.   There are numerous fellow VAs and other professionals you can call upon to help with an unfamiliar project. This can be done by either connecting your client with another VA or by acting as the go between yourself. In this case, the client lets you know what they need and you ask your associate for the help. More information on working with sub-contractors can be found in *Chapter 17 – Expanding Your Business*

Breaking the Ties

You may have tried everything you can to make a relationship with a client less maintenance, but there may be a reality that this will not work. If that becomes the case, then it is time to cut the strings and go your separate ways.

No matter how you choose to let your client know you do not feel your business relationship is working, be sure to keep the news professional. Do not fly off the handle or insult and belittle your client. Simply be honest and let them know that you feel someone else is better suited to be their assistant.

Keep Your Misfortune Private

One thing to keep in mind is to never ever slander a client in public or on public forums. If a high-maintenance client is something you want to warn others about that is your choice, but by using a public forum you are taking a chance of getting those on the forum or those who run it into trouble. If you insist upon giving someone the heads-up about how your relationship with a particular client was less than desirable, please do so in private.

> "Firing my first client was a very difficult thing for me to do because he was a friend and client. I repeatedly told him I was no longer interested in working for him and when I realized that he just wasn't "getting it", I thought perhaps a visual might work better. So I invited him over and returned all the files to him. As I handed him the pile, I said "these are all your records that you have left in my office for which I no longer will be responsible. It worked and I never heard from him again."
>
> *Denise Hill*
> *Divine Design Creative Services*
> http://www.divinepresskits.ca

Training, Upgrading and Certifications

When starting a business, each individual needs to ask themselves whether they have all the skills necessary to build a successful business. You might need to brush up on some skills, update your technical knowledge or you might need to start from the beginning and get a complete education.

If you are missing some key ingredients, then it's probably a good idea to take some training to fill in those gaps. If you have years of administrative experience but are just not sure how to run your own business, then some related courses would be helpful. If you are starting out with very little experience and really need a more complete education, then you would be better off looking at a more complete course or program.

Upgrading

There is a great deal of competition in the VA industry and you need to be at the top of your game to win and keep clients. As a Virtual Assistant it is important that you have current versions of the most popular software packages, and you must know how to use them. Each new version has improved technology and features and you should keep up to date. There are courses offered locally in the classroom as well as online courses. Research what's available in your area and find out what fits best with your needs.

There are also new technologies, programs and services that are offered on the Internet. It's a good idea to spend some time regularly searching out these offerings so that you are always offering your client base the most advanced technologies and services. Another good way to keep up to date is to belong to a VA discussion list like http://vanetworking.com, http://cvac.ca or http://ivaa.org. There are always discussions and suggestions about new programs or services that other VAs have discovered and found useful.

> "*Special courses or training*: Taking every secretarial course I could in high school and other related courses helped me to do the work. I would definitely recommend taking more computer courses and learning more about the Internet and how it works."
>
> *Francesca Frate, Owner/Operator*
> *AdminConcepts - Your Administrative Connection*
> *http://www.adminconcepts.net*

Training

There are many training courses and programs available. These courses vary in their implementation as well as focus and content. Some focus more on starting a business and others include administrative skills. The prices for these courses range between $200 and $5000.

We will provide an overview here of some of them, but your best bet is to do your own research and select the course that most closely meets your needs.

Virtual Business Start-up System (VBSS)
http://www.VirtualBusinessStartups.com

For aspiring and successful Virtual Assistants, this simple yet practical business startup system in a box will keep you both visually and intellectually stimulated on your exciting journey to entrepreneurship with your own successful Virtual Assistant business. It's an easy balance between short reading passages, writing exercises, helpful tips, templates and checklists. Includes everything you need to get started including a website package, business templates, 30 day step by step work book, reference books, coaching and many other resources all listed on the website. Here's some of what you will learn in the VBSS.

PHASE I: Business Sense

This phase of your virtual assistant startup will set the pace for the whole 30 days to come until you finish your VA startup. You'll receive the answers to many of your questions like: Will self-employment fulfill my needs? What's my motivation? What are my business goals? How organized am I? It will be a phase of self discovery and understanding of why you are starting up your VA business.

PHASE II: Business Description

This phase identifies what being a Virtual Assistant is all about. You'll work on defining your role as a VA, finding your target marketing and choosing your niche. You'll then start developing your business structure and pulling together all the loose ends like your business name, mission & vision statements to help you create your business milestones.

PHASE III: Marketing Kit

You can have the best business plan in the world but if you don't know how to market it, you might as well put it through the paper shredder. Tawnya Sutherland, a certified Internet Marketing Specialist and Business Strategist herself, will guide and help you (including templates) create a marketing kit that will stand out from your competition. From your business logo to getting your website ranking high in the search engines, she'll make sure you are seen by new clients from around the world.

PHASE IV: Operations:

This section covers all the legalese you'll come across in your business startup. From business insurance, hiring staff, bookkeeping or setting up your office space you'll learn how to find the resources you need to keep your operation running smoothly and efficiently without the typical business startup headaches & doubts.

PHASE V: Financial:

Having your financial goals in order is highly important in having a solid yearend revenue stream.   Tawnya will help you assess your expenses, set your pricing, determine how many hours you will work, teach you how to understand and chart your operational expenses. You'll wrap up this phase knowing you have your bookkeeping essentials in place.

PHASE VI: Business Plan:

By now you'll be ready to take on your business plan and develop it into the living bible that will be the tree trunk of your business forthwith. By the end of this phase you will have a completed business plan together with financials. You'll also learn how to become a Proactive VA, learning the 5 power keys to attain and keep your clients feeling like they can't do business without you!

PHASE VII: Maintenance:

Like a car that needs clean oil now and then, your business is no different. Tawnya will teach you how to maintain the momentum in your business week to week by teaching you how to choose a business coach to help motivate and guide you to success success stories of other Virtual Assistants. You'll be inspired by the success stories of others starting up just like you!

There are two levels of the VBSS with the first being the do-it-yourself level where you work through the system at your own pace. Or for those who want to pick up the pace with hand holding along the way, consider Tawnya's VA Intensive MotiVAtor Coaching Program. Visit the site for more info: http://VirtualBusinessStartups.com

Virtual Assistant Training Program
http://VATP.ca

The purpose of the Virtual Assistant Training Program is to be a resource and networking community for Virtual Assistants, while improving the quality of VA's in the community, and educating potential clients about their services.

Their mission is to create, develop and deliver a cost effective, convenient and high quality, training program for individuals who want to pursue the Virtual Assistant profession.

> **Module 1 - Tools of the Trade**
> **Module 2 - Enter the VA Community and Picture the Vision**
> **Module 3 - Client - Ready, Set, Go!**
> **Module 4 - Target Your Market**
> **Module 5 - Bullhorn Your Business**
> **Module 6 - The Buck Starts Here**
> **Module 7 - Time is of the Essence**
> **Module 8 - Next Steps to Raising the Bar**
> **Module 9 - Taking Care of Business**

To participate in the Virtual Assistant Training Program you need:

- 3 years previous administrative or related experience
- Intermediate knowledge of MS Office Suite
- Intermediate knowledge of the Internet
- A computer
- Reliable Internet access
- A noise cancelling computer headset
- And an open mind

AssistU

http://assistu.com

The Virtual Training Program (VTP) is a highly intensive, twenty-week program designed to guide you in becoming successful, long term, as a Virtual Assistant (VA). Using synchronous and asynchronous learning, coaching, and activities, the VTP is designed to give you the strongest start possible in creating, growing, and sustaining your business.

These are not skills like creating a better PowerPoint presentation, or web design, how to set up/maintain a shopping cart, or how to manage a client's social media strategy. The skills we give you may not be as sexy, but are absolutely more important than those. They are skills that will sustain you in your business and in relationships with clients regardless of the specific work you do, or don't do, with them. You have many of the task-related skills you need, already, and can learn others you may decide you need anywhere — and, in fact, many people learn what they need from other VAs in the AssistU community and others they belong to. The point is--you can get skills training from a thousand different sources. What we offer, you'll find nowhere else.

We also support the broadening of your understanding of virtual assistance and what you want for your business and yourself. Because it's so important to your success, we also spend time helping you understand how to create and sustain a solid small business. We take you from A to Z, giving you a road map of success!

Additionally, under the main curriculum, there are concurrent, and equally important sub-curricula:

Cyberskills — we show you what you need to know to be a power internet user, and introduce you and practice with you the use of technology that will allow you to better and more easily work and collaborate with your clients!

Writing Skills — we know what clients want from their VA, and strong writing skills are one of the hottest things requested. We help you strengthen your existing skills.

Extreme Self-Care — we know that, to have a terrific business, you need to have a terrific personal life. We also know that the corporate world doesn't care about you, and one reason you're considering being a Virtual Assistant is to get off that ever-spinning gerbil wheel. We help you work toward balance and taking time for yourself.

By the time you're finished, you'll have nearly 250 hours of training behind you, all designed to support your success as a Virtual Assistant, **and** you'll belong to the longest operating and successful communities solely for professional Virtual Assistants.

But don't take our word for it. Ask our grads--the people with successful practices, the ones who are living lives on their own terms. We're happy to connect you to them so that they can tell you about their work, their clients, and their experiences with us.

Or come to a call with our founder, Stacy Brice. She hosts a call every month for people who, just like you, are wanting to see big success and wondering about the best way(s) to get there. Her goal for that call is to give you the info you come for-- so you can ask her anything, and expect that she'll give you the straight scoop.

First step? Visit us online. If you like what you see there, talk to us. If you like what you hear, apply for our program. If you've gone all that way, we're probably the perfect people to take you on this part of your journey to having your own Virtual Assistance business, and work that contributes to your having a high-quality life!

Red Deer College Online Course
http://rdc.ab.ca/virtualassistant

Virtual Assistant Certificate
Certificate graduates are prepared to operate an office services home-based business. Graduates may also transfer into the Office Administration Online Collaborative Diploma.

Program Content (Total of Nine 3-credit courses)

> Core courses:
> | VA 100 | Document Formatting |
> | VA 110 | Communication Skills |
> | VA 120 | Basic Bookkeeping for Home Businesses |
> | VA 130 | Starting a Virtual Assistant Business |
> | VA 140 | Office Management for Virtual Businesses |
> | VA 150 | Marketing Your Virtual Business |
> | VA 160 | Virtual Practicum |
> | OADM 200 | Desktop Publishing |

> Approved option. Choose one of:
> | OADM 201 | Electronic Spreadsheets |
> | OADM 220 | Automated Accounting |
> | VA 170 | Web Design |

The VAinsider Club
http://VAinsiders.com

In 2005, Tawnya Sutherland decided that it was time to give Virtual Assistants an opportunity to become proactive and grow their VA businesses. She started the VAinsider Club to provide Virtual Assistants around the world with training, guidance and support as they grew their Virtual Assistant businesses.

Today the VAinsider Club is made up of both new and veteran VAs that truly care about the success of their business and the VA industry, as a whole. VAinsiders understand that creating a solid and successful business takes the support of others and the VAinsider Club is providing that support for them. The VAinsider club has become a place where members can get answers to their questions, celebrate their successes and just "hang out" with likeminded business owners in a fun, collaborative and exciting way.

With hundreds of members to date, VAinsiders is the fastest growing club of its kind for VAs looking to put their business on the fast track through motivational group training and resources.

The VAinsider Club membership includes three different levels to suit everyone's budget:

Every level will receive the **Monday MotiVAtor** to start off your week on the right foot in your virtual business. We also have pulled together some **fantastic discounts** on software and services from a list of premier partners for all VAinsider Club members and you'll receive **discounted advertising rates** at the well known VAnetworking.com website. AND, that's not all! To show credibility to your clients, to let them know you do invest in your business by joining elite and educational organizations for your business, you'll be able to sport our VAinsider logo.

VAinsider Booster:

This level is for the new entrepreneur who wants to be *"in the know"* in the VA industry and network with like-minded virtual business colleagues in a private environment to share and learn from each other. Includes full access to all our archived audio workshops plus it also includes a monthly ProactiveVA training workshop. (Read full benefits below)

VAinsider Get Clients:

This level is for the entrepreneurs who wants to **kick things up a notch and start filling their client base.** Includes everything in the Booster level plus full access to our job board and to our monthly Getting Clients ProactiveVA Series monthly workshop.

VAinsider Supercharge:

This level is for the entrepreneur who is **serious about their business and ready to invest in it.** This package includes everything in the above two packages plus much more. These entrepreneurs are looking to save time by not having to design their business templates or develop their business plan from scratch. They are ready to put together a strategic Internet marketing plan and follow through with it via online advertising online and the latest internet marketing techniques to put their business a step ahead of their competitors. They are looking for the support only an elite group of like-minded individuals can provide. This package also includes many other resources including a VA business plan, business templates, bonus advertising perks, access to VAnetworking's ebook Series, plus a collection of other resourceful business ebooks.

Whether you are a Virtual Assistant who needs a boost, new clients or a new strategic marketing plan, we have a package suited just for you.

Read full benefits at our website at http://VAinsiders.com

Virtual Business Training
http://virtualbusinesstraining.com

Virtual Business Training cultivates tomorrow's Virtual Associates through an accelerated, ten-week training program designed for those who are serious about starting or jump-starting a Virtual Assistant or Virtual Service Business. With our no-nonsense approach, client-simulation exercises and training from the best in the industry, students gain exactly what they need to launch a viable and sustainable VA business including the tools, tricks of the trade, software and hardware, pricing and marketing strategies utilized by the experts.

The 10 week program includes:

- Group and individual instruction, coaching and mentoring.
- Peer collaboration and client-simulation exercises in a dynamic learning environment.
- Presentations on topics crucial to the development and startup of a VA Business.
- Expert presentations and advice from Industry Leaders and Colleagues who own successful virtual service businesses.
- Extensive reference library, tools, and tips from other successful VAs.

Virtual Business Training is committed to ensuring the high standards of those offering their services virtually, to individual and industry integrity, and to producing top-notch virtual associates.

VAclassroom
http://www.cvac.ca/vaclassroom

VAclassroom offers a comprehensive skills training center for Virtual Assistants, Online Professionals and Consultants. The primary mission of VAClassroom is to equip new and existing Virtual Assistants and Online Professionals with the specific skills and knowledge that businesses are seeking today!

Watch the website for upcoming workshops on various skillsets demanded today of a Virtual Assistant like:

Internet Marketing Specialist Certification - Discover the specific Internet Marketing skills your clients are desperate for you to know. Further expand your Internet Marketing skills so you can further ignite your client and income opportunities for your business.

Social Marketing Specialist Certification - Discover some powerful new tools, skills and tactics to develop current, high demand social media services for today's market!

Virtual Event Specialist Certification - Discover the training that will have a new wave of clients banging down your doors, begging for your proven virtual event expertise and assistance!

Product Launch Specialist Certification - Get trained and certified in the Product Launch Support Specialist Training Program and watch your client and income opportunities soar.

Virtual Assistant Business Success Blueprint Training - Save literally months of time trying to create the right system for your business with this proven virtual assistant blueprint that was tirelessly developed by a six-figure virtual assistant extraordinaire over a ten-year period!

Online Video Marketing Specialist Training - Master an innovative and easy-to-implement system for delivering Online Video Marketing service packages to virtually any type of client!

Fantastic Facebook Pages Program - Master cutting-edge design and marketing skills to help your clients thrive and succeed in the largest media channel the world has ever seen!

Blog Marketing Tips, Tools & Tactics Course - Access a blog marketing blueprint that will take your blog site to new heights and make you look like "Blog Rock Star" with your clients!

Podcast Marketing Success Strategies - Access this innovative podcast marketing mini-course and develop cutting-edge skills to help your clients thrive and succeed in this new and unchartered mobile media frontier!

There has never been a better time to start or grow a virtual business than now! As many of you know, the Internet landscape continues to re-invent itself and businesses are in desperate need of talented Virtual Assistants. Consultants and Online Professionals to effectively service their evolving business and marketing support functions.

VA Training Site
http://VAtrainingSite.com

The VA Training Site was founded by Tawnya Sutherland and Lynette Chandler who seen a technical training need in the Virtual Assistant world that wasn't being met by other VA focused training programs online today.

Not only do Virtual Assistants need to be on top of their administrative skills like typing, internet research and Microsoft Word formatting, VAs also need to know, on the fly, how to help their clients with new business services they need right now!

There is a real and growing need for service providers who are able to support a businesses' day-to-day technical demands as the Internet matures and more businesses come online. Most do not need programmer level help, but someone who can handle the simple to intermediate issues. You can fill that need and once you do, you'll find yourself a cut above any other service provider off the street. Clients tend to value you more and you get recommended more often because others 'don't know how to do that tech stuff'.

Nowadays clients are asking more from their Virtual Assistants like:

- Do you know how to use Wordpress so you can set me up a blog?
- Can you set me up an affiliate center?

- Can you setup a help desk in Wordpress?
- Can you make my ebooks look sexy?
- Do you know CSS basics to help maintain my website?
- Do you know aMember so you can set up my membership site?
- Can you help me with my cpanel?

We know it's difficult to keep on top of all the new software coming out and the next social media craze. We know that as service providers, every working hour of the day is billable time. You can't spend too much of that time digesting courses 10 DVD's long. You need to cut to the chase so you can quickly apply your new skills and knowledge on a clients' job and be paid for it.

The learning modules you find here are created in bite-sized chunks, without stuff that complicate things. Some modules are built as kits complete with themes and frameworks so you don't have to start from scratch, crucial if you bill your clients by project because the more efficient you are, the more you earn.

Put an end to your learning frustrations...

We know how it feels to be lost in a sea of technical jargon or given cold answers by community support. Every training module at the VA Training Site is carefully developed to avoid jargon and confusing concepts so you won't be lost. Where difficult terms and concepts are inevitable, they are explained in as plain a manner as possible so you can grasp them and we'll support you so you never have to feel embarrassed about asking a question no matter how small.

You don't have to spend away all your profits to get the training you need in order to make more. You will find reasonably priced learning modules in our product line up so you can keep much needed expenses low and your bottom line healthy. The net result is, you get to keep more of what you work hard to earn to spend on things that are important to you and your family.

When you can support your clients with a range of services they really need, you are immediately more valuable than a service provider who can only do a small portion of work. Clients much prefer to work with people they already know and trust versus doing more recruitment. The more they value you, the more readily they will pay the price you ask. What this means is, you can boost your income without having to look for more clients or putting in more hours.

There comes a time when every Virtual Assistant needs that specific technical training that isn't easily found in affordable simple to learn modules. Check out our newest learning modules at http://VAtrainingSite.com

To Certify or not to Certify

Certifications are an issue of hot debate in the VA industry. Certifications either indicate the completion of a VA course or they are peer review based and may be fairly arbitrary. The most widely recognized certification is offered by VA Certified.

VA Certified

http://VAcertified.com

VAcertified.com is the go-to resource for Virtual Assistants who want credible, unbiased and international recognition for their skills, education, professional experience and industry contributions.

It's a fact that no matter how much you research a potential VA, there remains much guesswork in determining if a Virtual Assistant is in fact the experienced, skilled professional he or she claims to be. Yet top notch VAs work very hard to build and promote their businesses.

And that's why we created VAcertified.com. **No more will clients and prospective clients have to wonder**, "What does this certification really mean, and what does it take to get it?"

And no more will virtual assistants have to guess which certification program will give them a globally recognized and widely promotable credential.

VAcertfied.com provides VAs an unparalleled opportunity to put your skills, experience and contributions in front of an unbiased global review board of virtual assistants and virtual professionals.

Virtual Assistants who are VAcertified demonstrate to clients and prospective clients that:

1. Their products and services are relevant to how business is conducted in today's global economy.
2. They are committed to offering a level of professionalism in all that they do, both for their clients and the virtual assistance industry at large.
3. They are the VA they say they are. They represent themselves, their businesses, their offerings and the VA industry with integrity, honesty and respect for others.

When you have the **VAcertified seal on your website** and other key marketing materials, **any client from any country will have reason to trust in your ability to be the RIGHT Virtual Assistant to partner with.**

Unlike other certification programs made up of local business people, local organizations or individual training organizations, VAcertified.com has brought together a global panel of experts. These experts comprise our decision making board.

The VAcertified board worked together to agree upon the skills, training, and professional presence that are wanted, needed, and more importantly demanded by potential clients worldwide. This was not without much deliberation and debate, and we recognize that as the virtual assistance industry evolves, so must we along with it.

A Diverse Panel. A Diverse Perspective on What Makes a Great VA.

VAcertified.com drew upon the contacts of the world's largest VA social community (VAnetworking.com) and its relationship in the global market place to determine what today's client is looking for in a VA. It is those skills and abilities that are represented in the standards used to award the VAcertified seal to qualifying applicants.

We have found that not only do potential clients want to know what your skill sets are, they want to know where they came from. They want to know things like:

- Are your credentials from Government Certified Schools? Or from an online source?
- What kind of professional presence do you have, online and off?
- Do you give back to the community you live in? How about the one you work in?
- Are you professional successes verifiable?
- Do you understand the inherent challenges of succeeding in business today?

Your Hard Work and Dedication Elsewhere Counts.

VAcertified.com is the only Virtual Assistant certification program in the world that looks at everything that makes you YOU. That means you are credited for your unique skills and experience, **including what you accomplished before you were a VA.**

We are interested in the value of what you have done and who you have become. When you have earned the VAcertified.com seal, you have the endorsement of a global panel of experts who took the time to know every aspect of what makes you the VA you are today.

You can also be sure that prospective clients will take a second look. They will approach you with less doubt, less fear, and the confidence that you indeed have the skills and abilities you so market.

Certified Canadian Virtual Assistant

Offered at http://cvac.ca

CVAC has established the first Virtual Assistant certification program in Canada. Applications are open to *members of CVAC only.* Certification shows your potential clients and fellow VAs that your experience and professionalism is at a level that enables you to provide the best in services and assistance. It also shows that you are recognized by your peers as being exceptional in the industry and highly recommended for assignments that require your specialty. Your commitment to excellence and your passion for your business are a part of you that shines through in your assignments and customer service.

How to Apply:

There are several procedures that must be followed in order to apply for your CCVA Certification.

The first step will be to answer some Virtual Assistant industry and small business related questions. These questions range from the basic to specific questions for which the answers will prove your knowledge of the industry and the procedures needed to run a virtual small business.

The second step will be to provide some background information regarding your education and business experience.

The third step will involve writing a short essay relating why you started this business and what your aspirations are for the future.

The final step will be to put all the information together in professional format, and include a few other pieces of information to help establish your professionalism.

Below you will find a link taking you to the listing of documents that need to be filled in and returned to CVAC for consideration.

How will your application be judged?

Judges of your entry will include your fellow VAs, those who have established a presence as industry leaders. Each part of the application will be judged on a point system. Several judges will evaluate your entry and assign points for each part. These points will then be combined and averaged out to give you an average point total. That point total will determine whether you are eligible for the Certified Canadian Virtual Assistant accreditation. If your point total is not sufficient to receive the accreditation, we will provide you with reasons and tips for re-applying (if necessary). You are then welcome to re-apply at any time.

Certified Professional & Master Virtual Assistant – CPVA/CMVA
http://assistu.com

The CPVA designation is the first level of certification available to AssistU trained Virtual Assistants. The CMVA designation is the second level of certification offered. It is a Master's level certification, and the highest certification offered and available only to AssistU CPVAs. You must complete program instruction at AssistU to be eligible for these certifications.

REVA Institute

http://revainstitute.com

Certificate Program Learning Objectives:

A knowledgeable and trained Real Estate Assistant is in hot demand. We have the courses that cover it all. Take our courses individually to augment your current skills, or one at a time to work towards your certification as time permits.

In conjunction with REA University, the Real Estate Assistant Certificate Program covers a wide array of topics – Everything from the basics to niche services that you can learn to help you better assist your agents and make you a "hot commodity" in the real estate industry.

 To provide the student with the knowledge, skills and confidence necessary to effectively support real estate professionals by providing comprehensive theory and practical hands-on experience in our modules and accompanying audio training series.

We will also provide regular conference calls in order to answer your questions about the course material, and to mastermind with your fellow students.

International Virtual Assistant Association - IVAA

http://ivaa.org

The International Virtual Assistants Association (IVAA) is dedicated to the professional education and development of members of the Virtual Assistance profession, and to educating the public on the role and function of the Virtual Assistant.

Ethics Check Exam

The EthicsCheck Examination for Virtual Assistants assesses the Virtual Assistant's business ethics competencies in key areas, including:

- Billing Issues
- Conflicts of Interest
- Privacy and Confidentiality
- Ability to Perform the Work

Questions are formatted as either multiple-choice, case studies followed by a series of true-or-false or multiple-choice statements, or scale-rating scenarios (i.e., "Never"; "Almost Never"; "Seldom"; etc.).

CRESS Certification

The IVAA Real Estate Support Specialist Examination for Virtual Assistants assesses the Virtual Assistant's competencies in areas that are key when supporting real estate professionals, including: Legally Permissible Activities by Unlicensed Assistants.

- Real Estate Industry Terminology
- Privacy and Confidentiality
- Business Ethics
- Conflicts of Interest.

Questions are formatted as either multiple-choice, case studies followed by a series of true-or-false or multiple-choice statements, or scale-rating scenarios (i.e., "Never"; "Almost Never"; "Seldom"; etc.).

Moving Your Home-Based Business

Just mention the word moving and anyone who has ever done it will recall all the work that was involved and cringe at the thought of having to do it again anytime soon. The many hours of packing up boxes, disposing of unused items either in the garbage or donating them to charity, notifying contacts of your move, and then unpacking and finding a place for everything in your new home can add up to overwhelming stress and anxiety.

When you also have to move a home-based business, there is a lot more that needs to be done. In this chapter, we will cover items that will apply to moving a home and a home-based business. We will also cover moving a home-based business to a brick & mortar location.

Choosing the Right Home

Let's start at the beginning. If you run a home-based business and are considering moving to a new home, the first thing you will be doing is finding the perfect place. You will not only consider the comfort and aspects of the home for you and your family, but will also need to consider how your business will fit into your home. Your office area needs to be more than just a section of the living room or the kitchen table. For some, moving may be the first opportunity to have a designated office.

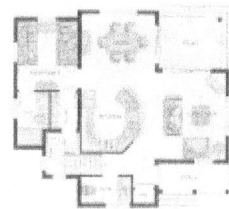

As your business grows, so will the need for more space. Multiplying file drawers and shelving will become the norm in your office. Although technology seems to be taking up less room these days, more and more gadgets and equipment are being developed that will take the place of certain equipment and add to your wealth of available services. You will inevitably want to get some of these new gadgets and will need adequate and appropriate room for them.

Also, if clients come in to your office, you should consider a big enough space to accommodate meetings. This will portray a positive and professional atmosphere to your visitors. However, we do realize that this may not be an option. In that case, do the best you can to provide an area somewhere else in your home that will be comfortable and won't create distractions or interruptions.

Location, Location, Location

As a Virtual Assistant with a primarily virtual client base, location may not be all that big a deal. However, many VAs have local clients who are an important part of their business and may require more hands-on work than virtual clients. For VAs who may be looking for a new home, location will be an important consideration.

If you have a tendency to travel to your client's place of business or if they often come to yours, you will need to stay in close proximity to where you are at present. The same applies if you tend to run errands for your clients. You want to stay in a range that will not mean spending more time out of your office doing these tasks.

However, as a virtual assistant, you can learn to adapt to new surroundings and the new challenges of being farther away from your clients. Your experience in the virtual world can be used to ease the transition and your client's piece of mind. Not to mention, if shopping for supplies or items for your clients is part of your service offering, you probably already know that you can get almost anything on the Internet and have it delivered directly to your home.

Staying within the Boundaries of Local Laws

You need to ensure that you are allowed to run a home-based business in your community. For an administrative business that doesn't have too many clients on the property, it is not usually an issue. However, in some areas there are legal issues that need to be considered. You should check with the municipality you are moving to and follow all their legislation.

Timing is Everything

It may seem like a silly thing to consider, but there may be times of the year that are either inconvenient to you or to your clients to be pulling up stakes and relocating to a new home office. Christmas time is generally one of the busiest times of the year for most people anyway, so moving a business around that time of year may not be recommended. Not to mention, due to weather considerations, moving in the winter isn't all that much fun.

If you have a client who has a busy time of year or if you have a busy time coming up, this may not be the ideal time to move. For example, preparing for trade shows takes up enough of your time without the added stress of moving or trying to find things that may be packed away in boxes. Of course, if the closing date on your new home is down the road a distance, you will not know what will be taking place in your business life at that time so avoiding a time conflict may be difficult.

Let Others Know You are Moving

This is when you will realize exactly how many people you come in contact with every day. The first thing you should do is make a list of the various people who need to be informed. This should be done several months in advance of your move to allow companies the time they may require for these administrative changes to take effect.

The obvious people or companies to contact include:
- Phone company; Utilities (gas, water, electric, etc.); Cable or satellite company

You will also need to advise your
- Child's school (both new & old if they will be changing schools); Child's bus company; Doctor, dentist, chiropractor, etc.

But the list doesn't end there. The following are some contacts that we don't want you to forget:
- Clients

- Lawyer
- Accountant
- Driver's Licence
- Insurance (business, automotive, etc.)
- Memberships in organizations (Chamber of Commerce, online associations, etc.)
- Subscriptions to magazines, newspapers, etc.
- Cell phone company
- Internet Service Provider
- Bank
- Credit companies, including any cards for stores
- The government for any payments you are entitled to (GST, child tax credit, income tax, etc.)
- Website domain and hosting companies
- Your website
- Courier companies you have accounts with
- Anyone you be expecting mail from (i.e. college alumni association, etc.), and
- Any place online that may have your contact information

There may be other people you need to contact and advise of your move. Be sure to add them to your list and start contacting them with advanced warning of your move. You can then worry about the others when you feel they need to be notified.

You should also arrange for a change of address notification with Canada Post. They offer two options… one for individuals and one for businesses. Unfortunately, as you run a small business and will need to include your business name on the change of address, you will inevitably have to pay more than when simply moving a household. Visit http://www.CanadaPost.ca for more information on their service.

Arrange for a Moving Truck

Whether your desire is to move your belongings with the help of friends and family or utilize the services of a moving company, you will need to arrange your transportation as far in advanced of the move as possible. Moving companies are very busy, especially during the first and last days of the month, so contact them well in advance to arrange for the truck. A good time to do this would be as soon as you have a firm date.

When speaking with the company, they will try to help you determine the size of truck you will need. Most do-it-yourself truck rental companies will base the size of the truck on the average furniture that fills a home (including a specified number of bedrooms). However, as you also have business equipment, you need to take into account every bit when figuring out the size of truck you will need.

Update Your Marketing Material

Be sure that you change your contact information on all of your marketing material. This includes business cards, letterhead, brochures, flyers, newsletters, and any templates you use during the operation of running your business.

Also be sure you change your information on your website and on any websites that list your contact information.

Err on the Side of Caution

We don't want to invoke fear in you or give the impression that being an independent business owner/Virtual Assistant is dangerous, but we feel it is important for you to be cautious in all aspects of running your business. Unfortunately, there are people out there that have nothing better to do with their time than to make others' lives a misery so, as they say... better to be safe than sorry.

Computer & Document Safety

Your computer will be the one place that will be open to intrusion and problems if you don't take precautions to minimize the dangers.

- Backup, backup, backup! Should any problems arise, you want to be able to regain your important information.
- Keep track of all usernames and password that you use. It is also a good idea to change your passwords every once in a while, and don't share your access information with anyone.
- Spam – No matter how hard any of us try, spam is a part of any computer owner's life, Internet connection and email. However, we can minimize threats they may pose by taking the following precautions:
    - Install a spam filter on your computer. If you are working with Outlook, the current and most recent versions include a Junk folder that can help to keep 'some' of the spam out of your Inbox.
    - Never click on a link that is included in any of these spam emails. Not only are you taking the chance that you will be taken to a website that adds cookies or spam to your computer, these spammers generally have a means of knowing when someone comes to their site from an email. As a result, these spammers are seeing visits and they will continue to send out these spam messages thinking they have a chance of selling their products.
    - Most spam is only a downright pain in the butt. It hits our Junk folders and is deleted at the click of a button. However, you may occasionally see some that are bad enough that they should be reported to someone. If you find that these emails are offensive (more offensive than the average spam that you get), you should either report it to the server company hosting the site or report it to your local police department.
- Viruses are also a threat to your computer. Again, you should never click on a link or open a document in an email from an unknown source as it may contain a virus. To keep a handle on viruses and stop them in their tracks, install an anti-virus program. Be sure to run a virus scan on your computer on a regular basis and also run it on new files that you receive from clients. You may trust them implicitly, but you never know when they have received a virus and not knowingly passed it on.
- Finally, if your computer has access to the Internet, you should consider having a firewall to stop intruders from gaining access. There are numerous security programs on the market that can help you with this. Some are listed in our Software List in the Resources section.

Physical Safety

There are not a lot of manual, physical disasters that can happen to a VA in comparison to many other occupations. However, injuries can and do occur as a result of not having the proper office equipment.

Going ergonomic can be a wonderful means of preventing physical ailments that may affect your job performance. By using the proper furniture and accessories, you can work comfortably all day without your body aching.

We recommend the following:

- Keep your monitor at eye level. You shouldn't have to raise or lower your head or eyes to see the center of your monitor.
- Your keyboard and mouse need to be at a level where your arms are at your sides and not extended out to reach the keys.
- Use an ergonomic chair that is on casters/rollers so you can move around as needed. Also, make sure your chair is at a height and angle that is comfortable for you and allows you to work with your keyboard and mouse, and correctly view your monitor.
- Use a headset on your phone so you aren't trying to work and hold the phone at the same time. Your neck, shoulders and arms will start to ache the more you try to hold the phone between your ear and shoulder.
- An ergonomic keyboard can also be an option if you find that your hands and wrists are feeling the stress.

Personal Safety

As a home-based business, it is best to be cautious when it comes to meeting with clients, especially new ones. We don't recommend having new clients come to your home office or you going to their home offices. It is best to meet in a public place, perhaps a donut shop or local restaurant.

If a client wants to meet with you at their home office, again… we don't recommend doing this. It is best to meet in a public location. Unfortunately, there have been reports of 'supposed' clients using the farce of needing an assistant in order to gain the trust of a VA and assaulting them instead. The bottom line is…be careful where you meet.

You may have a request to do work for a brick and mortar company. Use your discretion for these situations and, if it doesn't feel 'right' to meet in their offices, take someone with you (who can wait in the car) or suggest a more public meeting location.

Whenever meeting with a new client and, no matter where, be sure to tell someone where you are going and then check in with them when you return so they are aware you are safe.

Safety takes on many forms. This doesn't mean you can't have a successful business. You just need to heed any warning signs and use common sense.

Balancing Business and Family

When you first start your business and if you have a family, you may find that juggling day-to-day routines and making sure you have time for everything becomes quite the life drainer. And, as you become busier, it will only get more and more hectic unless you take steps to bring some organization to your daily activities.

Setting Boundaries

One of the first things you'll need to do when you start your home-based business is to educate your family and friends about what you're doing. Explain that even though you are at home, you are not available for visits. In order to build a successful business you must spend your 'office hours' working. It's difficult to turn your friend or neighbour away when they drop by for coffee at 10 am, but it gets easier. Once they understand that you're working, they'll limit their visits to outside of your working hours.

Dealing with Interruptions

Everyone deals with interruptions when they are trying to concentrate on something else. The daily grind of working for a living is also riddled with interruptions that are unavoidable. As home-based business owners, we have unique interruptions which are not experienced on the same scale by those working outside the home.

If you are going to make a living while working from home, you need to learn how to handle interruptions, and perhaps set some ground rules that both you and your family should follow.

One important thing that you can do to cut down on daytime interruptions is to NEVER answer your home phone during the day. Obviously if you use your home phone as your business phone this is tricky, but if you answer your telephone with your company name during 'office hours' and answer with a simple, 'Hello' outside of those hours, people will gradually get the message.

The most difficult people to teach about your need for silence and no interruptions are your children. If you are lucky enough to have children of school age, then you have an advantage, in that your children are in school for a good part of the day. However, there are school vacations that are unavoidable and you will have to make sure the children realize that although they have a day (or more) off, you still need to work.

Part of the charm of working from home is letting others see the whole picture. Many will completely understand the various background noises that they may hear when talking on the phone to you. However, if you answer phones for your clients, you need to take extra care in ensuring that everything sounds and appears as professional as possible.

Children need to read the signs. Of course, if they are ill or have some other issue that is keeping them home and they need your attention, then you will need to deal with these interruptions to the best of your ability. However, when they are home during regular working hours, it is important that your children learn to respect your needs.

> "*Balancing work/home life*: In the beginning I was constantly working on the business - it drove me. It was my reason for getting up in the morning; everything centered around my business. During the time that I was trying to establish myself I also had to deal with elder care, and many times I was torn. I had a husband who wanted my time, an aging mother and a new business that needed to be promoted. Needless to say, the one who really suffered was me. I forgot to take time for me.
>
> It's hard enough trying to balance every day, but when you add a business into the equation you're bound to reach a burn out stage. I really believe that we need to stop every now and then and take a day for ourselves, whether it's reading a book for the sake of reading, taking a few hours off to have picnic with yourself or just taking the dog for a walk. We have to remember that we are no good for the business, family or to ourselves if all we do is focus on one thing 24/7."
>
> *Francesca Frate, Owner/Operator*
> *AdminConcepts - Your Administrative Connection*
> *http://www.adminconcepts.net*

When the phone rings, they need to be taught to be quiet and wait their turn. The same holds true when you are concentrating on a project. Teach the children to do something productive while they are waiting to speak with you.

Keep the children busy with homework or chores. When you are unable to give them your full attention, be sure they have something else to keep them occupied and preferably this should be something productive.

If you have a child that is still too young to be at school for a majority of the day, you will have to deal with keeping the child entertained. Take advantage of nap times and use this time to return any phone calls that you may have missed or to work on a project that requires complete concentration.

If you find that someone comes to the door at an inopportune time, if you have a scheduled meeting, or if you have unexpected visitors who need some of your attention, be sure to have your answering machine set up to answer your calls. Better yet, if possible, arrange to meet with your visitors at a more convenient time.

For a minimal charge, most telephone companies will provide an Identi-call service where two phone numbers actually ring on the same line but with a different ring tone. This is a great way for you to be able to tell if the call is personal or business before you answer it.

Another feature commonly offered is to have extensions on your call answer feature. This way your message can say something like, "You have reached 555-1212, if you are calling for The Arnold Family, please press '1'. If you're calling for **V**alerie **A**rnold or Fictitious VA please press '2'.

If you find the need to let your answering machine take messages, you will eventually have to return the calls, so do so by prioritizing their importance. Then pick a suitable time of day to handle the not-so-important ones.

Another way to keep the kids occupied when you need to concentrate is to send them to a friend's house, allow them to invite a friend over, or use the services of a babysitter or caregiver. A few hours of uninterrupted work can be plenty of time to accomplish the important tasks that need to be handled.

As home-based entrepreneurs, we live to help others, so most of us find it hard to say no to anything. It is of utmost importance that you learn to do just that…say NO! If you find that someone is calling when you are trying to concentrate, or that they are calling regularly each day or week and taking your time away from your work, then it is best to be honest with them by telling them you are busy. Advise them that you will call them back when it is more convenient for you.

Set Office Hours

As we mentioned above, setting office hours can help keep your home-based life organized. A time for work and a time for family must be separated from each other and should be split based on what is usually considered regular business hours. This is the most logical for a service-based business such as virtual assistance.

Establishing office hours may be necessary if part of your service offering is to answer phone lines for your clients during specific hours. Of course, if you are based in one time zone and your client is in another, you may need to extend your regular hours, but there needs to be a "quitting time" for business tasks and a starting time for family tasks. Establishing office hours helps you, your clients and your family to stick to a routine and help cut back on those unwanted interruptions.

Housework vs. Work-work

When you're working from home, it's hard to ignore the various household chores that are on your list of 'things to do'. There always seems to be something that needs to be done. Taking care of household chores before settling down to work can sometimes be an unconscious method of procrastination, but if you set a period of time first thing in the morning to take care of personal errands or housework and then get down to work, that can be a great way to organize your day.

When it's time to work, leave your 'home' and go to your 'office'. If your office is in a separate room this is easier than if your office is at your dining room table. If your office is in a common room, then try to position yourself so that your back is to the room. You won't be constantly reminded of the chores that need to be done.

If you are the type of person who can multi-task (and aren't we all, to some degree?), then you may be able to take care of some of the household chores while you work. If you're on a lengthy phone call and you have a cordless phone and a headset you can walk around the house during the call allowing you to get some much-needed movement while straightening up, dusting or even putting in a load of laundry. It is very important to ensure that anything you're doing is NOT taking away from the needs of your client. If you can't concentrate on your phone call while taking care of these tasks, then don't. Leave them until 'after hours' and enlist your spouse and/or children to help out. After all, you wouldn't be expected to take care of household chores if you were away working at an office all day.

Don't Beat Yourself Up Over Lost Time

Even though we discussed the importance of setting regular office hours and sticking to them in order to gain some form of organization in your life, there will always be times that you may have to be away from your office during regular business hours.

If your child is sick and you need to tend to them, or if you have to pick them up from school due to illness or getting hurt, these are times when your family comes first. Hours or days later, you may feel guilty about taking that time away from your office, but don't! Most parents drop everything if there is a problem involving their children. You should be no different. Priorities need to be established, so please put your family first when necessary.

TRY to keep business hours as scheduled as possible, but don't beat yourself up about any instances where you need to leave your office to deal with other matters. If possible, make up for that lost time over the next few days and get yourself back on track slowly. Never let the fact eat away at you that you had to take some time away from your work. It's all a part of life and of being a parent with a career.

Be Good to Yourself

For many Virtual Assistants, day-to-day life is all about being good to your clients. We strive to offer them superlative service, no matter what the cost.

However, for VAs and many small business owners, the intensity of working long hours to provide the very best can take its toll, not only on our minds and bodies, but also on our businesses.

Owning and operating a small business is, in numerous ways, very different than being an employee. When you work for someone else and are not feeling well, you simply call in sick. However, when you are a small business owner and not feeling well, you know that things still need to get done so you tend to try to forget how you are feeling in order to complete tasks.

This is where you need to change our mindset. As a small business owner, if you aren't well, your business may suffer. Not to mention, if you aren't feeling well, your body is trying to tell you it's time to take a break. We will discuss ideas for taking a break later in this chapter.

> *"Finding time for 'you'*: Just as we schedule our clients work we also need to schedule time to learn, time to play and time to just sit back and do nothing. "
> *Francesca Frate, Owner/Operator*
> *AdminConcepts - Your Administrative Connection*
> *http://www.adminconcepts.net*

Reducing the Causes of Your Stress

As mentioned above, when you aren't feeling well, it's your body's way of sending you warning signs. Either you have a physical ailment that needs a doctor's attention, or your stress levels are playing havoc with your health. Those high stress levels could be caused by the numerous tasks you are trying to juggle. Studies have shown that work stress can contribute to the increased rates of heart attack and when you are stressed, there is a good chance you are also unhappy on some level.

The following are just a few ideas to help reduce your workload, and thus reduce your stress levels (which could be contributing to your body not feeling 100%):

1. Don't bite off more than you can chew. This cliché may seem like a given, but when running a VA business, saying no or turning away assignments can be quite difficult, especially during the start-up phase when you are trying to build a full practice.

2. Set reasonable office hours. When working from home, most of us tend to work much more than when we have to travel to our jobs. Try to restrain yourself and balance your life by setting regular business hours and sticking with them (except perhaps the occasional after-hours project). For more help with balancing work and home, see *Chapter 14 - Balancing Business & Family*.

3. You aren't superhuman, no matter how much you want to believe you are. When things are going well with your business, you may feel like nothing can bring you down and that you can accomplish everything that you have on the go. Again, learn your limits and remember that doing too much for too long WILL take its toll on you and your body.

4. Learn when to let a client or project go. No matter who you are or how dedicated you are to your clients, you will run into at least one person who will test your limits. No matter how profitable they may be, if you find that you have to calm yourself down each time you have contact with a client, it may be time to let them go.

5. Be sure to take breaks throughout the day. Even when you are an employee, you are entitled to a lunch break and perhaps other small breaks throughout your day. Just because you are an entrepreneur doesn't mean you aren't entitled to a break here and there.

6. If you do find that the workload is getting to be too much, outsource it. As VAs, our 'job' is to take the workload off our small business clients. However, we forget that we are also small business owners as well and there are VAs who are willing to help you, especially those who have a newer practice. For more information on expanding your business and bringing on sub-contractors, see *Chapter 17 – Expanding Your Business.*

Tips to Help Reduce the Stress

No matter how much we try to balance our lives (*Chapter 14 - Balancing Business & Family)* or reduce our workload (see above), we all suffer from some form of stress. With the fast-paced world in which we live, stress, unfortunately, is part of everyone's lives. We have more and more going on and the chances of staying stress free are slim to none.

Everyone has their own ideas and suggestions for helping to relieve some of the stress in their lives. The following are some suggestions of what you can do in your day-to-day lives to help tame the stress monster. Many of these ideas were offered to us by the members of CVAC:

1. Get plenty of sleep. How many times have you stayed up way past your bed time to get a project completed? This needs to stop. You need to ensure you get enough sleep to allow your body to relax and rest.

2. Eat regular, balanced meals. The vitamins and energy you get from a balanced diet can help your mind as well as your body.

   Breakfast is one meal that many of us skip in exchange for a good couple of cups of coffee or tea. However, some form of nutrients at the beginning of the day can get you started and get your brain working to capacity.

   Along the same lines, many of us tend to rush through our lunch hour (or half hour), if we stop at all. Eating at your desk is the wrong thing to do. Take the 30 minutes or more to walk away and enjoy your meal. It can help to rejuvenate you for the afternoon ahead.

When it comes time that you want a little snack, choose something nutritious. A favourite afternoon snack might be seedless grapes, an apple, a yogurt or some other treat that isn't completely laced with sugar and calories.

3. Exercise. We can see you saying to yourself right now, "Who has time to exercise?" Remember, exercise doesn't have to be a big workout. Going for a short walk can do wonders for your stress levels, not to mention the advantages it has on your body. The fresh air can help you feel rejuvenated and the motion of walking can help relieve tension in your back, neck and the rest of your body. Since you sit in front of a computer all day long, a 15-30 minute walk can help get the blood re-circulating and the heart beating stronger. Take the dog... he will love you for it. (Yes, dogs get a lot more excited about going for a walk than most humans do.)

4. Leave the laundry! Working from home is a constant reminder that there are things around the house that need to be done. Your first task is to separate work from home. Once you get the hang of that, it is time to decide if the family can live without the dirty clothes that are in the laundry baskets. If you are feeling like you just need to sit and relax, and the thought of doing the laundry or emptying the dishwasher make your blood pressure rise, just leave it.

5. Ask for help. If you are single and trying to run your VA business, there aren't a lot of people you can ask to help with the "home" chores. However, if there is a spouse around or children, ask them (or you might have to order them) to help. After all, where is it written that you are responsible for all the meals, grocery shopping, vacuuming, etc.?

6. When you do have to run out and do errands, try to make the most of your time and do more than one. For example, your main purpose may be to run to the post office, but on the way you can stop at Staples for your paper, Best Buy for your CDs, and so on. It takes much longer to run out three times than it does to go once and stop at three places. Then you could use the time you saved to sit and read a book or help your child with their homework.

7. Set up a schedule. Most VAs have or will have ongoing clients that require regular tasks to be done. Try to schedule time on a certain day to accomplish these tasks. As they say, "The best intentions..." There will be days or weeks when things don't go as planned and those schedules will go right out the window. However, do your best to accomplish those regular tasks when you originally intended to do them and in the time frame you allotted. (This also holds true for the regular family tasks that need to be accomplished.)

8. To Do Lists. It is easy to make a list and it will ensure that you get all the jobs done that are required, whether work or family related. Use the old-fashioned method of jotting down what needs to be done on a piece of paper or use software, such as Microsoft's OneNote or Outlook's calendar, to keep track of things and to remind you.

9. Change the location/environment where you do the work. Many homes have numerous computers, and thus a network is set up to get all those computers attached. If you have a laptop with a wireless connection, grab it and go out

on your deck. You will me amazed how just getting out of your office but still getting some work done can help your mindset, your mood and your stress levels.

Pamper Yourself

This is one of the hardest things for entrepreneurs to do. Most have a mindset of being in control of their businesses and, generally for women, control of the family too. As a result, being in control of ourselves usually takes a backseat and this can increase our stress levels tremendously. We are business owners, parents and spouses, but we are also "people" and people need to treat themselves every once in a while in order to feel like human beings again.

Some of the following ideas may not seem like they should be categorized as pampering, but anything that can help you feel like yourself again and give you a bit of a boost or break is definitely a little bit of a pamper.

1. Read a book. Many of us don't think we have the time to read anything that isn't business related. A good romance novel or anything other than business might be best. Either way, get away from the TV,, telephone and computer and just sit in a comfy chair and let your body relax.

    Many people, including Oprah, have been recommending inspirational books lately like *The Secret* by Rhonda Byrne and *A New Earth* by Eckhardt Tolle. Apparently they are both great reads with some wonderful life lessons. If you have nothing else that you fancy reading, perhaps one or both of these is the book for you. If not, maybe you can find some other inspirational book to fill your relaxation time.

2. Rent a movie (The Secret is available on DVD) or tape your favourite TV show. Then make some popcorn, grab a drink, find a comfy seat and just sit back, relax and enjoy the story. Even better, watch it alone so there is no threat of having to "remind" someone else to be quiet (which only adds to your stress).

3. Nothing feels better than a relaxing bubble bath. Let the family know you are not to be disturbed and then fill the tub, put in some of your favourite bubble bath and maybe even turn on some relaxing music, grab a glass of wine, and light some aromatherapy candles. Then slide into the tub and just let the warm water soothe your body. This might even be a good place to read one of those books we mentioned.

4. Play a fun board game with the kids or play catch with the dog. Don't worry about business and the housework; just concentrate on quality time with those you love.

5. Get away from it all, even if it is only for fifteen minutes. Take a short walk or jog around the block to clear your head. Take the dog for a run or run a simple errand that takes you out in the car. Nothing is that urgent that you can't take a few minutes to rejuvenate.

6. Get out of the house and go to your son's or daughter's hockey or soccer game. And make sure you cheer on your child...loudly! A great stress relief can be yelling at the top of your lungs.

   If the kids are into a more subdued sport, such as figure skating, go and either chat with the other parents at the arena or conversely, sit off to the side while watching your child and let the time alone help to unwind you.

7. Grab a cup of tea or a glass of wine and either sit on your deck or near a window and enjoy the outdoor views. This is good time to also read your book or do your favourite crossword or Sudoku puzzle.

8. Get a massage. This may only be possible if you go out to a masseuse, but perhaps your spouse or partner would be willing to try and work some of the knots out of your shoulders.

9. Sit down and listen to some soothing music. Again, you can read while listening, have a bath, enjoy a glass of wine, or anything to just allow the music to calm your nerves and soothe your soul.

No matter who you are or what you do, you will experience some level of stress, and we hope that the above ideas can help to alleviate the pressures you are feeling and allow you to function in your ever-increasingly busy life.

Running a VA Practice Part-Time

For many people, starting a VA practice on a full-time basis is just not an option. Some may still need to work a full-time "job" in order to have income while researching and getting their VA business off the ground. If this is your circumstance, you are not alone, but you will be limited to the number of hours you can work at marketing your business and working for your clients.

We all want to have a thriving business overnight but, to be perfectly honest, that will not happen. It takes a lot of hard work and many hours to get your business running at a level where you can quit your job and earn an income allowing you to live the lifestyle you may be used to. It is not impossible, as you can see by the number of successful Virtual Assistants running practices around the world, but it does take a great deal of passion, time and planning. Be absolutely sure you are ready to work full-time before you quite your job.

This chapter will help those of you who are starting a VA practice part-time or may need to go back to a part-time or full-time job to supplement your income while making a go of your business. You will learn some of your limitations and how to overcome them and find ways around those limitations until you feel ready to run your business full-time. Many of these suggestions are not only good for part-time practices, but also for full-time practices.

Your Current "Job"

1. Make sure you are **not putting your current job in jeopardy** by working elsewhere. Some companies have strict policies about their employees working elsewhere.

2. Some "jobs" aren't as busy as you would like them to be, so you may have **time on your hands during the day to do some of the work involved in running your VA practice**. However, make sure this is acceptable with your boss. You don't have to tell your employer that you plan to quit your job one day, but you may get into a lot of trouble if they see you working on something that is not related to their company.

3. If your employer is open to it, why not **see if you can do some of your work virtually for them**. You can take work home with you and as long as you get it accomplished, this new arrangement may be good for both you and your employer and eventually may help to transition you from employee to entrepreneur. Your present employer could become one of your first clients.

4. If your employer knows about your part-time business and is okay with it, **don't flaunt it and talk about it at your current job as** that may be pushing your luck, and you may find that your employer is not as open to the idea as you originally thought. Not to mention, some of your co-workers may accidentally spill the beans which could result in your dismissal and even theirs as well. It is best to keep a low profile when it comes to working at a job and running a business on the side.

Before You Start

1. **Be sure you have the support of your loved ones**. You will have enough stress to deal with trying to keep up with your current job as well as running your business. You don't need to have the added stress of having to deal with anyone who may not be supportive of your efforts. Talk it over and let them see the research you have found showing that it can be done. Perhaps if they are somehow involved, they will be more supportive. The stress of having to prove yourself is something you don't want to deal with, on top of everything else.

2. **Get the kids involved in your business**. Stuffing envelopes may seem like a monotonous job to you, but your kids may be overjoyed to be able to help you get your business off the ground. Not to mention, it will help take some of the work off your plate.

3. **Do your homework!** Don't try to take on clients right away, unless you are lucky enough to get started as the result of an employer wanting you to work virtually for them. You need to spend a great deal of time researching the industry and starting your business one step at a time.

4. **Join VA organizations** so you can start to learn from others. You will find that the VA industry is somewhat original. This is because we work together to help each other instead of considering each other as competitors. Joining these industry-specific organizations can give you a forum to ask specific questions and learn the dos and don'ts of those who are already running successful practices. Remember that you should try to limit your activity with these lists until after your regular job work hours.

5. **If possible, find a mentor** to help you. They may be more than happy to go over your marketing material and to just be there to discuss issues and bounce off questions with you.

6. **Plan your days and don't overdo it.** If you find that you are at your home office computer longer and longer, you may also find yourself half asleep during the day, and that can not only cause issues with your job, but also with your family. If you are extremely passionate about making this business a success, you are probably running on adrenaline most of the time and eventually that adrenaline may run out. Keep a plan of when you want to accomplish certain aspects of running your business and try to stick to it.

7. **Keep your family and your health in mind.** Don't let either of these take a backseat to your business. Again, you may want to have your business up and running as quickly as you can, but don't let your family and your health suffer along the way. Be sure to plan time to be with your family and get plenty of rest. If you aren't healthy, not only will your family suffer, but so will your job and your business.

Running Your Business

1. You will need to ensure that you **do not take on too many clients** if you are still working outside your home. Part of running a business is not only servicing your clients, but also marketing your business. Limiting the number of clients you take on will give you time to market your business and be with your family.

2. **Invest in a cell phone** so you can forward your home office phone number and/or email to it. Then, during your lunch break, you can respond to any inquiries. That may help to prove to your clients and potential clients that you are available during all regular business hours.

3. You need to **let your clients know that you are running your practice on a part-time basis**. This may deter some new clients, as they may think that you will not be available to them when they need you. However, with a cell phone and perhaps holding off for a short time period on telling them that you actually work full-time somewhere else, you can prove to them that it will not affect the speed in which you complete their projects. You may find that they are more than willing to give you a chance

4. Prove to potential and new clients that **you can handle the work they need accomplished** even if you are only running your business on a part-time basis. **Offer them a trial period** to show them you will make them feel like number one. Sometimes all they require when trying to contact you during the day is an acknowledgement that you have received their email and you will get back to them with a more detailed response later.

5. Prioritize your work as best you can. **Those emails can wait.** If you have a client who needs some work done, you need to put them at the top of the list and the emails can be read when you have time to tackle them without letting a client feel like you can't handle the project. Client work will generally be your highest priority.

6. **Carry a PDA, Blackberry or daily planner** with you so you can refer to it during your lunch hour and prioritize what needs to be done when you get to your home office.

7. If the work is just not coming in, **consider working for other VAs.** Many VAs have already spent numerous years establishing and growing their businesses. They may be at a point where they don't want to turn away projects, so they will sub-contract out to newer VAs. Remember that the other VA is doing all the work to get and keep the clients which means that you need to establish a sub-contracting rate that is less than what the VA you will be working for charges. It may seem like you are not getting what you are worth, but you are also not having to do all the work involved in attaining clients and keeping them happy.

8. **Pass on any projects for which** you know you don't have the time or expertise to another VA. As mentioned above, don't take on more than you can handle or more than you have the expertise to accomplish. You will

either end up not getting the project to the client on time or not giving them the final outcome that they thought they would get, which could result in losing a client. It is best to get the help of another VA for these types of projects.

Getting the Word Out

We will only get into a few ideas here, as a majority of the other marketing and networking ideas have been covered in other areas of this book. We recommend reading the entire book as it covers what ANY VA should be doing to get their business off the ground.

1. **One of the first pieces of marketing material that you should design is your business card**. This can be accomplished with any desktop publishing software and printed on your home inkjet printer, but investing in a professional printing house will help you to portray yourself as a professional business person.

2. **Take those business cards with you EVERYWHERE you go**. You never know when you will have the opportunity to pass your card on to someone who may need some assistance. You can even drop cards into business card drop boxes at local establishments or grab a tack and put them up on their bulletin boards.

3. **Do a mailing locally to small business owners**. You may need to do some research to gather the information for mailing, but to save on costs, consider doing a postcard mailing. Postage is generally less expensive for post cards than it is for letters. Outline the benefits of working with a virtual assistant and introduce yourself and your business. You won't have much room to do this so you will need to be creative. **And don't forget to follow-up.**

4. **Join your local Chamber of Commerce** and take advantage of being listed in their directory and going to their networking events. Get involved as much as you can, taking into consideration that you are working full-time. Perhaps you can offer an article for their newsletter or newspaper to show how a VA can help their members with their administrative overflow.

5. **Network, network, network!** There has to be some kind of organization in your area that offers a chance to network with fellow business owners and professionals. Try to find some and get out to their events.

6. **Do a press release in your local media,** keeping in mind that your boss may read it, so you may need to be careful where you try to get it published and how you word it. Press Release templates are available to members at http://www.cvac.ca

7. **Write an article for your local publications** about the benefits of working with VAs. An article, unlike a press release, does not have to mention the name of the person behind the business. Remember that an article should not be trying to "sell," but to inform, and it is in your byline at the end that people can contact you for more information.

8. **Tell anyone and everyone (except at work)** about your business and what you do. Ask them to help spread the word too, and even give them some business cards to hand out.

9. **Take out a listing in your local phone directory.**

10. If your budget will allow it, **take out a small ad** in your local paper or in a publication that targets your niche market.

11. **Get a website**! This is one of the essentials for a virtual business. It is 24/7 advertising at a fraction of the cost of print advertising which is not available 24/7.

12. **Respond to requests for proposals** that you receive from the organizations to which you belong and be sure you have an email form on your website for your visitors to request quotations from you.

13. **Be active on the email discussion lists to which you belong.** Perhaps one of the more veteran members will be impressed with your desire to learn and your ability to be professional. They may even approach you to see if you want to get involved in something on which they are working.

14. **Volunteer your time.** People will be able to see your work first hand and a paying project may come out of that.

Time to Become a Full-time Entrepreneur

Making the decision to give up the stability of a full-time job and that regular paycheque shouldn't be taken lightly. You must be absolutely sure that you are ready to become a full-time entrepreneur and are ready to take seriously all the commitments that come along with it.

So, when do you know that the time has come?

1. When you are turning away clients on a regular basis because you just don't have the time to get their projects done; that may be the time to think about quitting your job.

2. When you are sure that your finances are at a level where you can pay your bills and survive on the income you are generating; that may be the time that you are ready to become an entrepreneur on a full-time basis.

3. When your heart and your passion to make your new business a success becomes all that you can think about; that may be the time to officially open your VA doors to the world.

You may have to make some sacrifices in the beginning, but your passion will take over and you will wonder why you waited so long. However, be absolutely sure because once you become an entrepreneur, it will become a way of life and going back to a "job" may be the furthest thing from your mind.

Expanding Your VA Practice

When beginning your Virtual Assistant business, the thought of it getting to a stage where you will need to call upon the help of other VAs may seem like a dream. During the start-up phase, you are spending most of your time concerned with keeping your clients happy and making sure things are running smoothly.

Perhaps your plan is to keep your business at a level where you handle all of the projects yourself. That is fine and 80% of VAs do run their business that way, and very successfully. However, a new trend has taken shape in the industry where VAs are working together to provide a full range of services, all from under one company name.

If this is your goal, your first decision will be to decide on a business model. Do you want to continue keeping the hands-on approach by doing some of the projects yourself or do you want to take on more of a managerial role and simply acquire the projects and then designate them to the appropriate VA on your team? For some multi-VA company owners, this may be a gradual transition from one to the other.

Expanding your VA practice, no matter what business model you choose, can allow you to offer a multitude of services which can expand your market to include some of those projects that you wouldn't have been able to take on before or taking on many more that you have done in the past but now have more time and VA power to accomplish.

The advantages to your existing and new clients of working with a multi-VA business include:

- Clients only have to deal with one person instead of a different person for each task.
- Clients have a full range of services available to them, some of which they may not have known were available.
- Some clients may want to portray their businesses as being larger than they really are. They can give this impression quite easily and will appear as if they employ an entire office.
- Clients can take advantage of the usual benefits of working with a VA, such as not needing to supply extra equipment or office space and not worrying about government source deductions.

When to Consider Expanding

As previously mentioned, you may want to start your VA business as a multi-VA practice right from the get-go. However, you should consider perfecting your skills first and learn how to run a business before you take on some help.

The time to consider expansion is when you are working more than a 40-hour work week. If you are working too many hours, you may find that your business and your clients suffer. Having too much on your plate can cause feelings of stress and being worn out can cause a lack of quality expected by your clients. It can also mean that you don't have much time for a life outside your business. This is also a time to consider passing on some of your work.

Also, if you find you are getting requests on a regular basis for services that you don't supply, this may be the time to consider expansion. Just because you don't have the required expertise, doesn't mean that you can't offer the service. There are other VAs who do have the skills and would be happy to sub-contract through you.

Finding the Right Team Members

With the rapid growth of the VA industry and the rise in those wanting to find profitable work to do from home, enlisting help shouldn't be all that hard. After all, this is a great opportunity for new and aspiring VAs to get experience working on projects without all of the legwork needed to obtain new clients. Being on a multi-VA team is great for those who don't want to network and market their business, or for those who need a little extra income while they build their own individual practices. There are many successful VAs out there whose entire practice is built by subcontracting to other VAs.

However, when looking for members for your team, you don't want to take on someone who can just type; you want members to provide the excellence that your clients are accustomed to getting and in the time frame they need.

As with any hiring process (so to speak), you need to have a plan. First and foremost, you want to make sure the people who want to work with you have the necessary skills and will be available when you need them. The best way to start the process and learn about the prospective member is to have them fill in a questionnaire. This questionnaire should not only ask for the basic information (i.e. name, contact info), it should also ask for:

- Time zone and available hours
- What experience they have
- What software they work with
- What types of service they can offer
- And, of course, what kind of rate they will charge you.

We have included a sample questionnaire in the Appendices.

As with your clients, you want to build a relationship with your team members. However, there needs to be a line that shouldn't be crossed. Everyone involved should remember that this is a business relationship. That is why it isn't recommended to hire friends or loved ones as it can put a strain on your personal relationship should issues arise.

Ensuring You Have Contracts in Place

Once you have received the completed questionnaire and have determined that the person would be a good fit for you and your plans to expand, you need to set the ground rules of your relationship. This can be done by developing contracts between yourself and the VA. Some of the contracts you should have in place are:

- Sub-Contractor Agreement – outlines possible work the VA will do for you and over what period of time.
- Non-Disclosure Agreement – basically reiterates that any information acquired by the VA during the contract period will not be shared.

- Non-Competition Agreement – an agreement that the VA will not attempt to "steal" a client from you.

Again, we have included samples in the Appendixes. You may even want to amalgamate portions of each of the above into one contract.

Of course, it will be the work on and completion of the projects that you outsource that will determine if the relationship will stand up to your desired expectations. You may also want to include provisions for a probationary period to ensure that you both feel comfortable with how things are run and how projects are completed.

Managing Your Team

How you manage your team may be dependent upon the way you want each project to be handled. You may either want to be the person who handles all of the direct contact with the client or you may allow your sub-contractor to work directly with the client.

The good, the bad and the ugly can fall into play for each managerial structure. Let's have a look at them.

You are the sole contact for both clients and contractors:

> The Good:
> - You know exactly what is going on at all times.
> - You can ensure that the final result sent to the client meets your expectations.
> - You can be confident that no negative contact has taken place between your contractor and client.
> - You continue to build a relationship directly with the client.
>
> The Bad:
> - You have the sole responsibility of acquiring the clients needed to keep the contractors busy.
> - You are accountable for everything.
> - You have to spend time relaying messages back and forth.
>
> The Ugly
> - You have to be the good cop and the bad cop... if things aren't working out with a contractor, you are responsible to rectify or eliminate the problem.

You allow your contractors to have direct contact with your client:

> The Good:
> - You don't have to spend as much time being the go-between.
> - You have time to be able to have more direct involvement in a project.
>
> The Bad:
> - You don't know what is happening at all times between the client and the contractor.
> - You don't know if the projects are meeting your expectations.

The Ugly:
- You don't have as close a relationship as you would if the client was corresponding through you.
- There is the chance that you might lose the client to the subcontractor who has the better 'working' relationship.

So, as you can see, there are good and bad issues that need to be dealt with no matter how you decide you want to manage your team and your clients. Your preferences and how much control you like to have will determine if you want to be the only one each of your clients and contractors deal with or if you want to allow them to deal directly with each other.

Scheduling and Organizing

This section could be a book in itself. How you work with your contractors to keep things organized and ensuring that all the projects are being done and on schedule is a matter of preferences. We will only make some minor suggestions here and then you can decide how you prefer to handle things.

Keeping in touch:

Face to face contact is not an option for most Virtual Assistants, so you will need to keep in touch with your contractors by other means. The first two options are, of course, phone and email (and fax, if necessary).

Staying in touch by email can be done for the regular correspondence needed each day.

Phone contact can be done when you can't express your thoughts thoroughly in an email. However, if you do not have a long distance plan on your phone line, you may want to consider one of the VoIP services, such as Skype.

Skype can also be used to perform conference calls between you and your subcontractors, you and your clients, or you, your client and your sub-contractor.

If you need to make a visual presentation to the client or between you and your contractors, you may want to consider an online conference service, such as Talking Communities. See our list of recommended conference services in our Software List in our Resources section.

Sharing files:

When working with others, whether they are your clients or your contractors, there will come a time, and perhaps even numerous times, when you will need to share files. Sending them by email is the most common and widely used way to share some files, but once you get into large size files, email is not always the best choice. If the files are large, certain ISPs will not allow those files through.

There are a couple of online sources that can be used to send large files. One that we have used is http://www.sendthisfile.com.

For those sharing web design files, and even for other large file transfer needs, utilizing a File Transfer Protocol (FTP) or uploading to a web server may be a good option. We have a number of FTP programs listed in our Software List in our Resources section. If you use an FTP program, you can share the access details (username and password) with your contractor and they would just need to have an FTP program to download the files or you can simply provide them with a link to the file.

To upload to a web server through a browser, it is best to check in the control panel of your hosting plan. There may be an option to use a File Transfer feature. If you are unsure, ask your hosting company. Again, you can give your contractor access to the control panel of your hosting plan so they can download files themselves, which might not seem the best idea at first, or you can simply supply the URL link for them to download.

Staying on Schedule:

One of the most important tasks when it comes to working with contractors is to ensure that everything stays on schedule. Of course, there will be the occasional time that something may delay the completion of a project, but it is best for everyone to stick to a schedule, especially on tasks that are done on a regular basis.

As you begin working with contractors, it will be easy to keep to a schedule manually. Simply keeping in touch by email will tell you if things are running smoothly.

However, as you outsource more projects or tasks, you will need something to remind you of follow-ups or deadlines that need to be met. One way is to utilize the calendar that comes with Microsoft Outlook. For example, you can do such things as set reminders for hours or days ahead of an event and you can synchronize your calendar with your clients and contractors so you are all on the same page. It is best to check the help files of Outlook and their website for help with this as the features and instructions change depending on the version.

Online calendars can also be utilized. Have a look at our Software List in our Resources section for more ideas on calendars and other means to help you stay on schedule.

The decision to expand your business to include working with sub-contractors can be a frightening thought, but it doesn't have to be all that scary. Start slowly and gradually increase the help you get with your projects. Perhaps one day, you will be solely in charge of acquiring clients and organizing the tasks to be sure all of your contractors have work to do and everyone is happy.

Spreading the Word About Virtual Assistance

(Bonus chapter by Tawnya Sutherland)

What the Heck is a VA?

How many times have you heard this exact statement over and over again when you've explained what you do for a living to someone outside our industry? Heck, even my own mother still doesn't thoroughly know what I do?!?!

Virtual Assistance is a totally new concept and one that only about 1/15 will ever admit they even know anything about.

Our biggest barrier as Virtual Assistants is educating the public about us.

In order for the Virtual Assistant industry to grow, we must all duly take part in educating the public about us. By bringing awareness to virtual assistance as an administrative business alternative to the corporate world we will ensure our businesses continued growth and success.

For without clients, we make no money. Without money our business won't survive.

Education is the Key!

We can all start by educating our clients and the public media through various formats:

- Include educational content about our industry on your website.
- Offer a free eBook on how to partner with a Virtual Assistant.
- Write educational articles to put in your newsletter or better yet submit these articles online to other places looking for educational content like blogs, newsletters, article directories.
- Start an informational blog on how to Partner with a VA.
- Comment on another blog post about virtual assistance and how it can help small business entrepreneurs.
- Make a video and post on YouTube all about hiring a Virtual Assistant.
- Write a press release about how virtual assistance is taking over corporate America and submit to your news media venues.
- Speak at your local networking club about how to hire a VA.
- Wear a hat that says I'm A VA to initiate conversation about your business.
- Twitter about being a Virtual Assistant.

Remember, we won't be known if we don't start shouting so start yelling at the world about the Virtual Assistant industry!

To help you in spreading the word about virtual assistance, I've included some content from our blog called:

Partnering With a Virtual Assistant at http://VAnetworking.com/blog

Here you'll find here educational articles to help inspire you to get started teaching the world "What the heck a VA is all about!"   Enjoy!

Building a Solid Relationship with a Virtual Assistant

Today many entrepreneurs are beginning to put their faith in Virtual Assistants to assist them with their administrative needs. However, since the Virtual Assistant does not have a physical presence in their office, it can be a daunting task to begin to establish a strong foundation, let alone a solid relationship. Here are a few things you can put in place to ensure that you not only create a good foundation, but also build a solid relationship:

Establish a Good Line of Communication

The first step to establishing a good line of communication is determining the method of communication that will work best for both parties. Will it be via telephone, email or some other method? The next step is determining how often you will speak. Will you speak daily, weekly or as tasks arise? Finally you will want to make sure that your instructions are always precise and direct and more importantly are fully understood by your Virtual Assistant.

Become Open to the Possibilities

As you begin to work with your Virtual Assistant, remember that they, just like you, are a business owner as well. They understand the trials and tribulations, the ups and downs, that go along with running a successful business. You will find that many Virtual Assistants will offer ideas and suggestions based on situations that they have experienced within their own business and the businesses of their other clients. Always be open to the ideas and suggestions that are being presented by your Virtual Assistant and if you do not think the ideas are worthy of further consideration remember to offer reasons why.

Put Your Absolute Trust in Them

Just like any relationship, trust must be built and earned. You will find that the more trust you put in your Virtual Assistant, the more successful your relations will be. Remember that your Virtual Assistant will become involved in many areas of your business and will be privy to confidential information. Don't be afraid to "test the waters" with small tasks and as trust is built you can work up to larger, more demanding assignments.

Be Patient and Provide Guidance

Whether virtual or not, anyone that is new to your business with require a learning period. Please be patient with your Virtual Assistant as they learn about your business. Remember to provide your Virtual Assistant with guidance as they not only learn about your business, but as they learn what your needs are as well.

Relinquish Some of the Control

Many entrepreneurs have been going it alone for so long that relinquishing some of the duties and tasks is a hard thing to do. However, keep in mind that giving up control does not mean that your Virtual Assistant will be taking over your business, but simply will allow your Virtual Assistant to partner in your success.

Give a Little Respect Where Respect is Due

Remember that Virtual Assistants are professionals just like you and so much more than most secretaries or personal assistants. Through mutual respect and appreciation, your Virtual Assistant can become a vital part of the success and growth of your business.

By following these tips, you will be well on your way to building a solid relationship with your Virtual Assistant. Once you have established that relationship with your Virtual Assistant you will be able to get back to those things that attracted you to your business in the first place rather than worrying about all those administrative headaches. Finally, you can get back to concentrating on running your business rather than having it continue to run you.

A Virtual Assistant Can Do So Much More For You Than Just Type!

A Virtual Assistant can offer so many skills to a partnership with any business owner that many are often overlooked. Many entrepreneurs understand how Virtual Assistants can assist with basic secretarial jobs such as word processing, editing, proofreading and formatting of documents, but don't realize that there are so many other things a Virtual Assistant can assist them with.

A huge chunk of time, for any business owner, is spent on marketing. Having a Virtual Assistant that could assist you in putting your marketing plan and your marketing ideas into action is a huge asset for any company. Perhaps it is a simple marketing campaign which includes preparing and mailing flyers, brochures and newsletters or maybe it is a more complex undertaking such as creating an internet marketing campaign including article writing, press releases and social media marketing. Also, another thing to keep in mind is that many Virtual Assistants can take it one step further and conduct the research necessary to see what your competition is doing and ensure that you always stay in step with them, if not a step ahead!

For a business owner, not only is it important to get your message out there, but it is equally as important to follow up. However, due to the busy nature of being in a managerial role, it is not always as easy as it seems and is often that one task that goes overlooked or is pushed to the backburner. Having a Virtual Assistant that can take care of remembering anniversaries and birthdays, sending thank you notes and planning an annual customer appreciation night can be a huge asset in ensuring both client retention and loyalty. Also a Virtual Assistant can take the time to survey your clients and learn ways that they feel your business could be improved and then help you to implement those changes.

As an entrepreneur, there are so many tasks that we rely on our assistant to perform and because your assistant happens to work virtually, you forget that they can still assist with these tasks; it just takes a little more planning. Such things as travel arrangements, file conversions, purchasing and supply management, directory assistance, filing and bookkeeping can still be tasks you can be assisted with. Many times the Virtual Assistant is already completing these tasks for other clients and has a system in place to provide these services to you seamlessly.

Perhaps one of the best things about working with a Virtual Assistant is that they truly become your business support system. They can work behind the scenes to create an illusion that your business is larger than it truly is. From their home office they can check emails, manage your calendar, make appointments and conduct reminder calls. Without the knowledge that your Virtual Assistant is making those calls from their own home, your clients will be convinced that you have a team of people working in your office, which lends to credibility as a business. You can also provide your Virtual Assistant with an email address so they can answer inquiries of your existing clients and provide your potential clients with business information; essentially they become the first point of contact for your company and free up time for you to spend on other, more pressing matters.

Finally, remember that your Virtual Assistant can also work together with your accountant, graphic designer, web designer and any other professional you are currently working with. By allowing your Virtual Assistant to work with these professionals to ensure your wishes and instructions are being met and the project is completed on time, you will no longer have to worry about all the "behind the scenes" details of your business.

Good Communication is the Key to a Successful Partnership with a Virtual Assistant

The idea of working with an assistant that does not have a physical presence in your office can be a challenge to many entrepreneurs. As more people are willing to take the "leap" and are opening themselves to the concept of Virtual Assistance, they are realizing the importance of establishing a system of good communication. They are quickly learning that putting the tools in place to establish good communication is the key to successfully working with a Virtual Assistant.

First and foremost, it is paramount that a means of clear and concise communication is established. There are many different ways that you can communicate with your Virtual Assistant such as via email, telephone or any number of alternative methods. Establishing the best method of communication for both parties is an essential first step in establishing good communication. Remember to make this a part of your search for a Virtual Assistant because many have already established their preferred method of communication. If you prefer telephone consultations, find a Virtual Assistant that also prefers this method.

Just as important as figuring out how you wish to communicate is when and how often you wish to communicate. It is a great idea to set up a schedule for how often you would like to be in touch with your Virtual Assistant. Many entrepreneurs find it works well to establish a weekly phone call or email as a means of touching base and determining what is on each of their plates, what the status is of various projects and what projects are in the works. By establishing a regular routine it becomes a means for ensuring that nothing is overlooked or forgotten.

When you are in an office environment and utilizing an in-house assistant, many times throughout the day you will have face to face contact whereby you can check on the status of the projects and correct things as you go. With a Virtual Assistant, it can become a little more difficult because it isn't as easy to just pop by and see how things are going. When you are first starting with a Virtual Assistant, don't be afraid to ask your Virtual Assistant to break up your projects in smaller sections or bits and to ask them to check things with you as they go. In the same regard, don't be afraid to ask for progress reports until you are confident in them and the job they are doing for you.

As your Virtual Assistant begins working with you and until they learn your business and your expectations, there are sure to be many questions. Unlike an in-house assistant, there is not the ability to just pop into your office and ask a quick question. Your Virtual Assistant is likely to be communicating these questions to you via email or telephone, but if these telephone calls are redirected to voice mail many times it can be tricky to find the time to reply to these messages. Keep in mind that until you take the time to answer these questions, your project can not proceed. In the beginning it will be important for both parties to determine a schedule of expectations for the length of time it will take to answer these questions. Will you ensure that all questions are answered within an hour, within a few hours or within a day? Remember that as your Virtual Assistant learns your business and your expectations you will find that these questions will be fewer and farther between.

Finally and perhaps most importantly, is ensuring that any directions you provide to your Virtual Assistant are always precise and direct and that they are fully understood by all parties. Many times, instructions can be left up to interpretation, as is true with any Assistant, whether in house or virtual. Ensure that all expectations are understood and concerns are addressed immediately. If something is askew or you feel that a project has not been completed to your exact specifications, discuss it right away.

Of course as we suggested, the first step to working with a Virtual Assistant is being open to the concept of not having face to face contact, but once you put these tools in place and establish a system for good communication, you will find that the rest will all just fall into place.

Posted at VAnetworking.com/blog by Yvonne Weld of http://ableva.com

Understanding How a VA Operates

Most people who are searching for a VA have just heard of the industry and are overwhelmed when they find themselves faced with the task of hiring someone.

By understanding a few basics about Virtual Assistants, the entire process should be easier for you.

The first thing you should realize is that a Virtual Assistant is **not** an employee. You have to make that change in your mind from the start because it's not something that comes naturally to many people and VAs often take a great deal of offense to being thought of and/or treated like an employee.

When you work with a VA, you should look at it like hiring any other type of contractor; an accountant, a website designer (some VAs are website designers!), or a consultant.

The biggest benefit to the client/VA coupling is the relationship that's formed. A VA will become a business partner - a key player in the success of your company. A VA will learn all about your business and after working together on a regular basis will begin to anticipate your needs.

Because a VA is self-employed, they have a vested interest in the success of your business. The better you do with their help, the more that adds to the VA's success. There's a real incentive there to help you achieve your business goals.

The best way to reap this benefit of the client/VA relationship is to work with someone on a retainer basis. Each month, you have a set number of hours of the VA's time, guaranteed. Working in this manner through regular collaboration, you will get to know each other very well and you will really start to experience growth in your business if you've chosen the right VA!

Posted at VAnetworking.com/blog by Jaime Lee Mann of http://mannmadetime.com

Common Policies and Procedures of Virtual Assistants

There are a few key things to look out for when you initiate the process of working with a Virtual Assistant.

First of all, the VA should provide you with a contract or client agreement to sign before you start working together. This should outline his/her hours of operation, your rate, different policies and procedures which are put in place to protect both parties involved. Look at the agreement carefully and make note of payment terms, termination and non-compete clauses.

If your VA doesn't send you an agreement that's a bad sign!

VAs all bill a little differently. In the case of a retainer, almost without exception, these are billable on the first day of the month, for work to be carried out that month. Most VAs won't start work until payment is received. For project work, it's common that you'll be expected to pay a 50% deposit of the estimated cost to complete the project up front with the remainder due upon completion. For 'pay-as-you-go' arrangements, work is usually billed for on the last day of the month, and is due upon receipt.

All VAs track their time in some way, shape or form. Many use software for the task, others use manual stop watch methods. Whatever the case, if it's important for you to receive copies of this time log be sure to discuss this with the VA before you sign anything!

Some VAs don't believe they have a responsibility to show you their hours. If this is something that you want to have access to, just look for a VA who doesn't mind sharing that log with you. Most don't have a problem with it. If you wish to purchase a retainer you should specify to your VA that you'd like regular updates so you know when your hours are getting close to surpassing your retainer limit. Some VAs leave it

completely up to the client to watch their hours, while others will notify you if you come close to your limit early in the month.

As a general rule, a VA shouldn't be expected to be at your beck and call 24 hours a day, 7 days a week. Most keep regular office hours, and if you need work done outside of them, you will probably be charged a rush fee.

This is just a sampling of some of the items you will encounter when looking for a VA. Make sure you look for these things before you agree to work with a Virtual Assistant and carefully read any agreements before you sign them.

Posted at VAnetworking.com/blog by Jaime Lee Mann of http://mannmadetime.com

The Importance of Personality

Far more important than rates and almost equally important as skill when selecting a Virtual Assistant, is personality.

If you need website updates, assistance with your Internet marketing efforts and database management, you can find handfuls of VAs that provide those services and most will fall within the same price range.

How do you choose after you've narrowed it down to a couple of candidates?

The best thing for you to do is chat with each of these VAs on the telephone. It's important for you to get a sense of what it will be like to work with this person. You will learn more from a telephone conversation with these VAs than you would by looking at a page on the Internet. Some people have personalities that just don't work well together. It's better to find that out in the beginning than a few weeks down the road.

Many VAs will want to conduct a phone consultation with you to let you know how they operate and to get a sense of the services you require. This will be a great way to get to know one another and it's an extremely important step.

You should look out for this when you're searching a virtual assistant. Those VAs that conduct phone consultations with their clients are going to be confident in their services and help you tremendously during your transition to working with a Virtual Assistant.

Posted at VAnetworking.com/blog by Jaime Lee Mann of http://mannmadetime.com

Your Virtual Assistant Doesn't Have to Live Next Door

Whether you have an established VA or are looking to hire one, you must always be thinking forward. What type of work you will assign, how you will communicate the tasks and how the work will be done. You want a VA you can easily communicate with. A VA who can follow directions accurately whether delivered in writing, orally or through an instant message system.

With the speed of business today, one can be left behind with the simple click of a mouse. If you're not on top of your game, your competition will be. How do you get the jump on the competition? The secret is to hire a VA on the other side of the planet - or the country, or simply in another time zone.

Why does time zone matter?

Being on a different time schedule than your VA can actually benefit some businesses. A local VA will likely work the same type of hours as you do. Workflow takes a few days, as shown here:

        Day 1:   Assign the work to VA
        Day 2:   VA does the work
        Day 3:   Completed work returned and ready to use

If, however, your VA is hours away, it can take a day out of this scenario. While you sleep overnight on Day 1, the work is being done and will be on your desk ready to use on Day 2. This gives you a full day's jump on your competition; if they use local talent.

Don't misunderstand, I'm not suggesting you send work and expect it done immediately. A VA isn't on call 24/7! You must have a prearranged working agreement with your VA that they will do the assigned work in a set time frame. "On demand" work assignments can wreak havoc on a successful VA-Client relationship.

The time difference is very beneficial when your VA does work via remote log in to your computer. Suppose you have a VA updating your contacts twice weekly. You fax copies of the business cards, the VA logs in to your computer and enters the information directly into your Contact Management System. If you have a VA who lives in a time zone with a 5 hour difference, remote log in and updating can be done while you are sleeping - freeing up your computer for your workday. Or have your VA doing bookkeeping or checking your email for spam 3 hours before you wake up in the morning.

Get a jumpstart on your competition and get your work done earlier!

VAnetworking has the largest database of Virtual Assistant websites worldwide – you can find a VA anywhere in the world; from Australia to Nova Scotia, or Texas to the United Kingdom. Time zones can aid immensely in helping you and your VA work together and efficiently, while being far apart!

Check out the Virtual Assistant Search Engine http://VAsearchengine.com to find one in any locale!

Get Dozens of Skills with One Virtual Assistant

There are so many benefits to working with a Virtual Assistant. One of those is that in most cases you get a lot more brains than one!

No, Virtual Assistants aren't two-headed creatures, but most are very well connected through the VA networking forums, groups and associations they belong to.

Let me explain.

If you wanted to hire one employee who could maintain your website, manage your bookkeeping, design brochures, draft up sales letters and maintain your filing how much do you suppose you would pay that person if he or she did indeed exist?

When you work with a VA, we're not all able to do everything…actually nobody can do *everything*, but we have lots of colleagues.

If you hired a VA to handle your bookkeeping on top of your regular administrative tasks, that VA might not be able to maintain your website. Chances are that they will have someone in their back pocket to refer you to. Another way this can work is if you find one Multi-VA team to take care of your needs. A VA team is made up of lots of Virtual Assistants with different areas of expertise. You would work with the one who can best help you for each project, or you deal with the head VA who will be your main contact for everything so you deal with one person but get access to countless specialists.

Some people prefer the very special treatment they get when working with a solo VA who can refer others as need arises, where others like to work with a team that has lots of different skills to choose from while keeping it all on one bill.

So, if you've been considering a VA but can't find one who does *everything* I suggest you stop looking. Whoever you choose will be able to help find coverage in almost all other administrative areas.

Posted at VAnetworking.com/blog by Jaime Lee Mann of http://mannmadetime.com

Delegation Means More Control, Not Less

Many business owners have a difficult time delegating because they feel like they are giving up control. I'm here to tell you that giving up control couldn't be further from the truth! Delegating doesn't mean giving up control. It means gaining control.

As a business owner, you wear many hats, President and CEO, Director of Marketing, Bookkeeper, Public Relations Coordinator, and the list goes on and on. Doing all of those tasks every day means you have less and less time to focus on building your business, networking or even spending time with loved ones. You may become overwhelmed, feel out of control and wonder why you decided to go into business in the first place. But what if you could delegate some of that work to a skilled and trusted professional that you knew would get the job done leaving you more time to do all of those things you've been putting off? Wouldn't you feel relieved, energized, focused and even IN CONTROL?

A Virtual Assistant is that skilled and trusted professional you need to keep you moving forward in your business instead of wading through a black hole of "to do's" that may never get done because you don't have the time. Here are just some of the things you can delegate to a VA:

- Updating your blog or website
- Organizing and maintaining your contact list
- Creating and updating a monthly newsletter
- Designing your PowerPoint presentation
- Organizing a webinar or teleconference
- Research
- Formatting an eBook
- Marketing your business on the internet
- Creating marketing materials like postcards or brochures
- Monitoring your email
- Proofreading

Are these some of the things you're doing in your business or have thought about doing but can't seem to find the time?

Having someone you trust handle these tasks and others means that:

1. You are saving time by not having to do them yourself
2. You are focusing on money making activities in your business
3. You are saving money by not paying for overhead costs that come with an in house employee
4. You are able to set goals and do things that make you happy

All of this adds up to **MORE CONTROL!**

So the next time you are wondering whether or not to delegate something ask yourself one question, "Will delegating this task give me more control of my business by saving me time and money?". If the answer is yes congratulations! You're ready to take the next step and call a VA!

Posted at VAnetworking.com/blog by Jackie Nees http://integrityofficesolutions.com

How Outsourcing Can Make You More Accountable

It should be a given that hiring a Virtual Assistant will make you and your business more productive, right? But what about being more accountable for the tasks necessary to achieve your long range business goals? An incredible spin off benefit of hiring a VA is that you suddenly have someone who is "checking in" regularly to see if you've crossed any of those pesky to-dos off your list. Because let's face it, a Virtual Assistant can do a lot but she can't do everything for you!

When I hired my current Virtual Assistant back in July, (hi Ruth!), I told her upfront that she had carte blanche to boss me around whenever she felt it was necessary. Sound strange? Let me clarify.

Like any entrepreneur, I spend a lot of my time in what I call inspiration overwhelm. That is, I have more ideas than time. To bring my ideas to action in a somewhat premeditated fashion, I need more than someone to tackle my to-do lists. I need someone to actually wrangle my ideas into something more orderly than random emails to colleagues or scribbles in 10 different notebooks.

Now, when one of my projects or to-dos starts to linger a little too long on the back burner, I get a nudge from my VA (I love saying "my VA!"). Maybe she's not exactly bossing me around, but knowing there is someone else on my team (I love saying "my team!") who is waiting for me to do my part before she can either cross something off the list or move it to the next step, has a way of getting me off my proverbial butt. Suddenly I'm not just letting myself down by putting something off (because I'm being obnoxiously picky about perfecting it first which is another article entirely). Now I'm letting down a team member who is waiting for me to do my part so she can do hers.

Not to mention the powerful effect "otherness" has on the lone entrepreneur, the man or woman used to flying solo ALL of the time. When there is someone else watching you, observing you, waiting for your next move, you become self aware in a way that's just not possible all by your lonesome.

So, if you're putting off finding a Virtual Assistant because you don't want someone else to answer to, scrap that notion. It's misguided. It's counterproductive. It's really a bit high minded. You're special but you're not *that* special. Adding a new team member to your business might be just what the doctor ordered to cure symptoms you didn't even know you had.

Posted at VAnetworking.com/blog by Karri Flatla of http://snapwebmarketing.com

Let Your VA Be Your Eyes and Ears

As the old saying goes, "two heads are better than one". There is so much great information out there today whether it's a teleseminar, workshop or conference. You know you need to keep growing and learning if you want to stay on top of your game but who has the time? With everything you have to do on a daily basis you just can't squeeze in one more thing right? So why not let your VA be your second set of eyes and ears?

Your VA can do more than complete projects and perform daily administrative tasks. She can also be you when you're not available.

Virtual Events

If there's a teleseminar, webinar or online workshop coming up that you'd really like to attend, sign up and give the login information to your VA. Let her know the date and time so she can schedule the time to attend. She can ask any questions you'd like her to or simply take notes and present you with a report on the highlights.

Local or Long Distance Events

If you know of a conference in town or even in a different state, ask your VA if she would like to attend on your behalf. Not only could she get great information for you from the various speakers but also make valuable contacts for you by being a representative of your company. Some conferences that even suggest you send your VA or accompany her if time and budget permit. This option is especially helpful if you have two events happening at the same time and would like to attend them both but you can only choose one. Have your VA go to the other one and you can have a meeting upon returning to discuss what you learned.

Books and Programs

Do you have a stack of books you've been meaning to read but haven't been able to get to? How about programs or systems that you've purchased to help you in your business? Many of us are guilty of spending money on these products but never seem to find the time to get to them. Why not send them to your VA to read or go through? Your VA can give you the highlights of what she has learned and even work with you to implement strategies to help you build your business. You're not only getting good information for your own business but you're also helping her improve her business by giving her access to tools and resources which will only benefit you in the long run.

So the next time you wish you could clone yourself and be two places at the same time, know that you can with the help of a VA.

Posted at VAnetworking.com/blog by Jackie Nees http://integrityofficesolutions.com

5 Really Good Excuses for NOT Hiring a Virtual Assistant This Year

Hiring a Virtual Assistant can help your business succeed in so many ways it's hard to imagine why anyone would not at least give outsourcing careful consideration. Then again, why take bold and strategic steps forward with your business when you've got things like status quo and been-there-done-that to keep you warm and comfy? Just in case you're running out of excuses though, I've come up with a handy little list of trite excuses for *not* hiring your own VA today.

Print this list off and tape it to your desk. You just never know when you might have to turn down another opportunity to grow:

1. **I'm really not a planner.** If I hire a Virtual Assistant I will have to think about why I have a business and what I want to achieve this year and even 5 five years from now. Otherwise I'm just wasting her time and my money. And that just wouldn't be fair to either of us.
2. **How can I trust a VA with my business?** I mean, I'm over here and she's over there, *way* over there. How these VAs get any work done without someone looking over their shoulder is beyond me. It's just not good management. Besides, if I can't micromanage the details what will I do all day?
3. **No one could possibly do it as well as I can.** (And the way I do it is quite unlike anything you've ever seen.) I started this business because I have something unique and special to offer my adoring public. To think a Virtual Assistant could step in and competently assist with anything related to marketing or administration is, well, it's crazy talk.
4. **I don't have time to explain everything to a VA.** I'm too mired in paperwork and marketing and answering emails and God-knows-what-else to actually waste an hour or two a month with something as tedious as delegating. And like I said, what I do is *complicated*. Mysterious in fact.
5. **I can't afford to hire a virtual assistant.** Nope, not a single dollar left in my budget for getting the right things done at the right time. Heck, this computer system alone cost me thousands. I'd be nuts to spend another three hundred bucks this month on administration when I could just do it myself for nothing. I mean, the sales aren't exactly pouring in right now. (Though I'm not sure why.)
6. **Bonus Excuse:** Maybe next year I'll think about hiring a VA and getting ahead with my business. Right now I've just got too much to do.

There you have it. Six of the most widely used and abused excuses for not outsourcing all the crap that's getting in your way. Why choose silly things like productivity and purpose when you can defer to much easier choices like chasing your tail and working yourself to the bone?

Don't let a VA stop you from getting what you really want out of your business. It's just not worth it.

Posted at VAnetworking.com/blog by Karri Flatla of http://snapwebmarketing.com

Resources

All listed resources on the following pages are accurate as of date of publication. Should you arrive upon a "not found page" just do a simple search in Google for the name and if they has been moves, it will show up in the search engine results pages for you.

Listed in the section:

Virtual Assistant Organizations
Virtual Professionals Websites & Organizations
Virtual Assistant Groups, Communities & Websites
Virtual Assistant Directories
Administrative Professional Organizations, Websites & Other Resources
VA Training
Other Training Resources
VA Certification

Software List

Other Recommended Reading

Virtual Assistant Organizations

African Virtual Assistants Network (Afrivan) – http://www.afrivan.org

Alliance of UK Virtual Assistants – http://www.allianceofukvirtualassistants.org.uk

Australian Virtual Business Network (AVBN) – http://www.avbn.com.au

Be Virtual Assistant Wise – http://www.be-virtual-assistant-wise.com

Canadian Virtual Assistant Connection - http://www.cvac.ca/

Canadian Virtual Assistant Network - http://www.canadianva.net/

Colorado Virtual Assistants - http://www.co-vas.com/

Delaware Valley Virtual Assistants Association (DVVAA) - http://www.dvvaa.org/

DeskDemon – http://www.deskdemon.com

Home Secretarial Services – http://www.homececretary.com

International Virtual Assistants Association (IVAA) - http://www.ivaa.org/

International Association of Virtual Assistants (IAVA) - http://www.iava.org.uk/

Mid Atlantic VAs – http://www.midatlanticvas.com

Michigan Virtual Assistants – http://www.michiganvas.com

Military Spouse VAs - http://www.msvas.com/

Society of Virtual Assistants – http://www.societyofvirtualassisants.co.uk

UK Association of Virtual Assistants – http://www.ukava.co.uk

VAinsiders Club – http://www.vainsiders.com

VAnetworking.com – http://www.vanetworking.com

Virtual Assistant Groups, Communities & Websites

Coaches, Authors, Speakers Professional Assistant Assoc – http://www.caspaa.com

Real Estate Virtual Assistants Network (REVA) - http://www.revanetwork.com/

The Virtual Assistant Shopping Network – http://www.virtualassistantshop.com

The VAnetworking Forum - http://www.vanetworking.com/forum

Virtual Assistant Hub – http://www.virtualassistanhub.com

Virtual Assistant Directories

Alliance of UK Virtual Assistants - http://www.allianceofukvirtualassistants.org.uk/

Canadian Virtual Assistant - http://www.canadianvirtualassistant.com/

Desk Demon VA Directory - http://us.deskdemon.com

Elite Office Support - http://www.eliteofficesupport.com/

Shelancers – http://www.shelansers.com

VA4U - http://www.va4u.com/

VA Search Engine Directory - www.VAsearchengine.com

Administrative Professional Organizations, Websites & Other Resources

Association of Administrative Professionals New Zealand - http://www.aapnz.org.nz/

International Association of Administrative Professionals – http://www.iaap-hq.org

VA Training

Red Deer College VA Certificate Program - http://www.rdc.ab.ca/

VAclassroom - http://www.vaclassroom.com

VAinsider Club – http://www.VAinsiders.com

VA Trainer - http://www.vatrainer.com/

VA Training - http://www.vatraining.com/

VA Training Site – http://www.vatrainingsite.com

VBSS (Virtual Business Startup System) – http://virtualbusinessstartups.com

Virtual Assistant Training Program - http://www.vatp.ca/

Virtual Assistance U (VAU) – http://www.VirtualAssistanceU.com

Virtual Business Training - http://www.virtualbusinesstraining.com/

Virtual Training Program – http://www.assistu.com

VA Certification

VAcertified – http://www.vacertified.com

Certified Canadian Virtual Assistant (CCVA) – http://www.cvac.ca/

VA Certification (PVA & MVA) – http://www.vacertification.com

AssistU (CPVA & CMVA) – http://www.assistu.com

International Virtual Assistant Association (Ethics Check, CRESS, CVA) – http://www.ivaa.org

VAclassroom – http://www.vaclassroom.com

Software List

The following is a list of software that has been mentioned on various VA forums and email lists as a means to assist VAs with the decision of which software they may need when running their businesses. We do not necessarily recommend any of these software titles, but are simply providing a list of options for your reference. Also note that software and technology changes frequently, so we apologize if this list is not completely current and up to date.

Office Suites
(note: many of these offer various versions of their suites which have different software included in each.)

Microsoft Office - http://office.microsoft.com/
Open Office - http://www.openoffice.org/
Star Office - http://sun.com/staroffice
Corel WordPerfect Office -
http://www.corel.com/servlet/Satellite/ca/en/Product/1152105038419
Google Apps - https://www.google.com/a/
IBM's Lotus Symphony -
http://symphony.lotus.com/software/lotus/symphony/home.jspa

Word Processing

Microsoft Word - http://office.microsoft.com/en-us/word/FX100487981033.aspx
Microsoft Works - http://www.microsoft.com/products/works/default.mspx
Corel WordPerfect Office -
http://www.corel.com/servlet/Satellite/ca/en/Product/1152105038419

Desktop Publishing

Microsoft Publisher - http://office.microsoft.com/en-us/publisher/FX100487821033.aspx
Adobe InDesign - http://www.adobe.com/products/indesign/
Quark Express - http://www.quark.com
FreeSerif Software – http://www.freeserifsoftware.com

Data / File Management

Microsoft Access - http://office.microsoft.com/en-us/access/FX100487571033.aspx
Microsoft InfoPath - http://office.microsoft.com/en-us/infopath/FX100487661033.aspx
Microsoft Project - http://office.microsoft.com/en-us/project/FX100487771033.aspx
Filemaker - http://www.filemaker.com/
WebEx WebOffice - http://www.weboffice.com/
Folder Marker – http://www.foldermarker.com

Spreadsheets

Microsoft Excel - http://office.microsoft.com/en-us/excel/FX100487621033.aspx
AdventNet Zoho Sheet - http://sheet.zoho.com/

Accounting

Microsoft Accounting Professional - http://office.microsoft.com/en-us/accounting/FX100518171033.aspx
Intuit QuickBooks - http://quickbooks.intuit.com/
Simply Accounting - http://www.simplyaccounting.com/
MYOB - http://www.myob-us.com/getmyob/dr_continue.htm
Peachtree - http://www.peachtree.com/

Anti-Virus, Anti-Spam, Spyware Removal & Security

AVG - http://free.grisoft.com/
Norton - http://www.symantec.com/norton
McAfee - http://www.mcafee.com/us/
Webroot Spy Sweeper – http://www.webroot.com
Spyware Doctor – http://www.pctools.com
PC Tools Anti-Virus – http://www.pctools.com
Cloudmark – http://www.cloudmark.net

Time Management

Trax Time – http://www.spudcity.com
Easy Time Tracking – http://www.easytimetracking.com
Time Stamp – http://www.syntap.com

Email Program

Microsoft Outlook - http://office.microsoft.com/en-us/outlook/FX100487751033.aspx
Eudora – http://www.eudora.com
Thunderbird – http://www.mozilla.com/thunderbird/
GMail (Google Mail) – http://mail.google.com

Transcription

Express Scribe – http://www.nch.com.au/scribe
Start-Stop - http://www.startstop.com/home.asp

Web Conferencing

Adobe Acrobat Connect - http://www.adobe.com/products/acrobatconnectpro/
WebEx Web Conferencing – http://www.webex.com
Free Conference – http://www.freeconference.com
Arkadin Global Conferencing - http://www.arkadin.com/
Call-Fusion - http://www.call-fusion.com/index.jsp
Talking Communities - http://www.talkingcommunities.com/
No Cost Conference – http://www.nocostconference.com

Lead Management

Lead to Close – http://www.leadtoclose.com

Collaboration

Microsoft Communicator - http://office.microsoft.com/en-us/communicator/FX101729051033.aspx
Microsoft Groove - http://office.microsoft.com/en-us/groove/FX100487641033.aspx
Google Apps - https://www.google.com/a/
BackPack - http://www.backpackit.com/
SmartSheet – http://www.smartsheet.com

Contact Management

Microsoft Outlook - http://office.microsoft.com/en-us/outlook/FX100487751033.aspx

Instant Messaging

Skype – http://www.skype.com
ICQ – http://www.icq.com
MSN – http://www.msn.com
AIM – http://www.aim.com
Trillian *(a platform for multiple IMs)* – http://www.ceruleanstudios.com/

VoIP

Skype – http://www.skype.com

Presentation

Microsoft PowerPoint - http://office.microsoft.com/en-us/powerpoint/FX100487761033.aspx

Graphic Design

Adobe Illustrator - http://www.adobe.com/products/illustrator/
Adobe Photoshop - http://www.adobe.com/products/photoshop/family/
CorelDRAW - http://www.corel.com/servlet/Satellite/us/en/Product/1150981051301
Corel Paint Shop Pro - http://www.corel.com/servlet/Satellite/us/en/Product/1152105040688
FreeSerif Software – http://www.freeserifsoftware.com
Coffee Cup – http://www.coffeecup.com
Ifranview - http://www.irfanview.com/
GIMP – http://www.gimp.org/windows/

Animation

Corel Animation Shop - http://www.corel.com/servlet/Satellite/ca/en/Product/1152105040771
Adobe After Effects - http://www.adobe.com/products/acrobatpro/

Web Design

Microsoft SharePoint Designer - http://office.microsoft.com/en-us/sharepointdesigner/FX100487631033.aspx
Adobe Dreamweaver - http://www.adobe.com/products/dreamweaver/

Adobe Flash - http://www.adobe.com/products/flash/
FreeSerif Software – http://www.freeserifsoftware.com
Coffee Cup – http://www.coffeecup.com
PHP Designer Professional - http://www.mpsoftware.dk/phpdesigner.php
TopStyle Pro (CSS Editor) – http://www.bradsoft.com
Macromedia Studio - http://www.adobe.com/products/studio/index.html

File Transfer Protocol

WS FTP – http://www.ipswitch.com
CuteFTP – http://www.cuteftp.com
SmartFTP – http://www.smartftp.com
Core FTP - http://www.coreftp.com/
FileZilla - http://filezilla-project.org/
Coffee Cup – http://www.coffeecup.com

Backup

Nero BackUp – http://www.nero.com

Broadcasting

32bit Broadcaster – http://www.electrasoft.com
MailsBroadcast - http://www.mailsbroadcast.com/download.ecrm.freeware.htm
Emma - http://www.myemma.com/

Computer Maintenance

Registry Mechanic – http://www.pctools.com
CCleaner – http://www.ccleaner.com
Diskeeper Defragment – http://www.diskeeper.com

Media Players

Windows Media Player - http://www.microsoft.com/windows/windowsmedia/download/
Real Player - http://www.realplayer.com/
Quicktime - http://www.apple.com/quicktime/download/

PDF Creators/Converters

Adobe Acrobat Professional - http://www.adobe.com/products/acrobatpro/
Win2PDF - http://www.win2pdf.com
PDF995 - http://www.pdf995.com/
CutePDF - http://www.cutepdf.com/Products/CutePDF/writer.asp
Software 995 – http://www.software995.com

File Compression/Zip

WinZip - http://www.winzip.com/
Coffee Cup Zip Wizard - http://www.coffeecup.com/zip-wizard/
Zip Genius – http://www.zipgenius.it
Stuffit – http://www.stuffit.com

File Sharing

Microsoft OneNote - http://office.microsoft.com/en-us/onenote/
FX100487701033.aspx
Send This File – http://www.sendthisfile.com
Pando – http://www.pando.com

Process Mapping

Microsoft Visio - http://office.microsoft.com/en-us/visio/FX100487861033.aspx

Password Keeper

Passkeeper – http://www.passkeeper.com
KeePass – http://keepass.info

Learning/Course Management Software

Element K – http://www.elementk.com
Moodle – http://www.moodle.org

Miscellaneous

Read Notify – http://www.readnotify.com
(keep track of who is reading the emails that you send)

Picasa – http://picasa.google.com
(digital photo management)

FreeSerif Software – http://www.freeserifsoftware.com
(photo, drawing, web design, desktop publishing, etc.)

Coffee Cup – http://www.coffeecup.com
(All kinds of software downloads, generally web design related)

Download.com – http://www.download.com
(A great place to find software to download)

Xenu – http://home.snafu.de/tilman/xenulink.html
(Check for broken links on your website)

Adobe Reader – http://www.adobe.com/products/acrobat/readstep2.html
(PDF reader)

Shop'NCook – http://www.shopncook.com/menu.html
(Menu planner and create shopping lists)

CostGuard – http://www.costguard.com
(Food costing software)

QuickBase Project Manager -
https://www.quickbase.com/p/applications/project_mgmt.asp?ps=CW
(Client & project management plus calendar)

Other Recommended Reading

Books & Ebooks

Docu-Type's Business Building Ebooks – www.docutype.net/business_ebooks.htm
The Art of Follow-Up - https://paydotcom.com/r/10077/CVAC/423344/
Virtual Assistant – The Series - http://ww7.aitsafe.com/go.htm?go=www.va-theseries.com&afid=10449&tm=30&im=1
Virtual Business Start-Up System –
http://www.virtualbusinesssolution.com/cmd.php?Clk=494520
Executive Solutions for You (ES4U) – http://www.ES4U.com
Marketing Your VA Practice - http://www.The24HourSecretary.com
The Home-Grown Secretary - http://www.asecretary.com
The Virtual Assistant's Guide to Marketing - http://www.mjva.ca
The Virtual Assistant's Guide to the Multi-VA Business - http://www.mjva.ca

Newsletters

CVAC's Newsletter - http://www.cvac.ca/newsletter.php
Docu-Type's Virtual TidBits – http://www.docutype.net/news.htm
RSS Herald – http://www.rssherald.com
VAnetworking.com Newsletter - http://www.vanetworking.com/archives/
Virtual Assistant Business Newsletter –
http://www.virtualassistantbusiness.com/virtual-assistant-newsletter.html
Valley Virtual Assistant Newsletter - http://www.valleyva.net/

Blogs

Docu-Type's Small Business, Virtual Assistance & Web Design Blog –
http://www.docutype.org/blog
Partnering With a Virtual Assistant – http://www.vanetworking.com/blog
Virtual Assistant – The Blog About Our Industry - http://www.vadirectory.net/blog/
The Virtual Link Virtual Assistant Blog - http://www.thevirtuallink.com/blog/virtual-assistant-blog.htm
The Coach Virtual Assistant Blog - http://www.virtualaccuracy.com/blog/
OIVAC Blog - http://oivac.com/blog/
Assistant for Real Estate Blog - http://www.assistantforrealestate.com/blog/

Special Additions

VANetworking.com's Virtual Assistant Survey

Virtual Assistant Poem

VANetworking.com's 2008 Virtual Assistant Statistics

The Who, What, When, Where, Why & How of Virtual Assistants

VAnetworking.com is the largest membership base of Virtual Assistants online. The public media asked for our help and participation in putting together some general Virtual Assistant statistics for public consumption use in articles, stories, news and television related to Virtual Assistants. We hope these Virtual Assistant statistics will further help everyone understand more about this new career and the business entrepreneurs who call themselves Virtual Assistants.

Below are the answers to a few of the questions tabulated to date from 761 contributors who promote themselves as Virtual Assistants globally. You may view all the questions and responses on the website at http://www.vanetworking.com/survey.

Did you know that 96.8% of all Virtual Assistants are women and that 69.3% of these are married of whom 76.1% have children. 59.2% have college or trade school training with 82.5% starting their businesses after being in the workforce for some time.

32% of the VAs surveyed charge $31-40 per hour for their services with the majority of VAs putting in 31-40 hours of work per week. Amazingly, 43.6% of the VAs surveyed normally work on weekends.

93.7% of the Virtual Assistants surveyed stated that their clients are found through word of mouth referrals with 80.1% of VAs also marketing through a website online.

NOTE: You may freely use VANetworking.com's Virtual Assistant statistical data in any documentation both on and offline as long as you fully credit the VAnetworking.com at www.vanetworking.com as your reference source.

*Source: VAnetworking.com The Media Virtual Assistant Survey The Largest Global Meeting Place Online for Aspiring and Successful Virtual Assistants

These and many other statistics can be found in our survey results...VIEW the Virtual Assistant SURVEY RESULTS

Thank you,

Tawnya Sutherland
Founder of VANetworking.com

Courtesy of The VAnetworking.com   www.VAnetworking.com
All rights reserved 2008- Virtual Business Solutions 604.542.9664800-15355 24th Ave., Suite 393, Surrey, British Columbia, Canada V4A 2H9

Virtual Assistant Survey Questions & Responses

1. Gender

Female	96.8%	735
Male	3.0%	23

2. Marital Status

Single	13.1%	99
Married	69.3%	524
Divorced	13.0%	98
Common Law	4.5%	34

3. Do you have children?

Yes	76.1%	574
No	23.7%	179

4. If Yes, how many?

1	27.8%	161
2	39.4%	228
3	20.4%	118
4	7.9%	46
5 or more	4.3%	25

5. What is/are the age(s) of your child(ren)? Click all that are applicable.

1-5	30.6%	177
6-10	28.5%	165
11-15	31.3%	181
16-20	22.3%	129
Adults	37.0%	214

6. What's your educational background? Click all that are applicable.

High School	51.8%	392
College/Trade School	59.2%	448
University	32.2%	244
Online VA Training Program	19.8%	150
Online/Computer-based Courses	37.6%	285
On-the-Job Training	52.7%	399

7. Do you have any certifications? If so, which ones?

Yes	389
AssistU	27
Bureau Red VA Certification	6
Certified Insurance Virtual Assistant	1
Certified Virtual Bankruptcy Assistant	2
CRVA (Certified REALTOR.com VA)	1
GVA	8
IREAA	2
IREAA CCSVA	1
IREAA CREA	5

IVAA CRESS	28
IVAA CVA	16
IVAA EthicsChecked	37
JERPAT VA Coaching Certification	1
Military Spouse Virtual Assistant	1
Multiple Streams Dream Team 6-Day Intense VA Training Program	1
MVA	27
N/A	50
NAR REPA	17
Other - Non-VA-related	518
PREVA	19
Red Deer College VA Certificate	1
VA Certification in Marketing/Promotions - Santa Rosa Jr. College	1
VATP	3
VAtrainer Certificate	1
Virtual Professional	6

8. Did you start your business right after graduation? Click all that are applicable.

Yes	4.6%	35
After being in the workforce for some time	82.5%	622
After children were born	29.8%	225

9. Do you carry insurance for your business?

Yes	32.0%	240
No	67.9%	509

10. Why did you start your VA business? Click all that are applicable.

Wanted out of the corporate world	50.1%	379
Wanted to stay home with my children	41.0%	310
Wanted to own my own business	77.3%	585
Wanted flexible hours	78.7%	596
Wanted to make money	54.0%	409
Wanted independence	72.5%	549
Disability or physical reasons preventing you from working in the corporate world	7.4%	56

11. Is your VA business...

Full-time	58.9%	443
Part-time	41.0%	308

12. If part-time, do you also have another job?

Yes, part-time job	30.6%	70
Yes, full-time job	45.9%	105
Yes, other home based business (other than VA business)	29.7%	68

13. If it is part-time, do you intend to go full-time?

Yes	70.7%	217
No	29.3%	90

14. How long did it take before you had your first paying client?

They were already pre-arranged before my business started	23.2%	168
In the first month	30.9%	224
In the first 3 months	24.7%	179
In the first 6 months	9.7%	70
In the first 9 months	4.8%	35
In a year or more	6.6%	48

15. Do you use outsource work using subcontractors?

Yes	37.5%	276
No	62.4%	459

16. How do you market your business? (Please choose as many as you currently use in your business).

Online Networking via e-lists, forums, websites, etc.	70.4%	523
Online Search Engine Optimization Marketing	35.7%	265
Online Press Release Submissions	17.1%	127
Online Article Submissions	17.9%	133
Online Newsletter	14.5%	108
Online Banner Advertising	6.7%	50
Online Email Marketing Campaigns	15.1%	112
Online Affiliate Program	6.1%	45
Hand out Business Cards	74.0%	550
Newspaper or magazine ads	15.2%	113
Yellow page ad	14.0%	104
Cold calling	11.2%	83
Mail out media kits	6.3%	47
Mail or hand out flyers/brochures/postcards	38.9%	289
Networking at local community groups (Chamber of Commerce member, etc)	51.4%	382
Referral Program (referees of your services get a coupon or dollar amount) 22.7% 169		
I do not market at all	8.2%	61
Other marketing mediums:		151

Word of Mouth (friends, family, clients, former employers, self)
eBay
Website
Blog
RFPs
Public speaking
Online business directory listings
Professional networking
Radio
Car signage
Business magazine ads / Help wanted ads / Craig's list Work for free for a non-profit / charity
Flyers
Articles
Phone book

17. Do you have a...Click all that apply.

Marketing plan	62.3%	341
Business plan	88.1%	482
Contingency plan	25.8%	141

18. Which VA related organizations/groups do you belong to? Please list.

A Clayton's Secretary	42
ActiveRain	8
Alliance for Virtual Business	37
AssistU	60
Bureau Red	6
Colorado Virtual Assistant Association (CVAA)	8
CVAC	78
CVAN	39
Delaware Valley Virtual Assistants (DVVA)	7
DeskDemon	1
Digital Women	3
Elite Office Support	12
Home Secretaries	8
IAAP	7
IAVA	6
IAVOA	38
IREAA	39
Ireland VAs	1
IVAA	331
IVWCC	1
JER-PAT	3
Michigan Virtual Assistants	2
Mid-Atlantic Virtual Assistants	4
Military Spouse VA's	1
NAR REPA	2
NAWBO	1
None	13
Other	79
RemoteProfessionals.com	5
REVAnetwork	33
Ryze	7
Secretaries Int'l.	1
Society of Virtual Assistants (SVA)	14
Southeastern Virtual Assistants Group (SEVAG)	8
Southern California Virtual Assistants Group	3
Staff Centrix	1
Team Double Click	5
TopListed.net	2
UK Alliance of Virtual Assistants	5
VA Connection	5
VA Revolution	21
VA4U	30
VANETWORKING.COM	397
VAU	5
Virtual Assistants yahoo group	8
Virtual Biz Group (VBG)	7
Virtual Divas	2
Virtual Nation	6
Virtual Word Publishing	1
VirtualAssistantForums	4
VirtualAssistants.com	3
Virtually Yours	2
VirtualProfessionals.com	3
WAHM.com	3
Work The Web	1

19. Do you have employees?   (Not including subcontractors)

No	91.9%	688
Yes - full-time	3.1%	23
Yes - part-time	4.9%	37

20. If so, how many employees?

1 - Just Yourself	85.6%	292
2-3	12.6%	43
4-6	0.6%	2
7-10	1.2%	4
10 or more	0.0%	0

21. Do you niche market yourself? i.e.) Real Estate Virtual Assistant

Yes	43.4%	317
No	56.5%	413
Other		317

Other Niches:

Accounting	Documentation	Paralegal
Administrative Support	Ecommerce	Payroll services
Advertising copy writing	Editing	Performing artists
Affiliate Management	Editorial	Personal videos
		Pharmaceutical and healthcare
Agriculture	Engineers	market research transcription
Architects	Entertainment industry	Photo editing
Article writing	Entrepreneurs	Private investigators
Artists	Female solopreneurs	Project managers
Assist in setting up offices	Financial Planners	Promotional products
Association Management	Fitness industry	Proofreading
At Home Entrepreneurs	Ghostwriting	Prospect research
Audio transcription	Government	Public relations
Authors	Graphic design	Real estate
Baby Boomers	Health and disability	Sales
		Sales and Marketing support for
Bankers	Help desk	small manufacturers
Bankruptcy Preparation Services	High profile business people	SEO
Bilingual Services for Coaches		Sermon and testimony
and Conferences	Home businesses	transcription
Bilingual Virtual Assistant	Hospitality industry	Short sale negotiator
Bookkeeping	Hotel reservations	Show promoters
Building / Construction	Human resource assistance	Simulation analysis
		Small business importers and
Building Trade	Identity and branding for businesses	exporters
		Small business management
Business Coaches	Independent consultants	assistance
Business plan development	Independent professionals	Social entrepreneurs
Business plans and marketing	Insurance agents	Speakers
		Specialty foods, catering,
Career professionals	Insurance investigators	bakeries
Church groups	International	Sports
Claims billing	Internet marketers	Taxes
Coaches (life, business,		
personal)	Internet research	Technical assistance
Collection agencies	Invitations and announcements	Telemarketing
Commercial Lease	IT	Thesis writing

Administration

Community groups	Judgment Recovery Specialists	Tourism industry
Consultants	Law Firms	Trainers
Copywriting	Lawyers	Training
Corporate events	Legal and Conference (transcription)	Transaction coordinator
Corporate marketing support	Listing marketing coordination	Transcription
Court proceedings	Manufacturing representatives	Travel agencies
Court reporters	Manuscript typing/editing	Traveling sales people
Creative marketing	Media	Virtual Assistants
Creativity coaches	Medical	Volunteer board of directors
Customer service	Meetings and events	Web store management
Data entry	Mentoring	Website development
Database management	Music industry	Website maintenance
Deaf business owners	Non-Profit Association Support	Wordpress blog design
Dental/Medical Coding	Nursing students	Writing services
Design services	Organic SEO	Directly from my website
Desktop publishing	Organizing	RFPs from online job boards

22. How do you charge for services? Please check all that apply.

Hourly	87.7%	654
Retainer	60.7%	453
Project	50.5%	377
Other	6.0%	45

Other:

1 hour minimum, thereafter per minute
50% down and remainder due upon delivery or when invoiced
Actual time worked on project
All of the above, depending on the project/client
Always give one thing free or on a discount if applicable as negotiated
Based on Industry Production Standards
Bi-weekly
By line typed
By Project
Charge by the page.
Commission, when applicable
Flat fee
Flat Monthly Rate
Independent contract
Monthly
Number of words typed in a document
One time rate for creation of logos
Per page
Per recorded minute
Per transaction, per listing
Per unit
Percentage when necessary
Prepaid packages with discount
Service bundles
Special arrangements for some non-profits
Subscription
Work within client's limited budget

23. What is your hourly rate? (Amounts are based on a per hour USD rate)

Less than $10	1.3%	10
$11-20	10.3%	77
$21-30	30.2%	225
$31-40	31.9%	238
$41-50	17.6%	131
$51-75	6.8%	51
$76-99	1.5%	11
Over $100	0.1%	1

24. How long have you been in business?

Less than 1 year	37.8%	282
1-2 years	9.6%	72
2-3 years	21.6%	161
4-5 years	14.6%	109
6-7 years	5.9%	44
8-9 years	3.2%	24
10 years or more	7.2%	54

25. How many hours a week do you put into your business?

Less than 10	9.5%	71
11-20	22.3%	166
21-30	19.7%	147
31-40	23.9%	178
41-50	14.1%	105
More than 50	10.5%	78

26. Do you keep traditional work hours? (i.e., Monday-Friday, 9-5 plus or minus an hour)

Yes	38.6%	288
No	61.3%	458

27. As a rule, do you normally work on the weekends?

Yes	43.6%	326
No	56.2%	420

28. How many days a week do you normally work?

1-2	4.7%	35
3-4	25.6%	191
5-6	57.8%	431
7	11.8%	88

29. If you work nights, weekends, or holidays, do you increase your rate?

I do not work outside of normal business hours	18.1%	133
I work outside of business hours and do not raise my rate	62.2%	458
I work outside of business hours and do raise my rate	19.6%	144

30. Where is your office located?

Home office in a common room (i.e.: living room, dining room, bedroom, etc.)	31.1%	233
Actual home office in a separate room	66.1%	496
Office outside of home (rented space)	2.1%	16

Office outside of home (owned location)	0.5%	4

31. Where are you located?

United States	72.5%	542
Canada	15.1%	113
Australia	5.2%	39
Europe	4.0%	30
South America/Africa	2.3%	17
Asia	80.0%	6

32. Do you have a website?

Yes	85.3%	635
No	14.5%	108

33. If so, do you maintain your website yourself?

Yes	80.1%	526
No	19.9%	131

34. How do you find your clients? Click all that apply.

Word of mouth referrals	93.7%	697
Paper (magazines, newspaper, yellow pages)	23.8%	177
Electronic (Emails, banner ads, etc.)	31.5%	234
Directly from my website	49.6%	359
RFPs from online job boards	37.4%	278
Other	27.4%	204

35. How many clients do you normally have at any one time?

1-4	61.9%	451
5-7	21.4%	156
8-10	9.6%	70
11-20	4.4%	32
21-40	1.6%	12
41-100	0.8%	6
101+	0.1%	1

36. What percent of your clients do you turn over each month?

Less than 10%	78.2%	527
11-25%	8.8%	59
26-75%	7.4%	50
76-100%	5.5%	37

37. What timing system do you use to keep track of your clients?

Purchased time tracking software	47.6%	350
In-house designed program	11.1%	82
Traditional pen, paper, and stopwatch	24.9%	183
Other	21.5%	158

38. Are most of your clients...

Local to your area (1 hour drive maximum)	31.4%	231
Local to your state/province	11.3%	83
Within your home Country	46.5%	342
International	10.7%	79

Virtual Assistant

I am a Virtual Assistant, what is that you retort?
I'm the new age assistant, I'm happy to report.
Explain to me clearly, just what do you do?
Lend me your ear and I'll educate you.

I specialize in saving time, money and grief,
Professional resources beyond your belief,
I can clear off your desk and free up your mind,
From your administrative tasks of every kind.

We communicate by email, telephone or fax
Whatever means suits you to explain all the facts,
I work from my office with equipment I own,
You pay for my time and expertise, alone.

I can draft up your letters and mail them off too,
I can organize your database on a spreadsheet for you,
I can arrange your travel, your schedule or event,
I can create a PowerPoint presentation for you to present.

I can answer your calls while you're out for the day,
I can do your expenses, the virtual way,
I can edit your articles, papers and more,
You can optimize your business potential, like never before.

There are numerous ways that we can work together,
I'm there in an instant, no matter the weather,
No payroll, no downtime, no taxes, what have ya,
But realize this, I can't make your java.

There are so many areas that I can assist you,
Too many to list by this means, it's true,
Just visit my website or give me a call,
It's as easy as that...that's it, that's all!

Contributed by:
Karen Rossall
Copyright 2006
krossall@rogers.com

Input & Recommendations from Fellow VAs

Contributed by: Karen Shane, B.A., CPRW
Business Writing & Resumes, Toronto, Ontario.
www.resume4me.ca

Diversification is key to quiet times. When the phone isn't working, you have to investigate what is wrong. Try not to blame yourself, rather focus your energy and persevere to become skilled in software applications such as accounting programs, desktop publishing or digital transcription. Indulge in time to discover your hidden talents. Think add-ons and upselling services that could be directly related to what you do now.

The essential tools you need to sustain business are vital to the success of your organization. Improving your typing speed will enable you to become faster at your work. Equally important is learning how to proofread properly. By printing your document and placing this page to the right side of an original and comparing sentence by sentence will be the best method of choice. Should you submit documents to your client without checking for typos, you stand the chance that they will never tell you what is wrong with the document but they will not phone again for work to be processed.

What else can you do to create more business?
- invest more in advertising
- network with CVAC members to ask them to refer people to you
- contact small and medium sized businesses
- approach corporations but never rely on one client for your entire business income
- join professional associations
- find out what new companies are coming to your town/city from your local chamber of commerce
- raise your fees!
- create one niche for yourself in word processing or writing where everyone has to contact you for this one service you provide
- read Marketing publications and books from the experts
- consider re-naming your business
- get a registered business listing instead of going under your name only
- register for GST to look more professional so people take you more seriously
- improve your 30 second infomercial
- cold call, send out a postcard
- target market your audience
- purchase a colour printer
- think of innovative ways to encourage clients to return, i.e., offer an incentive in a percentage format, for example: 10% off your next order.
- set up a minimum fee that you would charge for each order
- read business sections in the newspaper
- reply to classified ads of companies who are in between, of hiring staff and do work for them temporarily
- place an ad in the Help Wanted section
- find out what words marketing experts rely on for selling: Save, Discover, Free.
- go out from the office and introduce yourself at breakfast meetings
- listen to what people have to say in terms of what they would want you to do

- learn more grammar, or how to type in another language.
- check your cash flow system and get money up front
- help other CVAC members with overflow
- join up with a mentor
- develop high impact presentation skills
- go to trade shows
- type memoirs for seniors
- diversify - for example, my niche became resume writing and I've become an expert in this area. You can locate an area and first call yourself a specialist and then when you're producing high calibre and quality work and feel confident you are an expert and others in the industry see you as one, you can call yourself an expert as well, but do not do this until you are well qualified.
- remain calm, do not get jealous of another V.A. making more money, keep persevering and you will become successful. Work extra hours; create a better business card; advertise more on line. You have to have the essential tools to reap the rewards of more income. You have to be passionate about what you do and know how to handle conflict and difficult clients so they don't wear you down.
- Finally: help your fellow CVAC members. Become a mentor, offer advice - share your education, offer goodness, never mislead another member, spread your goodness - what goes around comes around...back to you in a favourable way.
- Be honest, dependable, excellent in time management, precise, accurate and meticulous about everything.
- Freelance at an office for two days a week
- Tell the client the added value and benefits
- Focus and never give up.

Contributed by: Kate V. Kerans
Kerans Virtual Assistance
www.yourvirtualparalegal.net

Too many Virtual Assistants worry that by limiting their services, they are limiting their choices, when in fact, the opposite is true. By narrowing down your focus, you stand a much better chance of matching with a client while also getting to do something you enjoy. By choosing a niche, you have a specific focus, thereby making it easier to identify potential clients. Think of it like an arrow, long and narrowing to a point, so too should your focus be. Then, when you point it where you want it to go, you stand a pretty good chance of piercing the market where you aim it. On the other hand, if you have a broad choice of services and no aim, you are similar to a large block trying to penetrate a huge wall. The best part of using your 'arrow' is by doing so, your choices open up as soon as you penetrate that wall on the other side.

Contributed by: Francesca Frate, Owner/Operator
AdminConcepts - Your Administrative Connection
http://www.adminconcepts.net

Misconceptions you may have had about being a VA: That everyone, business owners would buy into the idea of hiring a VA. Having to educate people to realize that hiring someone like me was a great solution to help them take care of their administrative requirements.

Regrets about starting your business, waiting to start etc.: When I started my business in 2000 I was ready for it. I was unemployed not sure I wanted to become another worker bee in a large corporation. Starting the business helped me to grow as an individual. I've met a lot of great people and made some new friends. The only regret I have now is that after moving to a new city I didn't try harder to really market to my former clients. I let them drop me and I didn't try to show them that our working relationship could still work even though I would be over an hour away from them.

I regret wasting valuable time and not putting in an effort to really market myself once I moved to our new location. I didn't put in the same effort and time that I did the first time round. I just thought everything would fall into place. It didn't. It doesn't happen unless you are willing to commit the time and effort needed to re-introduce, re-launch and market yourself.

Benefits of being self-employed: Freedom to pick you own hours and not having to ask someone for time off. Seeing your self grow and learn all at the same time.

How you overcame difficulties: I can't say that I faced a lot of difficulties in my first life as a VA entrepreneur; I'm certainly experiencing some on the second go round. The main thing I thing is to stay focused and really push myself. Not to try and let things get to me and to always maintain a goal whether on paper or inside of me.

Feeling of loneliness/isolation associated with working from home: There were times when I missed having someone to speak with and bounce ideas off of. My husband became my mentor and joining business organizations and on-line groups such as CVAC helped me stay connected with others.

Sources of support: Taking the Self Employment Assistance program offered by Human Resources Canada Development was the best thing that I did. The training and education I received from the instructors was invaluable. Connecting with other VAs through on-line groups helped me to see that I wasn't alone. That other VAs, even seasoned ones were experiencing the same problems that I was. That VAs are truly a unique group because we are so willing to help one another. We don't see each other as competition but rather we see each other as a resource.

Is there anything you would do differently: My second time round I would definitely make changes. I should have started to research the companies in the area and made initial contact before moving.

Tips or advice for those just starting out: Learn everything you can about owning a business, find a mentor and surround yourself with positive people.

Contributed by: Karen Braschuk
Office Support 911
http://www.OfficeSupport911.ca

As a VA, I wanted to add my thoughts with regard to "firing your first client."

Often, as new VAs, we tend to accept pretty much anything and everything in terms of work. During the initial period of establishing ourselves, sometimes we have a misguided sense of gratitude and/or loyalty to certain clients just because they were with us at the very beginning—before we really got our feet off the ground.

What happened in my own VA business is that one client in particular took huge advantage of my initial sense of loyalty and gratitude. Because this client felt they had offered me mentorship and training in their business while I was green, they also felt that going forward, my work for them should have be done gratis (for free) for the most part. For many, many months, I continued to contribute to their business without any thought to my own business. Their time was valuable—mine was not.

After about a year working with this client, I realized that 90% of my time was being spent on them, yet they only contributed to 10% of my income as a VA. That's when I realized that as a VA, one must truly recognize and value oneself in terms of how much they contribute to the success of others.

I'm glad to report that I have since fired this client and gained others who truly appreciate how much true value I contribute to their business.

Just because you don't show up at a brick and mortar office every day doesn't mean you're not intensely focused and dedicated to the success of the business you are helping to succeed. My message to other VAs would be to never, ever underestimate the value of the services you provide, and if it comes down to needing to fire someone who doesn't recognize your value—do it. You have nothing to lose and everything to gain.

Contributed by: Charmaine Mitchell
Company- Office On The Run
http://officeontherun.ca/

Tips and advice for those who just starting out

Best advice for anyone starting out in this business, is to use the three P's rules I use to help me stay focus when I started this business.

- Perseverance- never giving up on your dreams and beliefs
- Patience- is the road to success only if you want it bad enough
- Passion- Loving what you day each day with conviction

Once you apply these rules you are on your way to be a successful VA

Appendices

Appendix I - Sample "Response to Classified Ad"

February 18, 2008

To Whom It May Concern,

I am writing to you in response to your classified ad in the (*name of publicat*ion) on Wednesday, February 16th, in which you mentioned your need for a part-time office assistant.

Have you considered a Virtual Assistant to help with your office overflow?

My name is (*your name*) and I am the owner of (*your company name*), located in (*location*). We specialize in providing virtual office assistance, desktop publishing and website design services on an outsourced, as-needed basis.

Our mission is to help small business owners (or your target market) meet and exceed the expectations of their customers.

I have included a copy of my company's brochure and some business cards. I invite you to visit our website at http://www.fictitiousva.com to learn more about our services and how we can assist you with your administrative tasks.

If you have any questions, please feel free to contact me at 905-555-1234 or by email at info@valeriearnold.com

Thank you for your time and I look forward to hearing from you.

Sincerely,

Valerie Arnold
Fictitious VA Business
http://www.fictitiousva.com
info@fictitiousva.com

Appendix II - Sample "List of Benefits" Flyer

BENEFITS OF HIRING A VIRTUAL ASSISTANT

1. No need to spend valuable time and money going through the resume screening, hiring and training processes.
    Our professional staff has the qualifications to get the job done!

2. No need to provide office space for an employee and their equipment.
    We do all the work in our office.

3. No need to acquire ANY additional equipment an employee is required to use.
    We have all the necessary equipment in our office.

4. Our clients have access to professional office assistance "when they need it"!
    We are just a phone call or email away.

5. No need to worry about source deductions, benefits, vacations, or loss of valuable office hours due to sick time.
    We handle our own expenses from our end.

6. Outsourcing some of your 'less important' or 'just can't get to' projects to *Fictitious VA Business* gives you the time to concentrate on more important tasks, like prospecting new clients and generating revenue.
    We take some of the overflow off your shoulders.

All in all, with just a phone call or email, you can:

**SAVE TIME
SAVE MONEY
&
GET PROFESSIONAL, ACCURATE HELP WHEN YOU NEED IT!**

OUTSOURCING = INCREASED PRODUCTIVITY & HIGHER PROFITS
We work with you to help meet & exceed the expectations of your customers!

Fictitious VA Business
TOWN, PROV/STATE, COUNTRY
PHONE: _____
FAX: _____
WEBSITE: http://www.**fictitiousva.com**
E-MAIL: info@**fictitiousva.com**

Appendix III - Sample Three-Fold Brochure

Located in Caledon, Ontario

As we are located in the beautiful town of Caledon, we are centrally located and therefore are able to provide personalized service to Brampton, Bolton, Caledon, Orangeville and all surrounding areas.

Also, with the advancement of technology use these days, we are able to provide assistance to clients worldwide.

Call today and let us help you meet and exceed YOUR customers' expectations!

PROUD TO BE CANADIAN OWNED & OPERATED CALEDON, ONTARIO

Why just keep up?...
Let us help you get ahead!!

Co-Founder and
Proud Member of:

Canadian Virtual Assistant Connection
http://www.cvac.ca

DOCU-TYPE Administrative & Web Design Services

Caledon, Ontario, Canada

Phone: _____
Fax: _____
Email: jbyer@docutype.net
http://www.docutype.net

DOCU-TYPE
Administrative & Web Design Services

Specializing in:
Professional, Creative & Affordable

Virtual Assistance
&
Web Design & Hosting

Enjoy all the benefits of an in-house employee without all the costs of hiring one!

Ph: _____
Fax: _____

Email: jbyer@docutype.net
http://www.docutype.net

BENEFITS OF HIRING A VIRTUAL ASSISTANT:

There are many benefits to outsourcing your projects to an off-site administrative assistance company.

Here you will find the

5 most important benefits:

1. No need to spend valuable time and money going through the 'resume screening', hiring and training processes. Our professional staff has the qualifications needed to get the job done!

2. There is no need to provide office space in your office to house an employee and the equipment they will need. We do the work in our office.

3. For that matter, there is no need to acquire that additional equipment that the employee will need to use. We have all the necessary equipment in our office.

4. Clients have access to professional office assistance *when they need it!* We are just a phone call or email away.

5. There is no need for the client to worry about source deductions, benefits, vacations or losing valuable hours due to sick time. We handle these at our end.

In other words:

With just a phone call, our clients

SAVE TIME,

SAVE MONEY

&

GET PROFESSIONAL,

ACCURATE ASSISTANCE

WHEN THEY NEED IT!

Why just keep up?...
Let us help you get ahead!!

Other services available:

Office Management,
Proofreading,
Transcription,
Databases,
Address Labels,
Internet Research.

Call today for your
Free Quotation

Or

Visit our website for more information

http://www.docutype.net

And, while you're there
Sign up for our Newsletter and submit your site for our Award.

DOCU-TYPE Administrative Services
Caledon, Ontario, Canada

Phone: _____
Fax: _____
Email: jbyer@docutype.net
http://www.docutype.net

Appendix IV - Sample Press Release

FOR MORE INFORMATION, CONTACT:
Valerie **A**rnold,
Fictitious VA Business
Phone: _____
Email: _____

FOR IMMEDIATE RELEASE

VIRTUAL OFFICE SUPPORT - THE WAY OF THE FUTURE

City, State/Prov, September 24, 2008—If you are understaffed or overloaded at the office, there is help out there for you! The newest way of the future in office staffing is outsourcing projects to a Virtual Assistant. Fictitious VA Business is an office assistance specialist. Owned and operated by **V**alerie **A**rnold, a veteran administrative assistant in the area, this company offers everything from professional word processing to small business web design.

Specializing in helping small business owners and entrepreneurs on an "as-needed" basis, Fictitious VA Business provides creative, expert assistance without the costs of hiring a full-time employee or the hassles of finding temporary help.

Projects can be forwarded by almost any means of communication (i.e.: phone, fax, mail, courier, e-mail, etc.) allowing Fictitious VA Business to not only help those in need of this service in (town/area) and surrounding areas, but all over the world. For more information, visit their Web Site http://www.fictitiousva.com, email _____, or contact **V**alerie **A**rnold at (*705-555-1212*).

— 30 —

Appendix V - Sample Invoice

I N V O I C E

DATE:
INVOICE #: 0033

BILL TO:

P.O. NUMBER	TERMS		
QUANTITY	DESCRIPTION	RATE	AMOUNT
Please make cheques payable to …..		TOTAL	$

Appendix VI - Sample Retainer Agreement

CONTRACT/RETAINER AGREEMENT

This Work for Hire Retainer Agreement ("Agreement") is made on this 28th day of June, 2007 between **V**alerie **A**rnold of Fictitious VA Business ("Contractor") and _____ ("Client").

1. Description of Services: Beginning on July 1, 2007, the Contractor will provide the Client with the following services:

- *Put in here a list of the services you will be providing the client*

2. Payment of Services: The Client will pay an initial Retainer Fee of $ _____ (US/CDN funds), which is based on $_____ (US/CDN) per hour for a total of ___ hours work. The Client agrees to pay the Contractor for the services set forth in article #1 above at the time of execution of this Agreement. Upon receipt of this initial Retainer Fee, the Contractor will begin the services set forth in article #1.

At the point when the initial payment and time frame (__ hours) has expired, the Client agrees to provide a second Retainer Fee in the amount of $___ for __ more hours of additional changes and ongoing maintenance. Again, work by the Contractor will continue upon receipt of this Retainer Fee from the Client. This procedure will continue in the same manor for any further expiration of Retainer Fees & changes, additions and maintenance to the website (i.e. Retainer Fee provided prior to conducting any further work).

3. Recognition: The Client shall allow the Contractor to insert contact and design information on the Client's site in the form of a small mention at the bottom of each of the pages with a link to the Contractor's website (*if you are doing website work for the client*).

4. Work Product Ownership: Any design material (i.e. graphics, HTML coding, etc.) shall remain the property of the Client with the Client allowing the Contractor to use said material for references and portfolio use.

5. Confidentiality: The Contractor agrees to keep all information provided by the Client in complete confidence. None of the Client's supplied material can be used by the Contractor for any other project they may take on. The same holds true in the reverse, the Client may not use any material provided by the Contractor for any reason other than that agreed upon in this Agreement. This provision shall continue upon completion of this Agreement.

6. Dissolution of Agreement: It is agreed upon by both the Client and Contractor that should this Agreement be dissolved and any portion of a Retainer Fee paid by the Client to the Contractor is still available, the Contractor shall provide enough additional services to cover that amount. As article #2 above states, there will not be any services performed by the Contractor prior to receipt of the Retainer Fee, therefore there will not be a provision necessary to cover outstanding work that needs to be paid for, as there will be none.

7. Entire Agreement: This Agreement contains the entire agreement of both the parties, and there are no other promises of conditions in any other agreement, whether oral or written.

_____
Signature of Client

_____
Signature of Contractor

_____
Date:

_____
Date:

Appendix VII - Sample Confidentiality Agreement

THIS AGREEMENT made as of November 5, 2012

B E T W E E N:

> (*Name of VA*), of (*VAs Company*)
> (the Contractor)
>
>   - and -
>
> (*Name of Client*), of (*Client's Company*)
> (the Client)

WHEREAS the Client and the Contractor have entered into or are about to enter into a business relationship for their mutual benefit;

AND WHEREAS as a condition of entering into and/or continuing such business relationship, the Client has required that the Contractor enter into this Agreement;

NOW THEREFORE IN CONSIDERATION OF the premises and other good and valuable consideration, the receipt and sufficiency of which is hereby acknowledged, the parties hereby agree as follows:

1.   **Definition**. Whenever used in this Agreement the following words and phrases shall have the following respective meanings:

    (a) **Confidential Information**@ means information in any form, not generally known to the public, disclosed to or acquired by the Contractor directly or indirectly from the Client or any clients, business partners or affiliates of the Client during the term of the Contractor's business relationship with the Client, including, without limitation:

(i)	information relating to the research, developments, systems, operations, clients and business activities of the Client or its business partners or Affiliates;
(ii)	information received from any clients, business partners or Affiliates of the Client;
(iii)	information specifically designated by the Client as confidential;
(iv)	information specifically designated by a client, business partner or Affiliate of the Client as confidential; and
(v)	information required to be maintained in confidence by the Client pursuant to an agreement with a client, business partner, associate or other person;

    but shall not include any information which was known to the Contractor prior to the date of the Contractor=s business relationship with the Client or which was publicly disclosed otherwise than by breach of this Agreement.

2.   **Confidentiality**. The Contractor acknowledges that (i) during his or her business relationship with the Client, he or she will be disclosed or will acquire Confidential Information; (ii) the Client has and will continue to enter into agreements with clients and others whereby the Client agrees to maintain the confidentiality of certain information; (iii) disclosure of Confidential Information to others with be highly detrimental to both the interests of the Client and its clients; and (iv)

Confidential Information is the property of the Client and/or its clients, business partners of Affiliates, as the case may be. Accordingly, the Contractor agrees that:

(a) the Contractor will not, at any time, disclose any Confidential Information to any other person not an Contractor of the Client, nor will the Contractor use Confidential Information for any purpose other than required by his or her contract; and

(b) the Contractor will not, at any time or in any way, take or reproduce Confidential Information unless required by his or her job. The Contractor will, upon ceasing to be contracted by the Client, return to the Client all Confidential Information in his or her possession or under his or her control whether such Confidential Information belongs to the Client or otherwise. The Contractor will also return all property then in his or her possession or under his or her control, which belongs to the Client or its Affiliates.

3. **Restrictions Reasonable**. The Contractor acknowledges that all restrictions in this Agreement are reasonable in the circumstances and hereby waives all defences to the enforcement thereof by the Client. In the event that any provisions of this Agreement shall be deemed void or invalid by a court of competent jurisdiction, the remaining provisions shall be and remain in full force and effect and the Contractor hereby confers upon such court the power to replace such void or invalid provisions with such other enforceable and valid provisions as shall be as near as may be to the original in form and effect.

4. **Irreparable Harm**. The Contractor acknowledges that breach by it of the terms and conditions of this Agreement may cause irreparable harm to the Client, which may not be compensable by monetary damages. Accordingly, the Contractor acknowledges that a breach by it of the terms and conditions of this Agreement shall be sufficient grounds for the granting of an injunction at the suit of the Client by a court of competent jurisdiction.

5. **Governing Law**. This Agreement shall be governed by and construed in accordance with the laws of the Province of Ontario.

6. **Entire Agreement**. This Agreement is the entire agreement between the Contractor and the Client relating to the subject matter herein and stands in the place of any previous agreement, whether oral or written. The Contractor agrees that no amendment to this Agreement shall be binding upon the parties unless it is in writing and executed by both parties.

THE CONTRACTOR ACKNOWLEDGES HAVING READ OVER THIS AGREEMENT AND UNDERSTANDS THE SAME AND AGREES TO BE BOUND BY ALL THE TERMS AND CONDITIONS THEREOF.

_____   _____
Witness   (Name of VA)

                                            November 5, 2012

Appendix VIII - Sample Non-Disclosure Agreement

This Agreement made as of (date)

B E T W E E N:

?????, of ?????

> (the "Discloser")

- and -

?????, of ?????

> (the "Recipient")

WHEREAS Discloser owns, possesses or controls certain trade secrets, and proprietary and confidential information acquired through the expenditure of time, effort and money, of a technical and business nature relating to ????? (collectively and individually described as the "Information"); and

WHEREAS Recipient desires to receive, and Discloser is willing to supply, the Information on the terms and conditions set out herein, solely for the purpose of investigating ????? (the "Purpose");

NOW THEREFORE THIS AGREEMENT WITNESSES that in consideration of the premises and the covenants and agreements herein contained the parties hereto agree as follows:

1. Discloser shall at its discretion provide such of the Information to Recipient as is required for the Purpose, verbally or in writing. Nothing in this Agreement obligates Discloser to make any particular disclosure of Information.

2. All right, title and interest in and to the Information shall remain the exclusive property of Discloser and the Information shall be held in trust and confidence by Recipient for Discloser. No interest, license or any right respecting the Information, other than expressly set out herein, is granted to Recipient under this Agreement by implication or otherwise.

3. Recipient shall use all reasonable efforts to protect Discloser's interest in the Information and keep it confidential, using a standard of care no less than the degree of care that Recipient would be reasonably expected to employ for his own similar confidential information. In particular Recipient shall not directly or indirectly disclose, allow access to, transmit or transfer the Information to a third party without the Discloser's prior written consent. Recipient shall disclose the Information only to those persons who have a need to know the Information for the Purpose and who have been approved by the Discloser to receive the Information. Recipient shall, prior to disclosing the Information to such employees and consultants, issue appropriate instructions to them to satisfy its obligations herein and obtain their written agreement to receive and use the Information on a confidential basis on the same conditions as contained in this Agreement.

4. The Information shall not be copied, reproduced in any form or stored in a retrieval system or data base by Recipient without the prior written consent of Discloser, except for such copies and storage as may reasonably required internally by Recipient for the Purpose.

5. The obligations of the Recipient under paragraphs 3, 4 and 5 shall not apply to Information:

(a) which at the time of disclosure is readily available to the trade or the public;

(b) which Recipient can establish, by documented and competent evidence, was in its possession prior to the date of disclosure of such Information by Discloser; or

(c) any Information which the Recipient is by law required to disclose.

6. This Agreement shall not constitute any representation, warranty or guarantee to Recipient by Discloser with respect to the Information infringing any rights of third parties. Discloser shall not be held liable for any errors or omissions in the Information or the use or the results of the use of the Information.

7. Recipient shall, upon request of Discloser, immediately return the Information and all copies thereof in any form whatsoever under the power or control of Recipient to Discloser, and delete the Information from all retrieval systems and databases or destroy same as directed by Discloser and furnish to Discloser a certificate by an officer of Recipient of such deletion or destruction.

8. When requested by Discloser, Recipient will promptly provide a list containing the full name and address of any person having access to or copies of the Information and the reason such access is necessary.

9. Due to the valuable and proprietary nature of the Information to Discloser the obligations assumed by Recipient hereunder shall (a) be unlimited in time or territory or (b) if it is held by a court of competent jurisdiction that this provision is illegal, invalid or unenforceable, shall apply only within those territories within which Discloser then carries on business and only up to 10 years after disclosure of such Information. If any provision of this Agreement is held to be invalid or unenforceable in whole or in part, such invalidity or unenforceability shall attach only to such provision or part thereof and remaining part of such provision and all other provisions hereof shall continue in full force and effect.

10. The Recipient shall indemnify and save harmless the Discloser from all damages, losses, expenses and costs whatsoever resulting from the breach of this Agreement by the Recipient.

11. This Agreement constitutes the entire agreement between the parties hereto with respect to the subject matter hereof and cancels and supersedes any prior understandings and agreements between the parties hereto with respect thereto. There are no representations, warranties, terms, conditions, undertakings or collateral agreements, express, implied or statutory, between the parties other than as expressly set forth in this Agreement.

12. This Agreement may not be assigned by either party without the prior written consent of the other party.

13. This Agreement shall ensure to the benefit of and be binding upon the respective heirs, executors, administrators, successors and permitted assigns of the parties hereto.

14. This Agreement shall be governed by and construed in accordance with the laws of the Province of Ontario.

IN WITNESS WHEREOF the parties have executed this Agreement as of the date first above written.

_____   _____
Signature of Discloser   Signature of Recipient

_____   _____
Date: Date:

Appendix IX - Sample Non-Competition Agreement

THIS AGREEMENT made as of November 5, 2012

B E T W E E N:

(*Name of VA*), of (*VAs Company*)
(the Contractor)
- and -
(*Name of Client*), of (*Client's Company*)
(the Client)

WHEREAS the Client and the Contractor have entered into or are about to enter into an business relationship for their mutual benefit;

AND WHEREAS as a condition of entering into and/or continuing such business relationship, the Client has required that the Contractor enter into this Agreement;

NOW THEREFORE IN CONSIDERATION OF the premises and other good and valuable consideration, the receipt and sufficiency of which is hereby acknowledged, the parties hereby agree as follows:

1. <u>Non-Competition</u>.

The Contractor acknowledges that he or she will acquire considerable knowledge about, and expertise in, certain areas of the Client's business and that he or she will have knowledge of, and contact with, customers and suppliers of the Client and its Affiliates (as hereafter defined). The Contractor further acknowledges that he or she may well be able to utilize such knowledge and expertise, following termination of his or her service with the Client, to the serious detriment of the Client in the event that the Contractor should solicit business from customers of the Client or its affiliates. Accordingly, the Contractor agrees that:

- during his or her contract and for a period of two (2) year after termination of his or her employment, the Contractor will not in any way be associated with or involved, directly or indirectly, with any person, firm, corporation or other entity engaged in any business which provides services substantially similar to the services provided by the Client or its Affiliates within the metropolitan area known as   and any area located within the vicinity of   miles from or within the vicinity of   miles from any other office of the Client, whether now operated by the Client or hereafter operated by it;

- he or she will not, for a period of two (2) years after termination of his or her employment, directly or indirectly, approach any customer or business partner of the Client or its Affiliates for the purpose of providing services substantially similar to the services provided by the Client or its affiliates; and

- he or she will not, for a period of two (2) years after termination of his or her employment, directly or indirectly, approach, solicit, entice or attempt to approach, solicit or entice any of the other employers of the Client or its Affiliates to leave the employment of the Client.

For the purposes of this Agreement, the word "Affiliate" shall mean any entity a majority of whose voting shares or securities are owned or controlled directly or indirectly by the Client or the shareholders of the Client, or whose control is held by the Client or the shareholders of the Client.

2. **General Provisions**.

- The Contractor acknowledges that all restrictions in this Agreement are reasonable in the circumstances and hereby waives all defenses to the enforcement thereof by the Client. In the event that any provisions of this Agreement shall be deemed void or invalid by a court of competent jurisdiction, the remaining provisions shall be and remain in full force and effect and the Contractor hereby confers upon such court the power to replace such void or invalid provisions with such other enforceable and valid provisions as shall be as near as may be to the original in form and effect.

- The Contractor acknowledges that breach by him or her of the terms and conditions of this Agreement may cause irreparable harm to the Client, which may not be compensable by monetary damages. Accordingly, the Contractor acknowledges that a breach by it of the terms and conditions of this Agreement shall be sufficient grounds for the granting of an injunction at the suit of the Client by a court of competent jurisdiction.

- This Agreement shall be governed by and construed in accordance with the laws of the Province of Ontario.

- This Agreement is the entire agreement between the Contractor and the Client relating to the subject matter hereof and stands in the place of any previous agreement, whether oral or in writing. The Contractor agrees that no amendment to this Agreement shall be binding upon the parties unless it is in writing and executed by both parties.

- This Agreement will ensure to the benefit of the successors and assigns of the Client.

IN WITNESS WHEREOF the parties have executed this Agreement as of the date first above written.

_____   _____
Signature of Contractor   Signature of Client

_____   _____
Date: Date:

Appendix X - Cease & Desist Letter Sample

Date

Owner of offending website

URL of offending website

I am the owner of {your company name and website address} which I have owned since {month year}. Everything on this website was developed by myself and is original content.

It has come to our attention that your {offending page(s) & URL(s)} contains content that is identical to the content on our {page} located at {page URL}.

While we realize that there are only so many ways that a Virtual Assistant can describe the benefits of utilizing our services {for example}, copying the content from another VA's website, word for word, is considered plagiarism and is not acceptable. Doing this not only shows a lack of imagination, it can also harm the placement of both your website and mine in search engines as they penalize websites that contain identical information.

We ask that you remove our content from your website immediately. Should you refuse, we will be forced to take further action.

Regards,

Your Name
Your Company Name
Your URL

Canada Revenue Agency **Agence du revenu du Canada**

REQUEST FOR A BUSINESS NUMBER (BN)

Complete this form to apply for a Business Number (BN). If you are a sole proprietor with more than one business, your BN will apply to all your businesses. **All businesses have to complete parts A and F.** For more information, see Pamphlet RC2, *The Business Number and Your Canada Revenue Agency Accounts*. If you have questions, including where to send this form, call us at **1-800-959-5525.**
Note: If your business is in the province of Quebec and you wish to register for GST/HST, do not use this form. Contact Revenu Québec. However, if you wish to register for any of the other three accounts listed below, complete the appropriate parts indicated in the following instructions.

₂To open a GST/HST account, complete parts A, B, and F.

₂To open a payroll deductions account, complete parts A, C, and F. ₂
To open an import/export account, complete parts A, D, and F.

₂To open a corporate income tax account, complete parts A, E, and F.

Part A – General information

A1 | **Ownership type and Operation type**

| Individual | Partnership Trust | Corporation | Other | (specify: |) |

Are you incorporated? Yes (a**l** **corporations have to provide a copy of the certificate of incorporation or amalgamation**)

Check the box below that best describes your type of operation:

Sole proprietor	Federal government (publicly funded)	Other government body
Society	Federal government (non-publicly funded)	Strata condo corporation
Employer of a domestic	Provincial government	Association
Foster parent	Municipal government	University/school
Religious body	Financial institution	Union
Hospital	Employer sponsored plan	

A2 | **Owner(s) information** – Complete this part to provide information for the individual owner, partner(s), corporate director(s), or officer(s) of the business. If you need more space, include the information on a separate piece of paper. The social insurance number is mandatory for individuals (sole proprietors) applying to register for a GST/HST account (Social Insurance Number Disclosure Regulations, *Excise Tax Act*).

Social insurance number (SIN)	First name	Last name
Title	Home phone – –	Home fax –
Occupation	Work phone – –	Work fax –
	Cell. phone – –	Pager number – –
Social insurance number (SIN)	First name	Last name
Title	Home phone – –	Home fax – –
Occupation	Work phone – –	Work fax –
	Cell. phone – –	Pager number – –

Contact Person – Please provide the name of a contact for registration purposes **only** (the contact name provided will not be considered an authorized representative). If you wish to authorize a representative to speak on your behalf about your BN account(s), complete Form RC59, *Business Consent Form*. See Pamphlet RC2, *The Business Number and Your Canada Rev* ***Appendix XI*** for more information.

Title	First name	Last name
	Work phone – –	Work fax – –
	Cell. phone – –	Pager number – –

RC1 E (07)

Canada

A3	Identification of business

Name

Physical business location	Postal or zip code

Mailing address (if different from the physical business location) c/o	Postal or zip code

Operating / Trading name

Language of preference   English   French

Are you a third party requesting the registration?   Yes (If **Yes**, provide your name and company name below)   No

Your name:

Company name:

A4	Major Business activity

Clearly describe your major business activity. Give as much detail as possible using at least one noun, a verb, and an adjective.
Example: Construction – Installing residential hardwood flooring.

_____

_____

Specify up to three main products or services that you provide or contract, and the estimated percentage of revenue they each represent.

	%
	%
	%

A5	**GST/HST information –** For more information, see Pamphlet RC2, *The Business Number and Your Canada Revenue Agency Accounts*.

Do you provide or plan to provide goods or services in Canada or to export outside Canada? If **No,** you generally cannot register for GST/HST. However, certain businesses may be able to register. See our pamphlet for details.	Yes	No
Are your annual worldwide GST/HST taxable sales, including those of any associates, more than $30,000? If **Yes,** you **have** to register for GST/HST. **Note:** Special rules apply to charities and public institutions. See our pamphlet for details.	Yes	No
Are you a public service body (PSB) whose annual worldwide GST/HST taxable sales are more than $50,000? If **Yes,** you **have** to register for GST/HST. **Note:** Special rules apply to charities and public institutions. See our pamphlet for details.	Yes	No
Are all the goods/services you sell/provide exempt from the GST/HST?	Yes	No
Do you operate a taxi or limousine service? If **Yes,** you **have** to register for GST/HST regardless of your revenue.	Yes	No
Are you an individual whose sole activity subject to GST/HST is from commercial rental income?	Yes	No
Are you a non-resident?	Yes	No
Are you a non-resident who charges admission directly to audiences at activities or events in Canada? If **Yes,** you **have** to register for GST/HST, regardless of your revenue.	Yes	No
Do you wish to register voluntarily? By registering voluntarily, you **must** begin to charge GST/HST and file returns even if your worldwide GST/HST taxable sales are $30,000 or less ($50,000 or less if you are a public service body). See our pamphlet for details.	Yes	No

Part B – GST/HST account information – Complete a separate form for each division of your corporation that requires a GST/HST account.

B1	GST/HST account identification – Check the box if the information is the same as in Part A3.

Account name

Physical business location	Postal or zip code

Mailing address (if different from the physical business location) for GST/HST purposes c/o	Postal or zip code

B2	Filing information – For more information, see Pamphlet RC2, *The Business Number and Your Canada Revenue Agency Accounts.*

Do you want us to send you GST/HST publications?　　　　　　　Yes　　　No

Enter the amount of your **sales in Canada** (dollar amount only)　　$　　　(If you have no sales enter $0)

Enter the amount of your **worldwide sales** (dollar amount only)　　　　　(If you have no sales enter $0)
$

Enter the fiscal year-end for GST/HST purposes.
If you do not provide a date, we will enter December 31.　　Month　　Day

Do you want to make an election to change the fiscal year-end for GST/HST purposes?　　Yes　　No
If **Yes,** enter the date you would like to use.
Month　　　　　　　　　　　　　　　　　　Day

Enter the effective date of registration for GST/HST purposes.　　　Y Y Y Y M M D　　See our pamphlet for information about when to register for GST/HST.
Year　　　　　　Month　　Day

B3	Reporting period

Unless you are a charity or a financial institution, we will assign you a reporting period based on your total annual GST/HST taxable sales in Canada (including those of your associates) for the preceding year. If you do not have annual sales from the preceding year, your sales are $0. If you wish to elect for a different reporting period, your options, if any, are listed below. Please indicate in the right column which option you wish to elect. For more information, see Pamphlet RC2, *The Business Number and Your Canada Revenue Agency Accounts.*

Reporting period election
Select **Yes** if you wish to file more frequently than the reporting period assigned to you.　　　Yes　　　No

Total annual GST/HST taxable sales in Canada (including those of your associates)	Reporting period assigned to you, unless you choose to change it (see next column)	Options		
More than $6,000,000	Monthly	No options available		
More than $1,500,000 up to $6,000,000	Quarterly	Monthly		
$1,500,000 or less	Annual	Monthly	**or**	Quarterly
Charities	Annual	Monthly	**or**	Quarterly
Financial institutions	Annual	Monthly	**or**	Quarterly

B4	Direct deposit information – The account holder identified below requests and authorizes the Minister of National Revenue to directly deposit into the account identified below, amounts payable to the account holder under Part IX of the *Excise Tax Act.*

　Complete the information area below or attach a blank cheque and write "VOID" across the front. This method provides a faster, more convenient, and dependable way of receiving refunds. The CRA will deposit your GST/HST refund into your bank account.

Branch number	Institution number	Account number

Name(s) of account holder(s):

Part C – Payroll deductions account information – Complete parts C1 and C2 if you need a BN payroll deductions account.

C1	Payroll deductions account identification – Check the box if the information is the same as in Part A3.

Account name

Physical business location	Postal or zip code

Mailing address (if different from the physical business location) for payroll deduction purposes	Postal or zip code
c/o	

Language of preference   English   French

Do you want us to send you the New Employers Kit, which includes *Payroll Deductions Tables* and information?   Yes   No

C2	General information

)   What type of payment are you making?
        Payroll   Registered retirement savings plan

        Registered   income fund   Other

)   How often will you pay your employees or payees? Please check the pay period(s) that apply.
        Daily   Weekly   Bi-weekly   Semi-monthly
        Monthly   Annually   Other (specify)

)   Do you want to receive the *Payroll Deductions Tables?*   Yes   No
      If **Yes,** select one of the following: Paper   compact disc (CD)

)   Do you use a payroll service?   Yes   No

      If **Yes,** which one? (enter name)

)   What is the maximum number of employees you expect to have working for you at any time in the next 12 months?

)   When will you make the first payment to your employees or payees?

Y	Y	Y	Y		M	M	D	D
						Month		Day
		Year						

)   Duration of business: Year-round   Season

      If seasonal, check month(s) of operation:

J	F	M	A	M	J	J	A	S	O	N	D

)   If the business is a corporation, is the corporation a subsidiary or an affiliate of a foreign corporation?   No
      Yes

      If **Yes,** enter country:

      Are you a franchisee?   Yes   No

      If **Yes,** enter the name and country of the franchisor:

Part D – Import/export account information – Complete D1 and D2 if you need a BN import/export account for commercial purposes (you do not need to register for an import/export account for personal importations). Complete a separate form for each branch or division of your corporation that requires an import/export account for commercial purposes.

D1 | Import/export account identification – Check the box if the information is the same as in Part A3.

Account name

Physical business location	Postal or zip code

Mailing address (if different from the physical business location) for import/export purposes c/o	Postal or zip code

Language of preference   English   French

Do you want us to send you import/export account information?   Yes   No

D2 | Import/export information

Type of account: Importer   Exporter   Both importer/exporter   Meeting, convention, and incentive travel

If you are applying for an exporter account, you **must** provide all of the following information.

Enter the type of goods you are or will be exporting:

Enter the estimated annual value of   are or will be exporting. $
goods you

Part E – Corporate income tax account information – Complete part E1 if you need a BN corporate income tax account.

E1 | Corporate income tax account identification – Check the box if the information is the same as in Part A3.

Name (as listed on your certificate of incorporation)

Physical business location	Postal or zip code

Mailing address (if different from the physical business location) c/o	Postal or zip code

Language of preference   English   French

Part F – Certification

All businesses have to complete and sign this part. You are authorized to sign this form if you are an individual, a partner, an officer of your business or a corporate director. If the Direct Deposit Information is entered, an authorized representative **may not** sign this form.

The person signing this form is the: Owner   ☐ Partner   Corporate director   Officer   ☐ Authorized representative

I certify that the information given on this form is, to the best of my knowledge, true and complete.

_____   _____
First and last names (print)   Title

_____   Year   Month   Day
Signature

IMPORTANT - READ CAREFULLY

RESEARCH YOUR CHOICES!

The Names Examiner searches the Corporate Register only. This register includes the names of corporations incorporated or registered extraprovincially in British Columbia. It does not include names of British Columbia firms, trademarks or corporations registered outside British Columbia. If you want to ensure your name is not used outside of British Columbia, you could also access the Trademarks database at www.strategis.ic.gc.ca, or you may wish to search other jurisdictions in Canada. Most public business and trademark registers in Canada are reflected in the NUANS database, which may be searched for a fee through private search firms.

The approval of any name is at the discretion of the Registrar. You are paying for three choices. Do not commit to any name before it is approved. Provide three choices for each company you wish to name, in descending order of preference. Check them out for potential conflicts through telephone listings, business directories and other publications.

Occasionally this office will reject all three of your choices. If that happens, it will be necessary for you to complete another Name Approval form with three more choices and submit it to this office with another reservation fee.

GENERAL

This form is used for the approval of all corporate and business names in British Columbia.

The first step in incorporation (company, society, cooperative association, financial institution) or registration of firms (partnership, proprietorship) or extraprovincial companies is the approval of the name through the Names Unit of the Corporate Registry.

Once your name is approved, it is reserved for you for a period of 56 calendar days. Any renewals of the reservation period will require payment of another reservation fee.

If you need assistance call our help telephone number at 250 356-2893.

Once your name is reserved, the next step is to submit the necessary information to incorporate a company or society, register a proprietorship, partnership or limited partnership or register a foreign entity as an extraprovincial company.

Please go to the Corporate Registry's Web site for information on how to incorporate or register, as well as information on other services provided by the Corporate Registry.

The Web site address is: www.fin.gov.bc.ca/registries.

Approval of a name by the Registrar for either a corporation or a firm does not provide a proprietary right or interest in the name under any circumstances. It is intended solely to protect the public interest by:

- preventing names of corporations which are so similar as to confuse or mislead; and
- providing a record which allows the public to determine which individuals are associated with a corporation or firm name.

A corporation or a firm name may be registered under the same name as another firm. As a result there are many duplications of firms names, however, a firm or a corporation name will **not** be accepted if it can be confused with another corporate name.

FIRM NAMES (partnership, proprietorship, limited partnership)

Registration of a firm does not provide any protection for that name and does not mean that the name will be available if you decide to incorporate a company using this name.

FEES

The payment of fees in advance is a mandatory requirement of doing all business with the Corporate Registry office. The fee to submit a Name Request to the Corporate Registry by mail is $30.00

Applicants are urged to consult the current Fee Schedule. Payment of the wrong amount is a common cause for the rejection of name requests. Cheques and money orders are to be made payable to the Minister of Finance.

PRIORITY SERVICE

Names are processed in the order of time of receipt. Upon request and on payment of an additional fee, an application will be processed in priority to others, normally within 24 hours of receipt.

PROCESS

This form allows you to make a maximum of three choices, **in order of preference,** for each name approval. If you wish to have more than one name approved, you must complete an additional form and pay another fee. Your first choice for a name may be approved, if available, and held for a period of **56 calendar days.** Any renewals of the reservation period will require payment of another reservation **fee. Your 2nd and 3rd choices are not examined unless the initial choice of name is not available.** Regardless of whether your three choices are all examined or not, the full fee is charged.

A name approval request may be made on this form, or in writing with the same information as is required on this form.

You can apply for your name in the following ways:

BY GOVERNMENT AGENT: Visit any Government Agent who will transmit the request to the Registrar. For locations go to www.govern mentagents.gov. bc.ca

BY ONESTOP KIOSK: Visit your local OneStop kiosk location. They will transmit the request to the Registries. User fees may apply. For locations go to www.bcbusinessregistry.ca

BY MAIL: Names Reservation Section, Corporate Registry PO Box 9431 Stn Prov Govt Victoria BC V8W 9V3

You can also apply for your name by visiting the Names Unit in Victoria, located on the 2nd Floor of 940 Blanshard Street.

Results will be confirmed in the same manner as the application was made.

NAME COMPONENTS

In assessing names, the Registrar's staff analyze them according to their constituent components. The form of name acceptable in principle consists of a distinctive element, followed by a descriptive element and ending with a corporate designation (if applicable).

e.g. ABC Manufacturing Ltd.

Distinctive	Element
Descriptive	Element
Corporate Designation	

DISTINCTIVE ELEMENT

The distinctive element serves to differentiate names having identical or similar descriptive elements, and for that reason, is the **most important** element to be examined in the name.

Names such as "Tire Shop Ltd." and **"Shoe** Store Ltd." lack an appropriate distinctive element and would be rejected for that reason.

They would be acceptable, if prefixed with an additional distinctive element (e.g. coined word, geographical location or personal name) that would distinguish them from all the other tire shops and shoe stores.

e.g. Vancouver Tire Shop Ltd.   **Sandell's Shoe** Store Ltd.

Coined and made-up words are acceptable distinctive elements, provided they do not conflict with others already registered.

e.g. Intertex Enterprises Ltd.   **Fabuform** Diet Centre Ltd.

A uniquely coined word, used in addition to a geographical location (e.g. Altrex Canada Ltd.), is normally considered sufficiently distinctive by itself that a descriptive element is not usually required.

DESCRIPTIVE ELEMENT

The descriptive element is useful in describing the nature of the business as well as expanding the options available. It allows for use of identical or similar distinctive elements, which might be desirable in developing a particular presence in the marketplace.

e.g. Victoria **Brake Shop** Ltd.   Victoria **Stationery** Ltd.

CORPORATE DESIGNATION

Incorporating companies **must have as the last word in the name,** the corporate designation, "Limited", "Limitee", "Incorporated", "Incorporee" or "Corporation."

For all purposes, using the abbreviations of these words (e.g. "Ltd", "Ltee", "Inc" or "Corp") is acceptable.

Extraprovincial companies may have "Limited Liability Company" or "LLC." as the last word in their name.

The corporate designation is not applicable to a firm name, society or cooperative name.

Firm names for partnerships and proprietorships **cannot** use "Ltd", "Inc" or "Corp" in their names, but they may use "Company" or "Co"

Firm names for limited partnerships **must** use "Limited Partnership" at the end of the name.

Firm names for limited liability partnerships **must** use "Limited Liability Partnership" or "UP." at the end of the name.

Societies should have the designation "Society" or "Association" as the last word in their name. Companies are precluded from the use of these words in their names.

Cooperatives should use the word "Cooperative" in their name and may also use "Association", "Society", "Union" and "Exchange."

SINGLE WORD NAMES

Single word names (such as International Limited) are normally not sufficiently distinct from other names containing the same word and generally will not be approved.

An exception may be allowed if the proposed, single-word name contains a coined word that has been trademarked and evidence of the trademark is presented with the name request. Each case will be determined on its merits.

Obvious contractions of common words (e.g. Petrochem, being a contraction of petroleum and chemical) are not considered to be coined words for the purposes of single-word names.

NUMBER NAMES

Numerals may be used in company names as the distinctive element. A year may be used in a name provided that it is the year of incorporation, amalgamation or registration.

e.g. 123456 Enterprises Ltd.   Pacific Enterprises (1997) Ltd.

The incorporation number may be used as the name of a British Columbia company. The accepted format is "345678 B.C. Ltd.."

A name reservation or fee is not required for B.C. companies using just their incorporation number. The name will be given according to the next available number at the time of incorporation.

Numbered companies from other jurisdictions, continuing into British Columbia and wishing to retain their numbered names, will be required to conform with the name requirements of this province.

PERSONAL NAMES

In most cases, a natural person's full name will be considered to be sufficiently distinctive and therefore acceptable.

e.g. Bill Brown Ltd.   John Smith Inc.

Two surnames, or initials with a surname, are normally accepted.

e.g. Brown, Green Inc.   J.R. Black Corp.

WELL KNOWN NAMES

Names, which include well known trade names and trademarks, will not be allowed without the advance written consent of the holder. e.g. Exxon, Xerox, Coke

EXTRAPROVINCIAL NAMES

Special consideration will be given to established extraprovincial companies applying for registration in the province, provided there is not a direct conflict in names.

SPECIAL CHARACTERS

The use of special characters (such as % or *) should be avoided in corporate and business names.

Some special characters may not be recognized by computer, will not print accurately and may not be allowed.
The "0" symbol will not be approved in a name under any circumstances.

NO SUGGESTION OF GOVERNMENT CONNECTION

The word "government" (in either its English or French form) will not be allowed. Other words which might imply connection with, or endorsement by, any government require written consent of that government. Examples of other words which imply government connection are "ministry", "bureau", "secretariat', "commission" and "certified."

The use of "British Columbia" or "BC" as the distinctive element in any name is considered to imply connection with the Government of the Province of British Columbia. Use will be accepted only on the written consent of that government, usually obtained from the Protocol Office, Intergovernmental Relations Secratariat, after the name has been approved by the Registrar.

Use of the words "British Columbia" and "BC" will be accepted without consent, if they are placed at the end of a name and before the corporate designation.

e.g. Pacific Warehouse Storage BC Ltd.

NO SUGGESTION OF CONNECTION WITH CROWN OR ROYAL FAMILY

A name which suggests or implies a connection with the Crown, any living member of the Royal family, or endorsement by the Crown or Royal family will not be accepted without the written consent from the appropriate authority after the name has been approved by the Registrar.

e.g. Prince Charles Tea Room Ltd.

This does not apply to references in a name to geographical locations such as Prince George, Prince Rupert and references to New Westminster as the Royal City.

The use of the words "Crown" or "Royal" in combination with another word(s) that does not imply connection with the Crown or Royal family may be allowed.
e.g. Triple Crown Painting Ltd.   Royal Star Holdings Ltd.

OBJECTIONABLE NAMES

Names that are considered to be objectionable on public grounds will not be accepted.

A name will not be approved if it includes a vulgar expression, obscene word or connotation, racial, physical or sexual slur.

The use of names of public figures will not be accepted without the advance written consent of the person named.

GUIDELINES

This abbreviated information is provided for convenience only. Corporate and business law is complicated, and there can be no substitute for sound professional advice. Neither the Corporate Registry nor the Ministry of Finance can accept responsibility for any errors or omissions in this information.

HELP IS AVAILABLE

For assistance or further information, please call 250 356-2893.

Please retain this sheet for your information

NAME REQUEST

**Ministry
of Finance**
BC Registry Services

Mailing Address:
PO Box 9431 Stn Prov Govt
Victoria BC V8W 9V3
Location:
2nd Floor - 940 Blanshard Street
Victoria BC

www.fin.gov.bc.cWregistries

NAME
APPROVAL NUMBER **NR**

*Important: Use this number on all documents and in
the electronic submission of documents.*

Phone: 250 356-2893 or
04 775-1044 (Greater Vancouver only)

ISTRUCTIONS:

Please retain the yellow copy for your records. If the
request is mailed, the Name Reservaton section will
notify you by letter once your request is completed.

Please type or print clearly.

SHADED AREAS ARE FOR OFFICE USE ONLY.

reedom of Information and Protection of Privacy Act (FOIPPA):
ersonal information provided on this form is collected, used and disclosed under
e authority of the *FOIPPA* and the *Business Corporations Act, Cooperative
ssociation Act, Partnership Act* or *Society Act* for the purposes of assessment.
uestions regarding the collection, use and disclosure of personal information can
e directed to the Executive Coordinator of the BC Registry Services at 250 356-
198, PO Box 9431 Stn Prov Govt, Victoria BC V8W 9V3.

PRIORITY REQUEST - *Additional fee required*

YES - This is a priority request and I have
enclosed an additional *fee for* this *service.*

ROUTING SLIP NO.   DEBIT BCOL ACCOUNT NO.

FOLIO NO.   DEPOSIT ACCOUNT TRANSACTION NO.

GOVT. AGENT TRANSACTION DATE			DATE RECEIVED		
VYVY	MM	DD	VYVY	MM	DD
GOVT. AGENT TRANSACTION NO.			GOVT. AGENT AMOUNT COLLECTED		
			$		

PPLICANT SURNAME   FIRST NAME AND INITIALS

DDRESS

TY   PROVINCE   POSTAL CODE

PPLICANT PHONE NO.   APPLICANT FAX NO.   CONTACT PERSON NAME

)   ( )

ndicate what the name request is for: (In order for this request to be completed, one box must be (✓) ticked)

CORPORATION (INCLUDES   PROPRIETORSHIP/   SOCIETY   FINANCIAL   COOPERATIVE
A FOREIGN CORPORATION)   PARTNERSHIP   INSTITUTION   ASSOCIATION

this request for a foreign corporation   IF YES, ENTER THE JURISDICTION   NATURE OF BUSINESS
ncorporated in another province or country?
    YES   NO

DDITIONAL INFORMATION

Jame Request *(first choice)* **PLEASE TYPE OR PRINT CLEARLY**

Jame Request *(second choice)* **PLEASE TYPE OR PRINT CLEARLY**

Jame Request *(third choice)* **PLEASE TYPE OR PRINT CLEARLY**

BRITISH COLUMBIA
The Best Place on Earth

Ministry
of Finance
BC Registry Services

Mailing Address:
PO Box 9431 Stn Prov Govt
Victoria BC v8w 9V3
Location:
2nd Floor - 940 Blanshard
Street Victoria BC

Appendix XIII – BC -
STATEMENT OF REGISTRATION
OF GENERAL PARTNERSHIP
OR SOLE PROPRIETORSHIP

PLEASE NOTE:

The registration of a business name under the *Partnership Act:*
- **does not provide any protection for that name, and**
- **does not mean that the name will be available if you decide to incorporate a company using this name.**

One of the primary reasons for registration of a Partnership or Proprietorship is so the public can identify and locate the individuals involved in the business. A proprietor or partner can be one of the following: an individual, corporation or other corporate entity such as a society, cooperative, etc.

Please have your name reservation approved before submitting this statement of registration. Name Approval Request forms are available from your nearest Government Agents Office or our Web site at: **www.fin.gov.bc.ca/registries** or by contacting this office. To **register online go to www.onestopbc.ca**

GENERAL INSTRUCTIONS

A. Name and Return Mailing Address:
All correspondence and documents will be mailed to this address.

B. Business Information:

Business Name: Enter the approved business name, not the owner(s) name.

Business Address: The location where the business is to be conducted in British Columbia. Enter the complete physical address. You may include general delivery, post office box, rural route, site or comp. number as part of the address, but the Registry cannot accept this information as a complete address. You must also include a postal code. If an area does not have street names or numbers, provide a description that would readily allow a person to locate your business (e.g., the 2nd house on the left side, 4 miles west on Central County Road, Creston, B.C.).

Mailing Address: Complete only if this address is different from the business address. A post office box or rural route number is acceptable as the mailing address.

Start Date of Business in British Columbia: **A date** must be entered. The date may be in the past, present or future.

Nature of Business: Provide a brief description of the nature of business (e.g., corner grocery store, automotive repair service, landscaping, etc.).

C. Proprietorship: Enter the full name of the proprietor. If a proprietor is a corporate entity, the corporation must have a registered address in British Columbia.

Residential or Registered Address: The address must be a physical location. You may include general delivery, post office box, rural route, site or comp. number as part of the address, but the Registry cannot accept this information as a complete address. You must also include a postal code. If an area does not have street names or numbers, provide a description that would readily allow a person to locate you (e.g., the 2nd house on the left side, 4 miles west on Central County Road, Creston, B.C.). If a corporation, the registered office must be in British Columbia.

D. Partnership: Enter the full name of all the partners. If there are more than three partners, you may attach an additional statement or a sheet of paper listing the partners' name and address. If a partner is a corporate entity, the corporation must have a registered address in British Columbia.

Residential or Registered Address: The address must be a physical location. You may include general delivery, post office box, rural route, site or comp. number as part of the address, but the Registry cannot accept this information as a complete address. You must also include a postal code. If an area does not have street names or numbers, provide a description that would readily allow a person to locate you (e.g., the 2nd house on the left side, 4 miles west on Central County Road, Creston, B.C.). If a corporation, the registered office must be in British Columbia.

If you need assistance to complete this form, please phone **250 356-2893** or **604 775-1044** (Greater Vancouver only).

Mail white and canary copies of this form to:

Ministry of Finance
BC Registry Services
PO Box 9431 Stn Prov Govt
Victoria BC V8W 9V3

To register a proprietorship or general partnership:

Name Approval	$30.00
Registration	$40.00
Total	$70.00

The above fees include one certified copy. Additional certified copies are $25.00 each.

Make cheque payable to the Minister of Finance.

Freedom of Information and Protection of Privacy Act (FOIPPA):
Personal information provided on this form is collected, used and disclosed under the authority of the *FOIPPA* and the *Partnership Act* for the purposes of assessment. Questions regarding the collection, use and disclosure of personal information can be directed to the **Executive Coordinator of the BC Registry Services at 250 356-1198, PO Box 9431 Stn Prov Govt, Victoria BC V8W 9V3.**

Mailing Address:
PO Box 9431 *Stn* Prov *Govt*
Victoria BC *V8W 9V3*
Location:
2nd Floor - 940 Blanshard *Street*
Victoria BC

**STATEMENT OF REGISTRATION OF
GENERAL PARTNERSHIP
OR SOLE PROPRIETORSHIP**

C O R P O R A T E

R E G I S T R A T I O N

G O V E R N . . .

. . .

N

Veb *site:* **www.fin.gov.bc.ca/registries**
Phone: **250 356-2893 or**
604 775-1044 *(Greater* Vancouver only)

NAME APPROVAL NO. - *If known*

N 1 R

A. Name and Return Mailing Address of person submitting this form

NAME

ADDRESS

CITY/
PROVINCE
POSTAL CODE

**Note: The registration of a business name under the *Partnership Act* does not
provide any protection for that name.**
Please **TYPE** *or* **PRINT CLEARLY.** Press firmly - *you* **are** making three copies.

B. Business Information - *This section must be completed by everyone.*

BUSINESS NAME

BUSINESS ADDRESS - ***Must be the physical location of the business in B.C., not just a general delivery, post office box, rural route, site, or comp. number*** ET

	CITY	PROVINCE	POSTAL CODE
		British Columbia	

ADDRESS - *Complete only if different from Business Address*

	CITY	PROVINCE	POSTAL CODE

START DATE OF BUSINESS IN
BRITISH COLUMBIA
YYYY/MM/DD

DESCRIBE NATURE OF BUSINESS (e.g., *grocery store,*
manufacturing)

C. Proprietorship - *This is to certify that no other person is associated with me in this
proprietorship.* PROPRIETOR NAME - *State owner's name in full*

RESIDENTIAL OR REGISTERED ADDRESS - ***Must be a physical location, CANNOT be just a general delivery, post office box, rural route, site, or comp. number***

D. Partnership - *This is to certify that the persons named in Section D are the only members of this partnership.*
PARTNER NAME - *State name in full*

RESIDENTIAL OR REGISTERED ADDRESS - ***Must be a physical location,*** *CANNOT be just a general delivery, post office box, rural route, site, or comp. number*

PARTNER NAME - *State name in full*

RESIDENTIAL OR REGISTERED ADDRESS - ***Must be a physical location,*** *CANNOT be just a general delivery, post office box, rural route, site, or comp. number*

PARTNER NAME - *State name in full*

RESIDENTIAL OR REGISTERED ADDRESS - ***Must be a physical location,*** *CANNOT be just a general delivery, post office box, rural route, site, or comp. number*

**It is an offence to make or assist in making a false or
misleading statement in a record filed under the
Partnership Act. A person who commits this offence .is
subject to a maximum fine of $5,000.**

FORWARD TWO COPIES TO THE REGISTRAR OF COMPANIES
PLEASE MAKE A COPY FOR YOUR RECORDS

FIN 707/WEB Rev. 2007/11 /8

Declaration of Trade Name

Partnership Act

I, _____
Name of Declarer

of _____
Resident Address in Full

declare that:

3.   I have been carrying on or intend to carry on the business of

Type of Business

in _____ , in the Province of Alberta, under
City, Town, Village

the name of

Trade / Business Name

Use of this name commenced on

Day / Month / Year

1.   No other person or persons are associated in partnership with me in this business.

Name of Declarer *(please print)*   Date of Declaration

Occupation   Identification

This information is being collected for the purposes of corporate registry records in accordance with the Partnership Act. Questions about the collection of this information can be directed to the Freedom of In formation and Protection of Privacy Coordinator for the Alberta Government, Box 3140, Edmonton, Alberta T5J 2G7, (780) 427-7013.

Declaration of Trade Name

PARTNERSHIP ACT

INSTRUCTIONS

The Declaration of Trade Name must contain the following information:

Item 1:
- Type of Business
- City, Town, Village where the business is located
- Trade / Business Name under which the Declarant carries on or intends to carry on business
- Date on which the use of the business name commenced.

The following information must be included:
- name of declarer authorizing (director/authorizing officer)
- occupation
- identification
- date

NOTE: Filing of a Declaration of Trade Name is required mainly to provide proof that the name is in use by a particular business. Filing of the declaration does not give any right of ownership of the name.

To assist you in making an informed decision on the proposed name, an Alberta Business Name Search Report should be obtained and assessed before you file this Declaration.

REG3018 (2003/05)

Appendix XV -

NEW BRUNSWICK / CERTIFICATE OF BUSINESS NAME OR CERTIFICATE OF RENEWAL OF BUSINESS NAME NOUVEAU-BRUNSWICK / CERTIFICAT D'APPELLATION COMMERCIALE OU CERTIFICAT DE RENOUVELLEMENT D'APPELLATION COMMERCIALE

THE PARTNERSHIPS AND BUSINESS NAMES REGISTRATION ACT (SECTION 9 AND 9.1)
LOI SUR L'ENREGISTREMENT DES SOCIÉTÉS EN NOM COLLECTIF ET DES APPELLATIONS COMMERCIALES (ARTICLE 9 ET 9.1)

1. Name or style to be registered / Appellation commerciale à enregistrer
2. Business activity or service to be carried on, in or identified by the registered name Nature de l'activité ou des services dont s'occupe la firme pouvant être évoquée ou identifiée par l'appellation commerciale enregistrée
3. Mailing address of corporation or business registering business name, giving street and number or R.R. number, and municipality. Adresse postale de la corporation ou de l'entreprise enregistrant l'appellation commerciale, donnant le numéro et la rue ou le numéro de la route rurale, et la municipalité. Postal Code/Code postal

4. Date of establishing business under the name and style / Date de constitution de l'entreprise sous l'appellation commerciale

Day/Jour	Month/Mois	Year/Année	Check if Renewal Cocher s'il s'agit d'un renouvellement	Telephone/Téléphone

5. Name of the corporation or person registering name / Nom de la corporation ou de la personne enregistrant l'appellation commerciale
6. Address where business is located / Adresse de l'entreprise Postal Code/Code postal

7. Signature of Director or Officer or Person Signature de l'administrateur, du dirigeant ou de la personne	8. Name and title of the Signing Official Nom et titre du signataire

Registrar Use Only / Réservé à l'usage du registraire

Reference No. / Nₒ de référence

Registration Date / Date d'enregistrement _ _____
                                                            Year/Année-Month/Mois-Day/Jour

Expiry Date / Date d'expiration   _____
                                                            Year/Année-Month/Mois-Day/Jour

This registration expires in five years, but may be renewed. Renewal is your responsibility. The registration expiry date will be shown in your Confirmation of Registration.

Le délai d'expiration du présent enregistrement est de cinq ans, renouvelable. Toutefois, la responsabilité du renouvellement vous incombe. La date d'expiration de l'enregistrement sera indiquée dans votre Confirmation d'enregistrement.

FORM / FORMULE 5
INSTRUCTIONS ON REVERSE SIDE / INSTRUCTIONS AU VERSO.

SN0295 (New) + SN0307 / 45-3502 (1 2/07)
SN0297 (Renewal) + SN0307 / 45-3502 (12/07)

INSTRUCTIONS	DIRECTIVES

ITEM 1
Print clearly the business name to be registered or renewed. For initial registration, we require an ATLANTIC based name search report (5 pages and covering letter) on your proposed business name.

A business name cannot have a legal ending, i.e. Ltd., Limited, Inc., Incorporated

ITEM 2
Indicate the business activity or service to be carried on.

ITEM 3
This should be the address where you wish correspondence from this office to be mailed. The address must be complete including a postal code.

ITEM 4
Indicate the date the business was established under the name being registered.

ITEM 5
Indicate the name of the person, corporation or partnership name registering the business name. **PLEASE NOTE THIS FORM IS NOT TO BE USED FOR A PARTNERSHIP NAME REGISTRATION.**

ITEM 6
Indicate the address where the business is to be located. A P.O. Box number is not acceptable. The address must be complete including a postal code.

ITEM 7
Only the person, officer or director of the corporation, or partner of the partnership, registering the business name is authorized to sign the form.

ITEM 8
Set out the name and title of the signing official.

POINT 1
Inscrivez lisiblement l'appellation commerciale à enregistrer ou à renouveler. Pour un enregistrement initial, vous devez annexer une copie du rapport de recherche de nom ATLANTIC (5 pages et la page d'accompagnement).

L'appellation commerciale ne peut pas comprendre une fin légale comme « limitée » ou « ltée », « incorporée » ou « inc. »

POINT 2
Indiquez l'activité ou le service commercial qui sera exercé.

POINT 3
Donnez l'adresse à laquelle nous devrions envoyer toute correspondance. L'adresse doit être complète et comprendre un code postal.

POINT 4
Indiquez la date d'établissement de l'entreprise sous la raison sociale enregistrée.

POINT 5
Inscrivez le nom de la personne, de la corporation ou de la société en nom collectif qui demande l'enregistrement de l'appellation commerciale. **CE FORMULAIRE NE DOIT PAS ÊTRE UTILISÉ POUR L'ENREGISTREMENT DES SOCIÉTÉS EN NOM COLLECTIF.**

POINT 6
Indiquez l'adresse de voirie de l'entreprise. (Un numéro de case postale n'est pas acceptable.) L'adresse doit être complète et comprendre un code postal.

POINT 7
Pour les fins de ce formulaire, le pouvoir de signature est réservé à la personne, le dirigeant ou administrateur de la corporation ou le partenaire de la société en nom collectif qui enregistre l'appellation commerciale.

POINT 8
Inscrivez le nom et le titre du signataire autorisé.

FEES
New registration: $112

Renewal: $62

Make payment to Service New Brunswick by cheque or money order. Fees include a mandatory publication fee in the Royal Gazette. DO NOT SEND CASH IN THE MAIL.

When completed, send the form and cheque to:

Corporate Affairs
Service New Brunswick
P.O. Box 1998
Fredericton, New Brunswick
E3B 5G4

DROITS
Nouvel enregistrement : 112 $

Renouvellement : 62 $

Veuillez annexer à votre demande un chèque ou mandat-poste libellé à l'ordre de Services Nouveau-Brunswick. Les droits comprennent les droits de publication obligatoires dans la *Gazette royale*. N'ENVOYEZ PAS D'ARGENT COMPTANT PAR LA POSTE.

Envoyez le formulaire dûment rempli et le paiement à l'adresse suivante :

Direction des affaires corporatives
Services Nouveau-Brunswick
C. P. 1998
Fredericton (Nouveau-Brunswick)
E3B 5G4

ADDITIONAL INFORMATION FORM: Business Name Registration

The following information must accompany your business name registration forms that are being sent to Corporate Affairs

---

1) Information on the Business Number (BN)

A. **Where the registrant of the business name has an existing BN,** please provide it here:

You will have a BN if:
You have a Canada Customs and Revenue Agency (CCRA) GST/HST account, an Import/Export account or a Payroll account.
Your business is incorporated.
Your organization is a registered charity.

B. **Where the registrant of the business name does not have an existing BN, SNB will obtain one on your behalf.**

If you are unsure if your business has a BN or you require information regarding the BN, please call the CCRA at 1-800-959-5525 or visit www.ccra.gc.ca/bn

2) Additional Information

A. **The registrant of the business name is:**
- Sole Proprietor
- Partnership
- Corporation
- ☐ Other

B. **Language preference for correspondence:**
- English
- French

B. **Person to contact regarding the application:**
Name:
Position:
Telephone Area Code: Telephone Number:
Fax Area Code: Fax Number:

The above information is used to generate or confirm the BN, which serves as a common identifier for federal and provincial purposes. The Government of New Brunswick and the CCRA have agreed to use the BN as a common business identifier. Over the coming months the New Brunswick government will continue to phase in use of the BN with provincial departments and agencies.

The following information, collected on the above form and on Service New Brunswick Corporate Affairs forms will be sent to the CCRA to confirm or create a BN:
- the business or corporate name
- registration or incorporation dates
- owner or director names and their phone and fax numbers
- ownership type; physical and mailing address
- business phone and fax numbers
- contact names and their phone and fax numbers
- language preference
  - This information, including the BN, will also be retained in the Business Registration Service information system of SNB for administrative purposes and to facilitate future registrations. Corporate Affairs will retain the BN, as well as information set out on its forms.

ADDITIONAL INFORMATION FORM: Business Name Registration

The following information must accompany your business name registration forms that are being sent to Corporate Affairs

---

1) Information on the Business Number (BN)

A. **Where the registrant of the business name has an existing BN,** please provide it here:

> *You will have a BN if:*
> *You have a Canada Customs and Revenue Agency (CCRA) GST/HST account, an Import/Export account or a Payroll account.*
> *Your business is incorporated.*
> *Your organization is a registered charity.*

B. **Where the registrant of the business name does not have an existing BN, SNB will obtain one on your behalf.**

If you are unsure if your business has a BN or you require information regarding the BN, please call the CCRA at 1-800-959-5525 or visit www.ccra.gc.ca/bn

2) Additional Information

A. **The registrant of the business name is:**
- Sole Proprietor
- Partnership
- ☐ Corporation
- ☐ Other

B. **Language preference for correspondence:**
- English
- French

B. **Person to contact regarding the application:**
Name:
Position:
Telephone Area Code: Telephone Number:
Fax Area Code: Fax Number:

The above information is used to generate or confirm the BN, which serves as a common identifier for federal and provincial purposes. The Government of New Brunswick and the CCRA have agreed to use the BN as a common business identifier. Over the coming months the New Brunswick government will continue to phase in use of the BN with provincial departments and agencies.

The following information, collected on the above form and on Service New Brunswick Corporate Affairs forms will be sent to the CCRA to confirm or create a BN:
- the business or corporate name
- registration or incorporation dates
- owner or director names and their phone and fax numbers
- ownership type; physical and mailing address
- business phone and fax numbers
- contact names and their phone and fax numbers
- language preference
    - This information, including the BN, will also be retained in the Business Registration Service information system of SNB for administrative purposes and to facilitate future registrations. Corporate Affairs will retain the BN, as well as information set out on its forms.

Appendix XVI -

NEW BRUNSWICK / CERTIFICATE OF BUSINESS NAME OR CERTIFICATE OF RENEWAL OF BUSINESS NAME NOUVEAU-BRUNSWICK / CERTIFICAT D'APPELLATION COMMERCIALE OU CERTIFICAT DE RENOUVELLEMENT D'APPELLATION COMMERCIALE

THE PARTNERSHIPS AND BUSINESS NAMES REGISTRATION ACT (SECTION 9 AND 9.1)
LOI SUR L'ENREGISTREMENT DES SOCIÉTÉS EN NOM COLLECTIF ET DES APPELLATIONS COMMERCIALES (ARTICLE 9 ET 9.1)

1. Name or style to be registered / Appellation commerciale à enregistrer

2. Business activity or service to be carried on, in or identified by the registered name
   Nature de l'activité ou des services dont s'occupe la firme pouvant être évoquée ou identifiée par l'appellation commerciale enregistrée

3. Mailing address of corporation or business registering business name, giving street and number or R.R. number, and municipality.
   Adresse postale de la corporation ou de l'entreprise enregistrant l'appellation commerciale, donnant le numéro et la rue ou le numéro de la route rurale, et la municipalité.

   Postal Code/Code postal

4. Date of establishing business under the name and style / Date de constitution de l'entreprise sous l'appellation commerciale

Day/Jour	Month/Mois	Year/Année	Check if Renewal	Telephone/Téléphone
			Cocher s'il s'agit d'un renouvellement ~	

5. Name of the corporation or person registering name / Nom de la corporation ou de la personne enregistrant l'appellation commerciale

6. Address where business is located / Adresse de l'entreprise

   Postal Code/Code postal

7. Signature of Director or Officer or Person Signature de l'administrateur, du dirigeant ou de la personne	8. Name and title of the Signing Official Nom et titre du signataire

Registrar Use Only / Réservé à l'usage du registraire

Reference No. / Nₒ de référence

Registration Date / Date d'enregistrement _____
                                          Year/Année-Month/Mois-Day/Jour

Expiry Date / Date d'expiration _____
                                Year/Année-Month/Mois-Day/Jour

This registration expires in five years, but may be renewed. Renewal is your responsibility. The registration expiry date will be shown in your Confirmation of Registration.

Le délai d'expiration du présent enregistrement est de cinq ans, renouvelable. Toutefois, la responsabilité du renouvellement vous incombe. La date d'expiration de l'enregistrement sera indiquée dans votre Confirmation d'enregistrement.

FORM / FORMULE 5
INSTRUCTIONS ON REVERSE SIDE / INSTRUCTIONS AU VERSO.

SN0295(New)-SN0297(Renewal / 45-3502 (11/05)
SN0307

INSTRUCTIONS

DIRECTIVES

ELECTRONIC FILING OPTION

You are now able to file your business name registration or renewal of business name electronically with Corporate Affairs. Please note certain conditions apply to on-line filing. Check our web site at http://www.snb.ca

ENREGISTREMENT ÉLECTRONIQUE

Vous pouvez maintenant soumettre une demande d'enregistrement ou de renouvellement d'une appellation commerciale en ligne à la Direction des affaires corporatives. Il faut cependant respecter certaines conditions. Pour de plus amples renseignements, consultez notre site Web à l'adresse http://www.snb.ca.

ITEM 1
Print clearly the business name to be registered or renewed. For initial registration, we require an ATLANTIC based name search report (5 pages and covering letter) on your proposed business name.

A business name cannot have a legal ending, i.e. Ltd., Limited, Inc., Incorporated

ITEM 2
Indicate the business activity or service to be carried on.

ITEM 3
This should be the address where you wish correspondence from this office to be mailed. The address must be complete including a postal code.

ITEM 4
Indicate the date the business was established under the name being registered.

ITEM 5
Indicate the name of the person, corporation or partnership name registering the business name. **PLEASE NOTE THIS FORM IS NOT TO BE USED FOR A PARTNERSHIP NAME REGISTRATION.**

ITEM 6
Indicate the address where the business is to be located. A P.O. box number is not acceptable. The address must be complete including a postal code.

ITEM 7
Only the person, officer or director of the corporation, or partner of the partnership, registering the business name is authorized to sign the form.

ITEM 8
Set out the name and title of the signing official.

FEES
New registration: $112

Renewal: $62

Make payment to Service New Brunswick by cheque or money order. Fees include a mandatory publication fee in the Royal Gazette. DO NOT SEND CASH IN THE MAIL.

When completed, send the form and cheque to:

Corporate Affairs
Service New Brunswick
P.O. Box 1998
Fredericton, New Brunswick
E3B 5G4

POINT 1
Inscrivez lisiblement l'appellation commerciale à enregistrer ou à renouveler. Pour un enregistrement initial, vous devez annexer une copie du rapport de recherche de nom ATLANTIC (5 pages et la page d'accompagnement).

L'appellation commerciale ne peut pas comprendre une indication du statut juridique comme « limitée » ou « ltée », « incorporée » ou « inc. »

POINT 2
Indiquez l'activité ou le service commercial qui sera exercé.

POINT 3
Donnez l'adresse à laquelle nous devrions envoyer toute correspondance. L'adresse doit être complète et comprendre un code postal.

POINT 4
Indiquez la date d'établissement de l'entreprise sous la raison sociale enregistrée.

POINT 5
Inscrivez le nom de la personne, de la corporation ou de la société en nom collectif qui demande l'enregistrement de l'appellation commerciale. **CE FORMULAIRE NE DOIT PAS ÊTRE UTILISÉ POUR L'ENREGISTREMENT DES SOCIÉTÉS EN NOM COLLECTIF.**

POINT 6
Indiquez l'adresse de voirie de la compagnie. (Un numéro de case postale n'est pas acceptable.) L'adresse doit être complète et comprendre un code postal.

POINT 7
Pour les fins de ce formulaire, le pouvoir de signature est réservé à la personne, l'agent, le directeur de la compagnie ou le partenaire de la société en nom collectif qui enregistre l'appellation commerciale.

POINT 8
Inscrivez le nom et le titre du signataire autorisé.

DROITS
Nouvel enregistrement : 112 $

Renouvellement : 62 $

Veuillez annexer à votre demande un chèque ou mandat-poste libellé à l'ordre de Services Nouveau-Brunswick. Les droits comprennent les droits de publication obligatoires dans la *Gazette royale*. N'ENVOYEZ PAS D'ARGENT COMPTANT PAR LA POSTE.

Envoyez le formulaire dûment rempli et le paiement à l'adresse suivante :

Direction des affaires corporatives
Services Nouveau-Brunswick
C. P. 1998
Fredericton (Nouveau-Brunswick)
E3B 5G4

NOVA SCOTIA
Service Nova Scotia
and Municipal Relations

Name Reservation Request

1. Search type please (check one):

" Atlantic region search	Fee: $42.60 + HST = $48.99
Federal search (required if name begins with 'Canada' or 'Canadian')..	Fee: $53.25 + HST = $61.24
Extra provincial corporation	Fee: no charge
" Society..	Fee: no charge

Requested name
Clearly describe your
business activities: _____

4. For Atlantic region and Federal searches, please indicate type of registration:

" Sole proprietorship	" Business name owned by a corporation
Corporation	" Business name owned by a society
Partnership	" Extra-provincial limited partnership
Co-operative	

Applicant / Business Owner Information

5. Name _____

_____
(civic number and street)   (suite / apt / unit)

_____
(po box)   (city)   (province)   (country)   (postal code)

_____
(Phone)   (fax)   (e-mail)

7. Sole proprietorships, partnerships and business names owned by a corporation may be able to register online. If your business qualifies you will receive a Registration ID by your preferred contact method.

What is your preferred contact method? ' mailing address   ' fax

8. Payment type: ' Cheque   ' Money Order   Please note:
                     ' Visa   ' MasterCard

_____
(credit card account number)

* if this name is reserved for your use, you will be required to register and do business using the exact name as registered
* if this name is reserved for your use, we will send you the results of our name search and an application for registration
* do not send a registration form with this reservation request form

_____
(expiry date)   (card holders name)

_____
(signature)

Nova Scotia Registry of Joint Stock Companies, PO Box 1529, Halifax, NS, B3J 2Y4

Need help? Contact us at 902-424-7770 (toll-free in Nova Scotia: 1-800-670-4357) or at www.gov.ns.ca/snsmr/forms/rjsc.stm

NR010   v0801

Saskatchewan Justice
Corporations Branch
200, 1871 Smith Street
Regina, Saskatchewan
S4P 4W5

Appendix XVIII -
Business Name Registration Kit
Instructions and Additional Information

Phone (306)787-2962
Fax (306)787-8999
E-Mail corporations@justice.gov.sk.ca

1. This kit includes Form A for registering a **Sole Proprietorship,** and Form A. 1 for registering a **Partnership, Joint Venture or Syndicate.**

2. **The fees to register are:**

Name Availability Search	$ 50.00	
Registration	$ 65.00	(or $55.00 if registered on-line)
Total	$115.00	(or $105.00 if registered on-line)

   - Documents are normally processed within 10 working days. You may request expedited service to have documents processed within 2 working days. The fee for expedited service is $100.00 if the Request for Name Search and Reservation has not previously been completed and $25.00 if the Request for Name Search and Reservation has been completed.
   - Make remittance payable to the Minister of Finance, (in Canadian Funds).
   - Payment can be made by:
     Cash/Cheque/Money Order or
     Visa/MasterCard.

3. You may fax the registration documents (plus authorize payment by Visa, MasterCard). If you fax the documents **DO NOT** mail the originals – keep them for your files. The faxed copy must be legible and suitable for imaging. <u>If the fax copy is not legible, you will be asked to submit the originals.</u>

   Your business name will not be registered until the completed documents, acceptable for processing, and fees have been received.

4. Send or bring your completed forms and fees to:

** Corporations Branch	Go to:
200, 1871 Smith Street	www.corporations.justice.gov.sk.ca **OR**
Regina, Saskatchewan	to register online
S4P 4W5	
Fax: (306) 787-8999	

   Corporations Branch public office hours are from 8 a.m. to 5 p.m., Monday to Friday.

IMPORTANT NOTES:

- If your forms are not completed correctly they will be sent back to you. Your date of registration will be effective the date the completed forms, acceptable for registration and all fees are received.

- **DO NOT** send cash through the mail.

- *WE RECOMMEND THAT YOU DO NOT USE YOUR PROPOSED NAME IN ANY WAY UNTIL THE CORPORATIONS BRANCH HAS ISSUED A CERTIFICATE OF REGISTRATION.*

PAYMENT FOR SERVICES

All services provided by Corporations Branch may be paid for by:

1) Cash/cheque/money order (do not send cash through the mail)
2) Visa/MasterCard
3) Debit Card (for walk-in customers only)
4) Deposit Account*
    * Applies only to those agencies who have an Account with Corporations Branch

For 1) Mail requests - include your cheque or money order, Visa/MasterCard number (including expiry date) or Deposit Account Number.

2) Fax requests - include your Visa/MasterCard number (including expiry date) or Deposit Account Number

Use the Client Payment Authorization Form below to authorize payment. This form will be destroyed once payment has been authorized.

CLIENT AUTHORIZATION PAYMENT FORM FOR PAYMENT BY:

_____

Deposit Account   Account #   _____

Visa/MasterCard   Card #:   _____

Name: _____

Complete Address: _____

Postal Code: _____

Saskatchewan
Justice
Corporations
Branch

Sole Proprietor
The Business Names Registration Act
[Clause 4 (1)(a)]

Form A

Please see reverse for instructions.

Please print (or type) clearly

Name of Business: _____

Location of Business: _____

(a box number is not acceptable)

_____
City, Town, Village or Rural Municipality (name and number)   Prov.   Postal Code

Mailing Address: ☐ Same as Above   **OR**

_____
Street Address or Box Number

_____
City, Town or Village   Prov.   Postal Code

I do hereby declare that,

a. **A** ☐ The applicant is carrying on   **OR**   **B** The applicant intends to carry on
              business in Saskatchewan;   business in
              Saskatchewan;

                                          AND

b. The applicant is the sole member of this firm.

5. 1) If the applicant is an individual, the applicant's full name, address including postal code and signature are
       required.

    2) If the applicant is a corporation, Indian Band or Limited Partnership, the name, entity number and
       signature of an authorized officer are required:

Date: _____

First and Last Name or
Name of corporation, Indian Band or Limited Partnership: _____

Address (for individuals only)
Entity Number (for corporations): _____

Signature of Individual or
Authorized Officer if the applicant is a corporation: _____

Sole Proprietor
Form A
INSTRUCTIONS FOR COMPLETION

This form is for use by sole proprietors only. Applicants that are partnerships, joint ventures or syndicates must use Form A. 1.

Item 1: Item 2:   Type or print the name of the business.

Enter the physical location of the business. A box number is not acceptable.

Item 3:   If the mailing address is the same as the location of the business, check the "Same as Above" checkbox. If the mailing address is not the same as the location of the business, enter the mailing address.

Item 4: 1) a)   If you have already commenced business under this name, check box **A.**

b)   If you will be commencing business in the future, check box **B.**

2)   A sole proprietorship may be an individual, a limited partnership, a body corporate or an Indian band. However, in order to register as a sole proprietor, the applicant must declare that no other entities (e.g. other individuals, corporations, partnerships, limited partnerships, joint ventures, syndicates, Indian bands) are associated with the firm.

Item 5: 1)   If the registrant is an individual, full name, address including postal code and signature are required.

2)   If the registrant is a corporation, Indian Band or Limited Partnership, name, entity number and signature of authorized officer are required.

NOTE: If the Owner is an individual who does not reside in Saskatchewan, the Owner must appoint a Power of Attorney. The Power of Attorney form is available at:

www. saskjustice.gov.sk.ca/corporations/forms

or by phoning Corporations Branch at (306) 787-2962

Completed documents, in duplicate, and the prescribed fee payable to the **Minister of Finance** are to be sent to:

Director, Corporations Branch
200, 1871 Smith Street

Please see reverse for instructions

Please print (or type) clearly

Name of Business: _____

Location of Business: _____

(a box number is not acceptable)

City, Town, Village or Rural Municipality (name and number)   Prov.   Postal Code

Mailing Address: ☐ Same as Above   **OR**

_____
Street Address or Box Number

_____
City, Town or Village   Prov.   Postal Code

4. 1) If the applicant is an individual, the applicant's full name, address, including postal code and signature are required.

2) If the applicant is a corporation, Indian Band or Limited Partnership, the name, entity number and signature of an authorized officer are required.

Date	First and Last Name or Name of Applicant	Address	Signature of Authorized Individual

We hereby declare that:

1) **A** We intend to carry on business in Saskatchewan as a: ☐ Partnership   ☐ Joint Venture   Syndicate ☐

OR

B We are carrying on business in Saskatchewan as a: ☐   Partnership   Joint Venture   Syndicate

AND

2) No one other than the applicants listed in item 4, above, are associated in business with the firm.

AND

3) [in the case of an application by a partnership] All of our partners who are individuals are at least 18 years of age.

Partnership, Joint Venture or Syndicate
Form A.1
INSTRUCTIONS FOR COMPLETION

Item 1: Item Type or print the name of the business.

2: Enter the physical location of the business. A box number is not acceptable.

Item 3: If the mailing address is the same as the location of the business, check the "Same as Above" checkbox. If the mailing address is not the same as the location of the business, enter the mailing address.

Item 4: 1) If the applicant is an individual, the applicant's full name, address including postal code and signature are required.

2) If the applicant is a corporation, Indian band or Limited Partnership, the name, entity number and signature of an authorized officer are required.

Item 5: 1) A) If you have not commenced business, check the box indicating the applicable description.

B) If you are a continuing business, check the box indicating the applicable description.

2) Only those entities listed in item 4 may carry on business in association with the firm

NOTE: If you are registering a Partnership whose Partners are all individuals and none of them reside in Saskatchewan, you must appoint a Power of Attorney. The Power of Attorney form is available at:

www.saskjustice.gov. sk.ca/corporations/forms

or by phoning Corporations Branch at (306) 787-2962

Completed documents, in duplicate, and the prescribed fee payable to the **Minister of Finance** are to be sent to:

Director, Corporations Branch
200, 1871 Smith Street

Request for Name Availability Search And Reservation

The Business Names Registration Act

Form G

Name (Typed): _____ Date: _____

Mail: _____

City: _____ Province: _____ Postal Code: _____

Attn: _____ Phone No: _____ Fax No: _____

(Where you may be reached between 8:00 a.m. and 5:00 p.m.)

This name is currently registered and I have a cancellation from the former owner(s). Please continue to enter the name and type of business. A cancellation, signed by the former owner(s) must be attached to the registration.

This name is to be used for:

☐ **Sole Proprietorship**   ☐ **Partnership**   ☐ **Syndicate**   ☐ **Joint Venture**

Saskatchewan Mandatory Search   **$50.00**
includes a search of names registered in Saskatchewan, Federal corporations and registered trademarks.

Service Options: (Results to be mailed unless fax option selected)	**Scope of Search:** (Select the scope of search preferred _____
Rush (extra $100 charge)	**Search all names** (A name search fee will apply to EVERY name)
Fax (extra $5 charge) Fax	**OR**
Number:	**Search to first available name**

Names to Search: (in order of preference) Each name requires a distinctive and descriptive term. A distinctive term distinguishes your name from anyone else in the same type of business. A descriptive term indicates what type of business you will be doing. Eg. Bob's Courier Service Ltd.. (If you have additional names, please attach a separate page. NOTE: You do not have to enter more than one name if you do not wish to).

_____

_____

_____

Type(s) of business the business intends to carry on: (please be specific, terms such as manufacturing, consulting, etc. need further clarification.)

_____

General location(s) in Saskatchewan where business will operate:

_____

** **Optional Searches Available (extra $60.00 fee)** To request a search for a trademark, federal name search or a search which contains similar names registered across Canada, contact Corporations Branch at (306) 787-2962 for further details.

STARTING A BUSINESS IN SASKATCHEWAN
LICENCE AND REGISTRATION REQUIREMENTS

1. Municipal or City Business Licence: - required in each municipality in which your business operates.

   CONTACT: Municipal Office or City Hall
   COST: depending on individual circumstances

2. Education and Health Tax Licence (also known as PST): required by all retail businesses selling tangible goods and services.

   CONTACT: Department of Finance
   Education and Health Tax
   2350 Albert Street
   Regina, Sask.
   S4P 4A6 Phone: 787-6645 or 1-800-667-6102

3. Goods and Services Tax Registration: (known as GST): required by most businesses.

   CONTACT: Regina Tax Services Office   OR   Saskatoon Tax Services
   Goods and Services Tax   Goods and Services Tax 340
   Suite 260,1783 Hamilton St.   – 3rd Avenue North
   P.O. Box 557   Saskatoon, Sask. S7K 0A8
   Regina, Sask. S4P 2N9 Phone: 1 -800-959-5525   Phone: 1-800-959-5525

   COST: No Charge

   You may also contact Canada Customs & Revenue Agency through their internet site at www.ccra-adrc.gc.ca

4. Employer Registration Number: required by all employers who make deductions for Income Tax, Unemployment Insurance, and Canada Pension.

   CONTACT: Regina Tax Services Office   OR   Saskatoon Tax Services 340
   Suite 260, 1783 Hamilton St.   – 3rd Avenue North
   P.O. Box 557   Saskatoon, Sask. S7K 0A8
   Regina, Sask. S4P 2N9 Phone: 1-800-959-5525   Phone: 1-800-959-5525

   COST: No Charge

   You may also contact Canada Customs & Revenue Agency through their internet site at www.ccra-adrc.gc.ca

5. Workers Compensation Coverage: required by most employers.

   CONTACT: Workers' Compensation Board
   200 - 1881 Scarth St.
   Regina, Sask.
   S4P 4L1
   Phone: 787-4370

6. If you are a motor dealer, auctioneer, collection agent, direct seller, credit reporting agency, provide training courses, or rent or sell videos, you should contact:

Saskatchewan Justice
Consumer Protection Branch
5th Floor, 1919 Saskatchewan Drive
Regina, Sask. S4P 3V7
Phone: (306)787-5550 or 1-888-374-4636 (in Saskatchewan)

*NOTE: Other licences may be required. You may check with:

Saskatchewan Industry and Resources at:
1-800-265-2001 or check their web site at www.ir.gov.sk.ca

Canada-Saskatchewan Business Service Centre at:
1-800-667-4374 or check their web site at www.cbsc.org/sask
for further information.

Form 1
Declaration for Registration of a Business Name
Partnership Act R.S.P.E.I. 1988, Cap. P-1
(Individual)

Canada
Province of
Prince Edward Island

I, _____
(owner's name)

of _____

_____
(postal code)

declare that:

1.   I have carried on, or intend to commence carrying on, business effective

20 _____

as _____
(nature of the business)

at

under the name of

2.   I have caused a search of the above mentioned business name by the Corporate Section of the Office of the Attorney General and understand the search results and am satisfied that it is not the name of any other known business or any name liable to be confused therewith or otherwise on public grounds objectionable.

3.   I am not aware of any other known business operating under this name or a name liable to be confused

therewith. And I make this declaration conscientiously believing it to be true.

_____   _____
(telephone)   (signature of owner)

_____
(date)

_____
For Departmental Use Only

Registration Date

Registration Number   _____

Expiry Date   Registrar

The Business Names Registration Act
REGISTRATION OF A BUSINESS NAME

Manitoba 🐃
Building for the Future

PLEASE PRINT OR TYPE.

1) Business Name

2) Name and Address (include postal code) to which duplicate should be returned and Renewals will be mailed	3) Contact person, if different from registrant
	Tel. (8:30-4:30)

4) (a) Does this business have a Business Number? (Please click on box to select.)

Yes   No

(b) If the answer to (a) is "yes," please set out the Business Number.

_____

5) The place of business is (full address, including postal code)

6) The date of start of business (cannot be more than 30 days in future)

7) The main type of business is

Declaration:

The business name being registered is not that of another known firm, company, corporation or unincorporated association, or a name liable to be confounded or confused with the other name, or otherwise objectionable on public grounds. No other firm, person or corporation is associated in partnership with the registrant(s).

8) If more than one registrant is listed in item 9, please answer the following question. (Please click on box to select.)

Is this a partnership?   Yes   No ☐

9) Registrant(s)

Full Name   Residence Address   Signature

_____

_____

☐ A schedule is attached with the names, addresses and signatures of additional registrants. (Please click on box to select.)

OFFICE USE ONLY		Cash Register Endorsement
Date of Registration:	_____	
Date of Expiry:	_____	
Registration Number:	_____	
Business Number:	_____	

Schedule of Additional Registrants

Registrant(s) Full Name	Residence Address	Signature
		_____
		_____
		_____
		_____
		_____

INSTRUCTIONS FOR REGISTERING A BUSINESS NAME
Under The Business Names Registration Act

STEP 1: RE SERVING THE NAME

Before a business name can be registered, a Request for Name Reservation must be filed to determine if the name is available for use. Please read the notes on the reverse side of that form.

Form Required	Filing Fee
Request for Name Reservation	$40.00

In addition to the traditional paper application that is still available, a Request for Name Reservation can be filed online at https://direct.gov.mb.ca/coohtml/html/internet/en/coo.html.

If your name is **reserved,** you will have 90 days to file the Business Registration forms by following Step 2 below. If your name is **rejected,** you must choose a new name and do Step 1 over again (including fee).

STEP 2: REGISTERING THE BUSINESS NAME

Forms Required (in duplicate)	Filing Fees
Form # 1 Registration of a Business Name	$45.00
Power of Attorney (if required)	$30.00

Notice under The Freedom of Information and Protection of Privacy Act

Information about this business is collected pursuant to *The Business Names Registration Act*. It is made available for public searching pursuant to that Act. Information will be shared with other government departments and the Minister of National Revenue pursuant to *The Electronic Commerce and Information Act* for the purposes of obtaining a Business Number (BN) for this company and administering a common business numbering and information system. If you have any questions about its collection, contact: The Director, Companies Office, 10 10-405 Broadway, Winnipeg, MB, R3C 3L6 or phone (204) 945-2500.

When is a Power of Attorney Required?

A Power of Attorney form will be needed if the registration form shows all the people registering the business name living outside of Manitoba. This person must be willing to accept all legal documents on behalf of the business in Manitoba. This person does not need to be a lawyer, but he or she must live in Manitoba.

Special Notes

- All forms must be typed or printed clearly and signed in ink.
- If your business is a partnership, the name, address and signatures of all partners is required.

PAYMENT OPTIONS

If you are filing the Name Reservation (paper applications only) and Registration forms together:

- If paying by **cheque,** please ensure there are two separate cheques (or **money orders),** payable to the **Minister of Finance.** If not, the office cannot process your forms and will need to send everything back.

- If paying by **credit card,** your signature on this form authorizes us to process two separate transactions.

If paying by **Credit Card,** please return this bottom portion with your forms

Name Reservation $40.00 ~   Registration $45.00 ~   Power of Attorney $30.00 ~

Visa ~   **MasterCard** ~

Card # _____   Expiry Date _____   Signature _____

Where to Send the Forms and Fees   **Any Questions?**

COMPANIES OFFICE   **Telephone:** (204) 945-2500   **Fax:** (204) 945-1459

Woodsworth Building   **Toll Free in Manitoba:** 1-888-246-8353

1010-405 Broadway   **E-Mail:** companies@gov.mb.ca

Winnipeg, MB R3C 3L6   **Website:** http://www.gov.mb.ca/finance/cca/comp_off/index.html

                                              Hours: 8:00 – 4:30 Monday to Friday

PLEASE NOTE:

These guidelines are to help in the completion of the registration of a business name. These guidelines are not a substitute for legal advice. Please read the attached instruction sheet for full information.

- Every section of the forms must be completed. If they are not, the forms will not be accepted.
- All forms must be typed or clearly printed.

SECTION 1 – BUSINESS NAME

1. The name of the business must be completed. The business name must match the reserved name exactly.
2. Except for a numbered business name, you must have a valid name reservation. Use **the** *REQUEST FOR NAME RESERVATION* form.

SECTION 2 – THE NAME AND MAILING ADDRESS

1. The name and address, including the postal code to which the duplicate should be returned and renewals will be mailed.

SECTION 3 – CONTACT PERSON AND PHONE NUMBER

1. A contact person and phone number (during working hours) must be shown.

SECTION 4 – DOES THIS BUSINESS HAVE A BUSINESS NUMBER? (BN) (The BN is assigned by Canada Customs and Revenue Agency (CCRA).

The registrant(s) of this business name may already have a BN if they answer yes to any of the following questions:

- Have you previously registered a business name?
- Have you registered to remit retail sales tax, health and post secondary education tax, or corporate capital tax?
- Have you ever collected GST?
- Have you ever had annual sales greater than $30,000?
- Will a corporation be the registrant of this business name?
- Have you ever had employees?
- Have you ever been in the import or export business?
- Will a registered charity be the registrant of this business name?
- Have you ever operated a taxi or limo service?

If you answered Yes to any of those questions, please ensure that the Business Number you already have, was assigned to same registrants as are currently registering for this business name. Business Numbers are assigned to sole proprietors, partnerships, corporations, or "other" business structures. For example, a BN assigned to a sole proprietor can not be used by a partnership, even if the sole proprietor is a partner.

- If none, write "not applicable" or N/A.

SECTION 5 – THE PLACE OF BUSINESS

1. The full business address must be shown.
2. We can accept a post office box, providing the form also shows one civic address. However if the location is a small town, a mailing address is acceptable, P.O. Box 34, Melita, MB R0J 0M0.
3. A place of business outside of Manitoba can be shown when there is no Manitoba address available.

SECTION 6 – THE DATE OF START OF BUSINESS

1. The date should be a day, month and year. It **cannot** be over 30 days in the future.

SECTION 7 – THE MAIN TYPE OF BUSINESS

1. The nature of business must be indicated. It must be specific and state the exact nature of business. e.g. miscellaneous is not acceptable.

SECTION 8 – IF MORE THAN ONE REGISTRANT IS LISTED IN SECTION #9.
Is this a partnership?

A partnership exists where two or more persons carry on a business in common, with a view of profit. Whether or not the relationship between the persons registering this business name constitutes a "partnership" is a legal question. If you are unsure, please speak to your lawyer

SECTION 9 – FULL NAME OF REGISTRANT(S)

1. Must show the full name (not just initials) and residential address of all registrant(s). An officer or director must sign on behalf of the corporation.
2. If there are no registrants residing in Manitoba, a Power of Attorney form must be filed in duplicate with an additional fee of $30.00.

Disclaimer

While every effort was made to collect the most up-to-date, correct information, we cannot guarantee that all information is correct at the time of publication. Please double check all information, especially the information regarding registering and licensing your business to ensure that you are following the correct procedures for your area.

Also, we are not lawyers. All contracts are simply suggestions. In order to ensure that you are legally protected you will need to talk to a lawyer in your area.

Conclusion

Owning and operating a virtual assistant business is extremely rewarding. If things are going well, we can take full credit for the success. If things are challenging, we learn from these challenges and thus grow our businesses while knowing what to avoid the next time.

You will go through both highs and lows (we hope the lows are few and far between), but if you have the skills, knowhow and passion, your Virtual Assistant practice can be one of the most rewarding parts of your life which will make those challenges much easier to deal with.

We hope that the information we have offered in *How to Build a Successful Virtual Assistant Business* will help you to take your business to a level beyond your expectations. We also hope that you will call upon this book as a reference through all aspects of running your business.

Be sure to share in the giving by visiting our website and sharing your thoughts on the different aspects of running a virtual assistant practice.

Continued success!

About the Authors

About Janice Byer

Janice Byer founded Docu-Type Administrative & Web Design Services (www.docutype.net) in September of 1998. She has over 25 years of experience in administrative, web design and office management skills.

Janice is a Certified Canadian Virtual Assistant (CCVA), Certified Master Virtual Assistant (MVA), and the recipient of several awards for her business. She is also a Co-Founder (since 2002, along with Elayne) of the Canadian Virtual Assistant Connection (www.cvac.ca) and is active in many Virtual Assistant related organizations and initiatives.

As an author of hundreds of articles on the subjects of virtual assistance and small business, as well as self-help ebooks for VAs, working on *How to Build a Successful Virtual Assistant* Business was just a natural and logical progression for her. Janice is looking forward to helping many more interested parties to find success in the VA field she loves.

Janice's personal message:

"I am so glad that Elayne and I decided to write this book and I sincerely hope that it helps to alleviate some of the concerns of both new and established VAs during the various transitions of running a VA practice. I hope you find all the information helpful and I wish you tremendous success in this exciting and rewarding career choice!"

Janice D. Byer, CCVA, MVA

Owner: Docu-Type Administrative & Web Design Services
Websites: http://www.docutype.net
                http://www.docutype.org
                http://www.docutype.org/blog
                http://www.equinewebdesign.ca

Co-Founder: Canadian Virtual Assistant Connection
Website: http://www.cvac.ca

Author: Business Building Ebook Library
Website: http://www.docutype.net/business_ebooks.htm

About Elayne Whitfield-Parr

Elayne Whitfield-Parr began Executive Assistance in 2000, transitioned her company to a successful multi-VA practice offering a full complement of business support services in 2002, and then incorporated Executive Assistance Business Solutions Inc. in 2006. In 2007, EA Design (www.eadesign.ca) was formed to handle the website and graphic design component of the business.

Canadian Virtual Assistant Connection (cvac.ca) was co-founded by Elayne who is also their director. CVAC was created to inspire and support VAs of all levels of expertise. It is a place where over 500 members from across Canada can gather together to find support, education and benefit from the vast array of available resources.

Speaking regularly to groups regarding the Virtual Assistant Industry is one of Elayne's principal responsibilities as the co-founder of CVAC. She is a graduate of the University of Western Ontario, a Certified Canadian Virtual Assistant (CCVA), a Master Virtual Assistant (MVA), a Professional Real Estate Virtual Assistant (PREVA), and a member of several related associations.

Elayne lives in Barrie, Ontario with her husband Tim and her sons, Taylor (15), Cameron (10) and Braedan (5). When she's not working or volunteering in her community, she can be found on her boat in Georgian Bay with her family and friends.

Elayne's personal message:

"When I started my business I put, literally, hundreds of hours into research and educating myself about the Virtual Assistant industry and all aspects of starting a business. I hope this book cuts down on that learning curve for VAs just starting out as well as VAs who are ready to bring their business to the next level. I truly hope that you are as fulfilled and completely happy with your business as I am with mine."

Elayne Whitfield-Parr, CCVA, MVA, PREVA

Owner: Executive Assistance Business Solutions Inc.
Websites: http://www.executive-assistance.ca
  http://www.executiveassistance.org
  http://www.eadesign.ca

Co-Founder: Canadian Virtual Assistant Connection
Website: http://www.cvac.ca

Index